"With truly masterful use of humor as a coping strategy, SHUT UP ABOUT YOUR PERFECT KID authors Gina Gallagher and Patricia Konjoian address the challenges, the heartbreak, and the touching victories of parenting children with disabilities today. The book is a valuable and insightful resource for any family member or friend of a child with special needs. It conveys a wealth of practical information with a warmth and compassion that helps parents realize they are not alone."

DEIRDRE E. LOGAN, PhD, psychologist, Children's
Hospital Boston, and assistant professor of psychology,
Harvard Medical School

"Anyone who has ever laughed while raising a child will love this book! Gina and Patricia really find the humor in special needs parenting—and they validate us all."

SUSAN SENATOR, author of *Making Peace with Autism*
and *The Autism Mom's Survival Guide*

Shut Up About Your Perfect Kid

A SURVIVAL GUIDE FOR ORDINARY PARENTS OF SPECIAL CHILDREN

Gina Gallagher &
Patricia Konjoian

THREE RIVERS PRESS | New York

Published in the United States by Three Rivers Press,
an imprint of the Crown Publishing Group,
a division of Random House, Inc., New York.

www.crownpublishing.com

Three Rivers Press and the Tugboat design
are registered trademarks of Random House, Inc.

A previous edition of this work was published in the
United States by Shut Up Industries, Inc., in 2006.

Grateful acknowledgment is made to the following for permission to reprint
previously published material:
LeeAnn Karg: Material reprinted or revised from kargacademy.com, reprinted by
permission of LeeAnn D. Karg, MEd, Disability Specialist.
Emily Perl Kingsley: "Welcome to Holland" by Emily Perl Kingsley, copyright ©
1987 by Emily Perl Kingsley. All rights reserved. Reprinted by permission of the
author.

Library of Congress Cataloging-in-Publication Data

Gallagher, Gina.
    Shut up about your perfect kid : a survival guide for ordinary parents of special
children / Gina Gallagher and Patricia Konjoian. —1st Three Rivers Press ed.
        p. cm.
    "Originally published in the United States by Shut Up Industries, Inc."
    1. Parents of children with disabilities. 2. Children with disabilities. I. Konjoian,
Patricia. II. Title.
HQ759.913.G35 2010
649'.152—dc22   2010010572

ISBN 978-0-307-58748-0

Printed in the United States of America

Book design by Cindy LaBreacht
Illustrations by Katie Gallagher and Daniel Terrasi

10 9 8 7 6 5

First Three Rivers Press Edition

To all the "special" parents,

grandparents, and guardians
who feel sad, overwhelmed, and isolated.

You are not alone.

And to our own special parents,
Vi and Tony Terrasi,
who remind us of that every day.

CONTENTS

CONTENTS

FOREWORD

Welcome to *Shut Up About Your Perfect Kid*.

First, the good news: I really like this book. Now, the bad news: I really don't like the title, and only partially because I don't love the words *shut up*. The main reason I don't like the title is that this book really isn't about other people's kids being perfect. This book is about the journey of two moms—one whose child is diagnosed with Asperger's syndrome, the other whose child is diagnosed with bipolar disorder—as they struggle to understand their kids' differences and keep their heads above water in a world that still doesn't understand individual differences very well at all. It's not easy out there for kids with social, emotional, and behavioral challenges, and it's not easy for their parents, either. These two moms (and their kids) somehow find their way, though, and this book is about their journey.

The other good news is that the wisdom they gather along the way is packed into this book as well. Though they are more favorably inclined toward psychiatric diagnoses than I am, they've made no attempt to transform themselves into mental health professionals in telling their stories. One of the best parts of the book is that these two moms sound like . . . well, two *moms*. And two very funny moms at that. So you're going to laugh (a lot), and cry (a little), and you're going to hope for the best, and you're going to pray that someone can help their kids, and best of all you're going to know that you're not alone.

So if you were hoping for a dry, predictable reading experience, I'm quite certain you've selected the wrong book. Kids with social, emotional, and behavioral challenges aren't dry and predictable, so hang on to your hat and bring along some tissues.

Finally, if you were hoping for a long foreword, wrong book again. You need to start reading!

Ross W. Greene, PhD, author of *The Explosive Child* and *Lost at School*; founder of Lives in the Balance (livesinthebalance.org)

IMPERFECT AUTHORS' NOTE

WHEN WE BEGAN the journey of writing this book, we had no idea where it would lead us, though we certainly had our share of fantasies. We dreamed about making entrances at our next high school reunions ("So what if we've gained fifteen pounds since graduation! We wrote a book!"); jetting off to exciting places ("Pat, maybe we'll go to Chicago and meet Jerry Springer"); even amassing a world-class financial empire ("Should we build the Shut Up Industries' skyscraper in Boston or in Providence?").

But neither of us ever—not in our wildest dreams—imagined the riches this book would bring us.

To be honest, we weren't even looking to write this book. We were looking for therapy; a way to cope with the challenges and frustrations of raising daughters with **autism** and **bipolar disorder** in a society hell-bent on perfection. (See Glossary on page 229 for definitions of terms in bold.)

"Why do people have to stare at Katie like that? She can't help it if she flaps her hands."

"You think *that's* bad. Yesterday, we pulled up next to a mother we know at a traffic light. I swear she hit the door locks when she saw Jenn."

We felt completely and utterly alone—like no one understood our kids or us.

Fortunately, we were blessed with each other and a gift that's been handed down by generations of our kooky family members—the ability to find humor in almost anything. ("So you had a good time at that wake, too, Pat?") This gift helped us see the absurdity in the way parents judge their children, and the ridiculous ways they brag about them. ("Patty and Gina, did I tell you my daughter, Misty Blue, led the preschool soccer team in scoring?")

With that, we came up with a brilliant idea (which is pretty amazing because anyone who knows us knows neither of us is that bright). We would write and self-publish our first book—a book that explores the humorous, heartwarming side of raising an "imperfect" child in a world preoccupied with perfection. An honest-to-imperfectness book that shows parents of "imperfect kids" that they are not alone and provides the insights, information, and inspiration they need to help their children succeed. A book we just felt compelled to call *Shut Up About Your Perfect Kid*.

When we pitched the idea to other parents of children with disabilities with whom we shared an "imperfection connection," they were all over it. "You have to do this! We're so sick of people bragging about their perfect kids and never asking about ours!" Fueled by their support, we consulted Gina's disability specialist, LeeAnn Karg, MEd, and began writing our book. (We will include many valuable tips from LeeAnn on the following pages.) We also created and trademarked The Movement of Imperfection to encourage people to openly talk about why they're proud of their imperfect kids.

Word of our book and The Movement of Imperfection spread. Before long, we received our first invitation to speak for the Parent/Professional Advocacy League (PAL), a highly respected organization that promotes a strong voice for families of children and adolescents with mental health needs.

We were shocked and scared to death when they asked us to be the keynote speakers at their annual dinner in front of 250 families and professionals.

"Are you s-s-sure th-they said, s-s-speakers, Pat?"

Even our husbands were amazed. "Let's get this straight. Someone actually wants to pay to listen to you?"

We were worried about what we would tell the audience (and whether we would bore them to tears) when a dear friend gave us some valuable advice. "Gina and Patty," she said. "Just tell your stories. Speak from the heart. That's all they want."

And that's precisely what we did. We laughed and cried with the audience, recounting the pain of discovering our daughters' disabilities, joking about our frustrations with our perfection-preoccupied society, and sharing the many gifts our daughters have given us. When we were done, we were shocked to find a line of about fifty people waiting to speak with us.

Soon after, we began receiving requests to speak at parenting, mental health, and autism conferences in Massachusetts and in other exotic parts of the country.

"Pack your bags, Gene! We're going to Akron, Ohio, the birthplace of rubber and oatmeal."

"Pat, I thought it couldn't get any better after speaking in Southern Illinois, home of the world's largest catsup bottle."

Wherever we traveled, people patiently lined up to talk to us and share their stories. Though we were flattered by it all (and still are), we eventually realized that The Movement of Imperfection was no longer about our kids or about us. *It was about all the disabled individuals and their caretakers who have so desperately wanted to talk and be heard.* We're not quite sure when, but somewhere along the line, we realized we weren't really there to speak, but to listen. And we have.

We've listened to mothers:

"My son is twenty-seven and bipolar. I really wish The Movement of Imperfection had been around when he was growing up. I felt so alone."

"Are you kidding me? I would have loved to have beaten a bragging mother over the head with this book just last week."

We've had the opportunity to hear from fathers, who too often hold in their feelings:

"This was so helpful to me. My wife goes to support groups, talks to complete strangers, and feels better. Guys don't share that kind of stuff. I have no one to talk to about my daughter's autism."

We listened to grandparents:

"Its really hard on me. I have to watch my daughter and granddaughter suffer. Their lives are so hard."

We've even talked with parents who have experienced what we all fear most—the loss of a child to suicide. They've amazed us with their courage and willingness to help others.

"It's too late for my son, but I'm here to help other parents who might be able to save their kids."

We also had the privilege of attending a National Alliance on Mental Illness (NAMI) gala and hearing announcer, actor, and former NFL star Terry Bradshaw speak eloquently about his battle with depression.

He said, "I'm a man with a lot of issues. But it's not my issues that define me. It's what I do with them."

Perhaps nothing impacted us more than our conversation with Todd, a man with a mental illness who approached us at the NAMI Pennsylvania state conference and said, "I want to thank you. Your children are lucky. My parents dealt with my illness by trying to beat it out of me."

There's no question, this remarkable journey has made us richer in ways we never thought possible. It's led us to kind, honest, real people from all walks of life whom we never would have met otherwise. People who have had the courage to openly share their proudest moments and their darkest days, and have taught us how to embrace differences in ourselves, in our children, and in others.

And to think, we thought we were alone. Maybe we really aren't that bright.

Okay, we'll shut up now.

WARNING!

Shut Up About Your Perfect Kid is a high-speed, turbulent ride with sharp turns and sudden drops.

Readers with high-blood pressure, heart disease, neck problems, motion sickness, or general poor health may find their condition aggravated by this reading adventure.

Please remain buckled in at all times and enjoy the imperfect ride!

Shut Up About Your Perfect Kid

The Movement of Imperfəction

They are here. There. And everywhere. You can hear them buzzing at spelling bees. Running at the mouth at track meets. Even trumpeting at concerts. They are the parents of those "perfect" kids. You know them—those people you meet in life who love to tell you how smart, athletic, gifted, and talented (blah, blah, blah) their kids are without your ever even asking.

"Nice to meet you, Gina. What do you do for a living?"

"I'm a freelance writer."

"Speaking of writing, my four-year-old son is already writing in cursive."

So how exactly are you supposed to respond to these child-worshiping chatterboxes? Especially when you have kids who (How can we say this delicately?) aren't exactly poster children for perfection.

Kids, well, like ours.

We probably should explain up front that though we refer to them as our kids, we're not married or life partners (not that there's anything wrong with that). We're actually sisters. Not the kind you find in habits, though we certainly have our share of bad ones. We're the other kind—the DNA- and childhood-bedroom-sharing kind. (For visualization purposes, you might think of us as Mary Kate and Ashley minus the twinness and the thinness.)

And in addition to sharing the same parents and a lot of the same imperfect traits—sloppiness, disorganization, lack of discipline, immaturity (in the spirit of saving paper and the forests, we won't list

[1]

them all)—we have something else in common. Something that a lot of sisters don't share.

We're both raising daughters with disabilities.

And that's not so easy to admit these days. Because whether we like it or not (and we don't), we live in a perfection-preoccupied society. A society that admires people who live in perfect houses, are married to perfect spouses, have perfect bodies, and of course, above all, have perfect children. (For those of you keeping score at home, we're both batting .000.)

For many of us parents, this perfection-palooza starts early on in our parenting careers. Usually from the moment our kids are born— when we look for creative ways to make our children stand out and be admired by others.

"That's a nice-lookin' baby, Patty. So tell us, how did she score on the **Apgar**?"

"Well, Michael and I were pleased with the results, though they did take some points off for her conehead and **jaundice**."

"Oh, that's too bad. Our little Mandy aced hers. The doctor said he's never seen such a perfect baby."

We should point out that this pattern doesn't occur only with parents of young children. No sir. We've met parents who brag about their children at every stage of life.

"Did I tell you my son, Malcolm, just got a fellowship for his work with garlic?"

"Would you believe my son, Albert, still has all his teeth at age seventy-eight?"

Nor does it happen with "perfect" strangers. Even our own loving, but nonetheless perfection-crazed mother has been known to brag about us, which is particularly amusing, since she knows better than anyone how vastly imperfect we are.

"I told all the seniors at the flu shot clinic that you guys signed a publishing deal with Random House!"

"Ma! Stop doing that! It's embarrassing!"

"Yeah, Ma, have you forgotten the name of our book?"

"Oh, stop it. I'm a mother; I'm supposed to brag about my smart girls. Now both of you do me a favor and grow your nails. You don't want to be signing books with them looking like that."

Ask Us About Our Kids

For the record, we're not saying we don't want to hear parents talk about their high-achieving kids anymore (though we certainly see how some could make that leap from the name of our book). We just want them to ask about *ours*. Because even though our kids may not be gifted athletes, students, or musicians (or room cleaners), they've given us plenty of reasons to be proud. Reasons most people don't even think about.

Patty, for example, the older sister, is proud of Jennifer, her seventeen-year-old **bipolar** daughter, for her courage and maturity.

"Jenn, are you sure you want to get up and speak in front of all those people at that suicide prevention fund-raiser?"

"Well, Mom, I am nervous, but I want to do this. Sometimes I feel like no one can relate to me. This is my chance to be heard."

And Gina, an avid athlete, is proud of Katie, her fifteen-year-old daughter with **Asperger's syndrome,** not for the way she bounces a ball, but for the ways she bounces back from adversity time and again.

"Mom, it's okay that I didn't get invited to that party with my friends. I'm just lucky to have friends."

Because we've struggled so much trying to find a place for our kids in this perfection-obsessed society, we become frustrated when other parents don't share the same struggles, and often resent the fact that they don't understand ours.

"Jenn's been so depressed and anxious. We were so relieved when we learned the hospital had a bed available for her."

"Oh, Patty, I know just how you feel. I was a nervous wreck waiting for Rumer to get into that elite soccer camp. Thank God we got the last spot!"

Sometimes, we even feel like we're on a completely different planet from these parents.

"Gina, you're so lucky your kids don't play sports. The fees are outrageous."

"And you're lucky your kids don't have issues. Therapy is no bargain, either."

But even though our children have different strengths, challenges, and ways of thinking, don't we all want the same things for our kids? Like for them to be happy, successful, and accepted?

Our daughters with disabilities have helped us see that. And through their beautiful blue eyes (if we may be so bold as to brag), we've been able to view the humor, irony, and absurdity in the ways so many parents judge and live through their children.

"Sorry, ladies, I can't go out for drinks tonight. I have to work on my chocolate volcano for the science fair."

And to openly admit how far we all are from perfection.

"Gina, your house is so clean. How do you manage to keep it that way?"

"Oh, I just throw everything in the closets and under the beds."

For us, it's all very ironic. As parents, our job description calls for us to teach our kids and help them become better people, yet our daughters are the ones who have taught us and made us better. Their courage and resilience have given us the strength to do what we've been so reluctant to do our entire lives: to be real and to accept and embrace imperfections in ourselves, in our kids—and in others.

And so with tribute to these blissfully imperfect young ladies, we created this imperfect book and started speaking around the country to introduce The Movement of Imperfction. This long-overdue movement invites parents to come out of their messy closets and celebrate the joys, gifts, milestones, and even quirks of their imperfect children. And, of course, to finally do some bragging. Here. There. And everywhere.

"May I take your order?"

"Yes, I'd like a Whopper. And speaking of whoppers, my autistic child just told his first lie!"

We invite you to join The Movement of Imperfction by talking openly about your imperfect child and helping this wacky world see what our daughters have now made so clear to us—that the true beauty of our children lies not in how many goals they score or A's they earn, but in who they are inside.

Sounds like an imperfectly good idea to us. (We would know.)

The Truth About Lying and Children with Autism

As our disability specialist, LeeAnn Karg, MEd, explains, lying is a milestone for many children with autism spectrum disorders (ASDs):

Developmentally, most children with autism view the world from a single, *concrete* perspective: everyone shares exactly the same thoughts and feelings. Lying requires several perspectives: the true details of the event, the created lie, the realization that thoughts are private, the understanding that every choice has a consequence, and the discovery that one can still choose a negative behavior. Therefore, lying can be viewed as reaching new developmental milestones . . . and as a real reason to celebrate!

Not to brag, but *all* our children seem to have mastered this skill. Yeah, yeah, we know you want us to shut up about our lying kids!

For more information on this and other disability topics, visit LeeAnn's website, kargacademy.com.

The Movement of Imperfǝction encourages people to be honest and real and, above all, to face their imperfections. We were excited to learn that people have really embraced it, particularly when they visited our website (www.shutupabout.com) and completed the following sentence:

You Know You've Got Issues When . . .

✔ Your Asperger's son tells you he "missed having lunch with the principal today."

✔ Telemarketers call your house and hang up *on you*.

✔ Your idea of a family vacation is to gather around the kitchen island.

✔ Without remembering requesting them, you begin receiving e-mail newsletters from *Psychiatric Times*.

✔ The entire pharmacy staff knows your name, your address, and the name of your first pet.

✔ You've diagnosed Amelia Bedelia with a nonverbal learning disability.

✔ Your son gets a sticker at Wal-Mart and then proceeds to eat it.

✔ Your child's occupational therapist tells you your voice is "probably annoying to your child."

✔ You come home from a quiet, getaway weekend with your spouse and discover that your house is wrapped in crime scene tape.

And finally . . .

✔ Each one of your children has his or her own attorney.

PART I

The Loss of a Perfect Dream

We must embrace pain and
burn it as fuel for our journey.

—KENJI MIYAZAWA

Welcome to Holland

BY EMILY PERL KINGSLEY

I am often asked to describe the experience of raising a child with a disability—to try to help people who have not shared that unique experience to understand it, to imagine how it would feel. It's like this . . .

When you're going to have a baby, it's like planning a fabulous vacation trip—to Italy. You buy a bunch of guide books and make your wonderful plans. The Coliseum. The Michelangelo David. The gondolas in Venice. You may learn some handy phrases in Italian. It's all very exciting.

After months of eager anticipation, the day finally arrives. You pack your bags and off you go. Several hours later, the plane lands. The stewardess comes in and says, "Welcome to Holland."

"Holland?!?" you say. "What do you mean Holland?!? I signed up for Italy! I'm supposed to be in Italy. All my life I've dreamed of going to Italy."

But there's been a change in the flight plan. They've landed in Holland and there you must stay.

The important thing is that they haven't taken you to a horrible, disgusting, filthy place, full of pestilence, famine, and disease. It's just a different place.

So you must go out and buy new guide books. And you must learn a whole new language. And you will meet a whole new group of people you would never have met.

It's just a different place. It's slower-paced than Italy, less flashy than Italy. But after you've been there for a while and you catch your breath, you look around . . . and you begin to notice that Holland has windmills . . . and Holland has tulips. Holland even has Rembrandts.

But everyone you know is busy coming and going from Italy . . . and they're all bragging about what a wonderful time they had there. And for the rest of your life, you will say "Yes, that's where I was supposed to go. That's what I had planned."

And the pain of that will never, ever, ever, ever go away . . . because the loss of that dream is a very very significant loss.

But . . . if you spend your life mourning the fact that you didn't get to Italy, you may never be free to enjoy the very special, the very lovely things . . . about Holland.

CHAPTER 1

Snowflakes and Disney World

Out of the World of Parent Fantasy
Comes the Scary Reality

When does it happen? That precise moment when you realize that despite your best-laid plans, you've completely and utterly lost control of your life? It's a question we often pose to each other, though in a more direct and simple way.

"Hey Pat, when did our lives take that left turn into Crazyville?"

"Oh that's easy, Gene; when we had kids."

It's not like we made plans to go there, or ever, in our wildest dreams, imagined our lives would head in that direction. Like a lot of prospective parents, we had plans—dreams and expectations for our future children's lives. We wanted them to enjoy the same happy, relatively normal childhoods we had. For us, being challenged meant finding a way not to upset our loving, generous, and sometimes forceful Italian grandmother.

"Gina, come here and finish your drink."

"But Nana, I don't like highballs. And besides, I'm only six."

Yes, easy, carefree childhoods. That was the plan, until that painful moment when we realized our children's lives—and the lives of our entire family—would never be "normal."

Gina's "Chilling" Dose of Reality

Some things just aren't funny.

The snowflake essay Gina uncovered in her then ten-year-old-daughter Katie's backpack sure wasn't. Gina had always thought of

[11]

snowflakes as light and airy. But the one in this essay? It was dark and heavy.

As she read it, Gina instantly felt the weight of the dark words before her:

> *If I were a snowflake falling, I would be sneaky and clever, too, and when I fall I would strike. . . . After I am going to my school, it is time for revenge. As I'm walking down, I ran into the principal and knocked her over. Oh no, I ran over the principal. Oh well, I'll just leave her there. The students are working, not for long. Here I go. Fear me, ha ha ha. I charge right into the school and damage everything before my school blows up 5, 4, 3, 2, 1. Bye, school. I won't be missing it. I flow away fast. Now what should I do next now that my school is gone? World and I have a present for all, a bomb. And also one last thing: beware of me.*

Oh, it's not like Gina wasn't warned about it. Earlier in the day, while she was working comfortably in her warm home office, she'd received a call from Katie's fifth-grade teacher. When the phone rang and the name of her school district flashed on the caller ID, Gina knew something was wrong. The letters may have appeared small, but to Gina, they lit up like a nuclear meltdown warning: "Danger, Will Robinson!"

Almost instantly, Gina felt a familiar burn in her stomach. "Oh no! Not again!" she cried out, startling her little dog, Max, who was napping by her feet.

Gina had no idea what the call was about this time, though she knew it wouldn't be good. They never were.

"Mrs. Gallagher, it's the school **psychologist.** Katie had another meltdown today."

"Mrs. Gallagher, it's the school nurse. Katie's here with another stomachache."

"Mrs. Gallagher, Katie's hand flapping has really increased. The other kids have noticed."

Over the years, the calls from the school had been relatively sparse, maybe one or two every few months. But in the first few months of

Katie's fifth-grade year, Gina had received more calls than the Jerry Lewis telethon.

With a disorder that affected her ability to relate to other children, Katie was different from other kids, and the struggles of dealing with her differences were escalating along with the school calls.

Remember to breathe, Gina reminded herself as she shakily put down her cocoa cup, picked up the phone, and braced herself for the bad news that was sure to come.

"H-H-Hello?" she stuttered.

"Mrs. Gallagher, this is Katie's teacher."

"Yes, what is it? What's wrong?"

"Well, something very upsetting happened at school today."

"What was it?" Gina asked, impatiently.

"Well, for the holiday break, I asked the class to write a snowflake essay . . ."

It might have been stress or her warped sense of humor, but Gina started to giggle.

"Mrs. Gallagher, are you there?"

"Yes, it's just that I fail to see how anything upsetting can come out of a snowflake essay."

"Well, this is *very* serious."

"Go ahead, I'm listening," Gina responded, fighting back laughter.

"Mrs. Gallagher, in her snowflake essay, your daughter threatened to blow up the school."

"Come again?"

"You heard me. Katie wrote a snowflake essay and threatened to blow up the school."

Gina couldn't help but laugh.

"We have to take these things very seriously, Mrs. Gallagher."

"I'm sure you do, but you can't honestly think Katie would hurt anybody? She wouldn't hurt a fly. She doesn't even like eating animal crackers."

"Believe me, Mrs. Gallagher, I'm not afraid of Katie."

"You shouldn't be. I'm not sure she knows how to build a bomb. She barely has her multiplication tables down," Gina responded, tipping back in her chair and twisting the phone cord around her fingers.

"I've made the principal aware and she doesn't think we need to alert the police."

"The police? You thought about calling the police?" Gina asked, straightening up in her chair, as she pictured her sweet ten-year-old in prison stripes.

"Yes. As I said, we have to take these things seriously."

"Can I see a copy of this essay?" Gina blurted out.

"Of course. I'll send it home in Katie's backpack."

By the end of the school day, Gina was frantically pacing at the bus stop, waiting for her "Little Unabomber" to come home.

"Hi, Mom," Katie said, climbing off the bus in her usual awkward way of two feet on a step.

"Give me your backpack! I need your backpack!" Gina demanded.

"Sheesh. Here!" Katie replied, slowly shrugging it off her little shoulders.

"Hurry up! Hurry up!" Gina shouted, wiggling her anxious fingers in Katie's face.

Holding the backpack in front of her as though it were a dirty diaper, Gina raced into the house and took the backpack into her office, where she opened it, extracted the weighty essay inside, and started to read. A part of Gina had thought it was all a mistake or a joke, but when she saw her daughter's name above the dark words on the page, she was smacked with the reality of it.

Oh my God! I have no idea what's going on in my daughter's head. Is she suicidal? Does she want to hurt others?

Distraught that she could be having these thoughts about a child she'd raised, Gina immediately confronted Katie.

"Katherine, did you write this?" she asked, staring down at her daughter and using Katie's formal "you're in trouble" name.

"Yes, Mom. Are you mad? Am I in trouble? Do I have to go to the principal?" Katie asked, tears falling down her face, leaving red blotches on her sensitive cheeks.

"Katie, why did you do this? Do you know how serious this is?" Gina cried.

"Mom, I didn't mean it. I did it to be funny. The boys next to me were talking about hurting the principal and I just wanted to make them laugh."

"Why? Why would you do that?"

"I wanted to fit in, Mom. I'm different! I hate being different. All I want to do is fit in! The kids all think I'm weird! I can't take it anymore, Mom!" Katie said, bursting into full sobs.

"Oh, honey, don't say that! You're not different! You're just like everybody else," Gina said, but deep in her heart, she knew her daughter was right. And it hurt her like no other hurt she had ever experienced.

Gina hugged Katie and walked her to her room. "Honey, Mommy has some things she needs to take care of. We'll talk about this later." Then she went into *her* room, closed the door, and cried like a baby, silently asking God, *Why did you give my daughter this disability? Why? Why does she have to suffer? And why me? I'm not strong enough for this! I can't handle this!*

For the first time in her thirty-eight years of living, Gina Gallagher felt like she wanted to die. She couldn't bear the thought of being there to watch her daughter struggle for the rest of her life.

Patty's "Wild Ride" into Reality

Our mother always said, "There must be nothing worse than losing a child." Patty never understood what she meant until she had a child of her own, and thought she might lose her, though in a different way.

"Don't leave me! Come back! Mom, help me!"

"Keep walking, Michael! Don't look back!" Patty commanded her husband, tightly squeezing his hand as they walked together down the cold, sterile hallway.

She paused as Michael stopped and removed his steamed-up glasses to wipe away the tears flowing beneath them.

What are we doing here? Patty wondered to herself. *This can't be happening!*

She had, after all, led a happy, normal childhood. The only hospital in her childhood was *General Hospital*. Now here she was leaving her eleven-year-old daughter, Jennifer, all by herself in a real hospital. A *mental* hospital.

At that moment, Patty wasn't sure if she had lost her daughter forever. But the truth was, she had been losing Jennifer for a few years.

She actually knew something was terribly wrong when Jennifer was just eight. Patty and her family were on a dream family vacation in Disney World—"the Happiest Place on Earth."

The evening parade had just ended. Mickey, Minnie, and the gang had floated away into the sunset, leaving Patty's family and her favorite characters—our mom, dad, brother, and Gina—behind. Patty couldn't help but smile as she looked up and down the colorful streets at all the families grinning from mouse ear to mouse ear.

That is, until she was interrupted by an all-too-familiar and painful screech.

"Why do they have to leave? Why!" shouted eight-year-old Jennifer, who was sitting on the curb, hugging the Minnie Mouse on her sweatshirt and flailing her legs.

"Oh that's just great! It's even happening here!" muttered Patty,

Why In-Patient Hospitalization Was Necessary

Patty brought Jennifer to the hospital for two reasons. First, she wanted to ensure Jennifer's safety and the safety of her two other children. Secondly, she wanted to get an accurate diagnosis for Jennifer. LeeAnn Karg, MEd, explains why in-patient hospitalization was necessary:

In-patient hospitalizations are essential for effective emergency psychiatric consultation. They provide the safest environment for the greatest number of specialists to simultaneously evaluate your child under controlled environmental and medical conditions.

helplessly realizing that the Magic Kingdom, the place where "dreams come true," was about to turn into her personal nightmare.

It really shouldn't have surprised her. Over the past few months, Jennifer's moods had become increasingly unpredictable. She would cry for hours and become violent about the smallest things.

"Why? Why can't I wear my jelly shoes?"

"Because, Jenns, it's thirty degrees outside and snowing."

"WAAAAAHHHH! I hate you!"

She was also becoming alarmingly destructive.

"Jennifer Marie! What are you doing with my scissors and the family picture?"

"I'm cutting myself out. I don't want to be part of this family anymore."

And during that dream vacation to Disney—the one Jennifer had been excited about for months ("How many days till we go, Mom? Tell me! Tell me!")—her moods were just as unpredictable. Somehow Patty had actually thought Jenn's problems would disappear, but instead of seeing Snow White, Patty saw her daughter magically transform into Grumpy, Saddy, and Angry.

"Why do I have to go in the haunted mansion? I already have a witch for a mother."

The sadness was the hardest part. Jenn seemed to have no interest in the places the family went or the people who accompanied us.

"No, Mommy. I don't feel like riding Mr. Toad's Wild Ride with Nana!"

"How about going for a swim? Your cousins are all in the pool."

"No, thank you. I want to stay here in the hotel room."

As Patty dragged a screaming Jennifer ("I hate you! I'm going to kill myself if we leave!") through the massive crowds toward the exit to the park, she glanced over at her four-year-old son, Mikey, who was resting comfortably in his stroller. *Why can't Jennifer be more like him? He's so easy!* Patty thought, while Jennifer hissed, "I hate you for making me leave!" and hurled a stuffed Minnie Mouse at Patty's head.

"Jenns, honey, it's okay," said Patty's husband, Michael, bending down to pat her back. "Mickey and Minnie just have to go home now, and so do we. We'll come back. I promise."

"It's all her fault," Jennifer screeched, pointing at Patty.

"You stupid jerk, Jennifer!" shouted her "sympathetic" big sister, Jules. "Don't talk to Mom like that!"

"Jules! Please shut up!" a stressed-out Patty yelled. People in mouse ears stopped to give her looks of disgust. Oh, she knew what they were thinking—*Hey, bad mother, why don't you just smack that spoiled rotten kid?* Before she had Jennifer she would have thought the same thing. Now she knew not to judge. She also knew she had to get Jennifer out of there—fast. The last thing the Disney PR people needed on their happy streets was a real-life Cruella De Vil screaming at her kid.

Dragging Jennifer ahead with newfound purpose (*I've got to get this bratty kid the hell out of here!*), Patty tried to calm herself. She began humming her favorite Disney songs to maintain her sanity.

Both a little scared . . . Beauty and the Beast.

Twenty minutes later, when Jennifer had screamed herself into exhaustion, Patty's family exited the tram to the parking lot and walked toward their rental car. When they got to the car, an exhausted Patty climbed into the passenger seat and told her husband, "Michael, let's get the hell out of here. I can't stand to spend one more minute in the Happiest Place on Earth."

Our Neighbors in Crazyville

At the time we experienced these life-altering incidents, we thought we were alone and no one understood our struggles. Since then, we have met hundreds of parents who have experienced their own painful realizations about their children. Parents who have had to commit their children or see them locked up in prison. What's amazed us is how these people have managed not only to survive these experiences, but also to learn from them. We discovered this at our first speaking engagement when a lovely woman announced, "Yeah, my bipolar son is in jail again."

"That's terrible. We're so sorry," we said.

"I'm not. At least I know he's safe, off drugs, and getting three squares a day."

We're pretty sure her parental fantasies never involved her son in an orange jumpsuit, but somehow she's managed to focus on the positive and make the most of her time in Crazyville.

CHAPTER 2

Straight Hair to Straightjackets

Where the Dreams of Parental Perfection Started—and Fell Apart

A t one point or another, long before they enter the wondrous world of parenthood, people fantasize about what their future children will be like. Prima ballerinas and star quarterbacks often come to mind. Even we, the self-proclaimed poster sisters of imperfection, had picture-perfect images of what our kids' lives would be like.

Gina's Story: Boys Will Be Girls

Gina definitely had detailed plans for her future children, which she shared with Patty one evening in the confines of our shared, cramped bedroom (on one of those rare childhood occasions when we got along).

"Pat, my kids are going to be great students and athletes like me. But unlike me, they will be boys."

"Well, you kinda do look like a boy."

But on the day her firstborn entered the world, Gina realized things don't always turn out the way you plan.

"Congratulations, Mr. and Mrs. Gallagher. You have a healthy baby girl!" the doctor announced.

"A what?" Gina asked the doctor, who had a tendency to mumble.

"A baby girl," he said with remarkable clarity.

"There must be some mistake. I'm having a boy. I can't possibly have a girl. I won't know how to do her hair."

But when they placed the warm eight pound, six ounce pink bundle in her arms, Gina had to admire her work.

"I have to say, she's pretty cute. And look at those long fingers," she remarked to her husband, Mike. "I bet she can palm a basketball already. How about we name her Katherine after your mother?"

As Gina looked more closely at Katie, she was hit with a rush of panic. "Mike, this kid can't be mine. She's got blue eyes, frosted blond hair, and long, thin legs. They must have mixed up the babies, and somehow we ended up with Christie Brinkley's kid!"

"No, Gene, I already checked. Her bracelet matches yours."

As the days and weeks progressed, Katie became the love of Gina's life. She was such a happy, easygoing baby. Gina would put her in her Exersaucer (a stationary play toy, not a scary movie staring Linda Blair) and Katie would hop up and down for hours. Even our parents were amazed at how easy Katie was.

"You got a great one, Gene. She's such a good kid."

"Yes, most babies her age are into everything. We can't believe how long she can sit still."

Our wise, loving Italian grandmother, Nana Terrasi, was enamored with Katie, too; at least, that's how Gina interpreted her words.

"Gina, I love all my great-grandchildren. But this one is different. I'm telling you, this baby is special."

Gina definitely didn't need convincing Katie was special. In fact, she was fairly certain Katie was gifted. By eighteen months, Katie was speaking in sentences and arranging her toys in fascinating and creative patterns. When she was just three, she lined all her stuffed animals in a row up and down the stairs and said, "Look, Mommy! I made a roller coaster." And one day when she spotted Katie feeding herself alternating using her right and left hands, Gina was over the moon.

"Look, Mike! She's gonna be a switch-hitter! I knew she was athletic."

As she grew, Katie became increasingly beautiful. Her hair, which started out with highlights, went completely blond, and her eyes remained a beautiful blue. Gina fell so in love with Katie, she eventually overcame her fear of doing Katie's hair.

She did notice that Katie had a few quirky habits—like constantly jumping up and down, shaking her hands in front of her, and watching TV out of the sides of her eyes. But in Gina's mind, these things just added to her baby's charm. ("She does the cutest things!") One of Gina's close childhood friends (also a mother) wasn't as impressed by it. "Genie, why is she doing that? Don't you think that's strange?"

She's just jealous because Katie is so beautiful, Gina thought.

Others seemed to want to criticize Katie, too. Like the owner of the day care center Katie attended when she was four. On Katie's last day at the center, the owner turned to Gina and said, "Your daughter has problems, and you're not helping."

"Excuse me?" Gina asked, sure she was hearing things.

"Trust me. She's got some needs, and you're not helping her. You're constantly picking her up and carrying her. You just wait and see."

Concerned, Gina turned to her husband. "Mike, do you think there's something wrong?"

"Gene, don't listen to her. She's just bitter because we're taking Katie out of her day care. Katie's perfect. Just look at her!"

PRESCHOOL PREMONITION

When Katie was four, Gina was excited to start her in preschool. Not even a month or so into the school year, Gina was pulled aside by one of Katie's teachers, who looked like she was about twelve.

"Mrs. Gallagher, we need to talk," she said, reminding Gina of those times when her husband looked at the credit card bill first.

"What's my little prodigy up to now?" Gina asked, beaming.

"Well . . . she has a cutting problem," the teacher blurted out.

"Dear God! I saw a special about self-mutilation on MTV. I had no idea Katie was doing that."

"No, not that kind of cutting," she said, holding up a paper gingerbread man that looked like it had gone a few rounds with Jaws.

Big deal, she can't cut, Gina thought. *So she'll never be a hairstylist or a plastic surgeon.*

"It's not just cutting," the teacher continued, barely getting the words out. "She has a poor pencil grip, too."

So she won't be a bowling scorer, either. Who cares? Gina rationalized to herself.

"I'm sorry, Mrs. Gallagher, but these are signs of motor difficulties."

Gina had to laugh. She was starting to think teachers were just looking to find things wrong with Katie. First the day care owner had told Gina that she hugged Katie too much, and now this teacher was pointing out problems with Katie's pencil grip, of all things. Was Katie so perfect that this was all they could come up with? Gina wanted to tell them to stop nitpicking about Katie and help kids who had *real* problems.

By the end of the school year, Katie's cutting and pencil holding had improved, and Gina and the teacher decided Katie was ready to move on to the big show—kindergarten.

On the day of the kindergarten screening, Gina was a nervous wreck, doing her best to prepare her daughter.

"Okay, Katie, if Thomas the Train leaves the station at two o'clock and another train rolls into the station—"

"Mom, stop! You're confusing me!"

To Gina's delight, Katie passed the screening. *Everything is fine,* Gina thought, taking a deep breath.

THE WHEELS ON THE BUS GO ROUND AND ROUND (THEN COME OFF)

On Katie's first day of kindergarten, Gina felt like a mother sending her soldier child off to war.

"Bye-bye, Katie. I love you, honey! I'll miss you!"

"Mom, can you get off the bus now?"

Gina was beside herself. For the first time in five years, she had no idea what Katie was up to. Every day when Katie returned home from school, Gina would rummage through her Scooby-Doo backpack, searching for a shred of information about Katie's "secret life" at school.

Not even a few weeks into the school year, Gina found it—an impersonal form letter from Katie's teacher requesting permission for Katie to undergo some testing. Gina was devastated. *Oh no! Not this again!* Immediately, she picked up the phone and called the teacher.

"What's this testing all about? Why didn't someone tell me?" Gina cried.

"I'm sorry about that, Mrs. Gallagher. We just noticed that Katie has really been struggling with the day-to-day routines and interacting with the other children. And her pencil grip is poor."

Not the damn pencil grip problem again, Gina thought. *What's wrong with these people?*

Gina was shattered, but she decided to grant permission for the testing, seriously thinking the whole thing was a terrible mistake.

Within a few weeks, Gina was invited to discuss the results in a **team meeting.** For those unfamiliar with this concept, a team meeting is like a celebrity roast without the jokes. You are thrown into a room with five, six, or sixteen hundred teachers who tell you everything that's wrong with your child (the celebrity). (See chapter 7 for more information, including valuable tips for managing team meetings.)

At first, everyone seemed very friendly and complimentary of Katie. "Oh, she's so adorable. And we love her clothes."

"Thank you." Gina beamed with pride. *This is going to be fun,* she thought.

Then they proceeded to go through test results and use terminology Gina had never heard, including mentioning some kind of test called a Wechsler Intelligence Scale for Children, or **WISC.** Silly Gina thought WISC was laundry detergent.

Gina sat there in a state of complete confusion until the "master of ceremonies," or team leader, broke through and said, "Your daughter's social and academic struggles may indicate a **learning disability** of some sort."

Gina's head started to pound. Clearly, she was no longer having fun.

"But she passed the kindergarten screening. Everything must be okay," Gina rationalized.

At that, one of the administrators said, "Yes, she did, but we thought her presentation was awkward. She got all the answers right, but she made poor eye contact."

Gina just sat there in silence, stunned.

"Mrs. Gallagher? Mrs. Gallagher? Are you okay?"

"Uh, yeah. I'm fine," Gina responded, desperately trying to hold in the tears that were now flooding her eyes.

"So do you have any questions?" the team leader asked, putting a box of Kleenex in front of Gina.

Gina had a million. Like why were they all looking at her funny?

And speaking Klingon? And passing each other glances? But all she could muster was: "What do you think is wrong with her?"

"Mrs. Gallagher, we're not able to diagnose your child," the team leader said. "Only a **neuropsychologist** can do that. But we can put her on an **Individual Education Plan,** or **IEP.** In fact, we'll work on that right now."

"That's wonderful news," Gina said, blotting her eyes and silently asking herself, *What the hell is an IEP?*

What seemed like three days later, Gina was sent on her way with a pile of papers that would have made an IRS auditor cringe. She felt completely overwhelmed and sick to her stomach.

When she got home, she immediately picked up the phone to call her husband.

"Mike, it was awful. I felt like I was on another planet. They were using words I never even heard of. And they told me they want to put her on something called an IUD."

"Birth control? Why the hell would they want to do that? She's only five!"

"No, it's not that. It's an I-something. Oh, I forget. It was so confusing. They were speaking in code," Gina cried. "I think it means Katie has special needs."

"Special needs? Where did they get that? Did they tell you what they think is wrong with her?"

"They wouldn't say, but they think she's really bad off, Mike. I can tell just by the way they were looking at each other. What are we going to do? How did this happen?" Gina cried.

"Calm down, Gene. It's probably nothing. I had some trouble when I was that age. I turned out all right. We'll figure something out."

Gina couldn't wait for that to happen. She didn't know what to do, until a friend suggested she call another mother who was a parent of a child with autism. "You should call her. She's been through all this stuff."

Gina called immediately.

"They told me there's something wrong with my daughter, and my husband and I have no idea what to do."

"Get her tested," the mother said.

"But they already tested her," Gina said, glancing at the pile of test results on her desk.

"No, you need to get an **independent educational evaluation** from a neuropsychologist. That way, you'll have documentation when you fight them for services."

"What's a *neuropsychologist*?" Gina asked, a bit perturbed that this woman, too, was speaking Klingon.

"It's a doctor who studies psychology and understands the different types of disabilities. We went to a wonderful one at Children's Hospital. You should call right away because it took us a year to get our appointment."

"A year? I can't wait a year. I need to find out what's wrong now!"

TESTING . . . 1, 2, $3,000 TESTING

Gina asked the school to provide a list of neuropsychologists and settled on one in Worcester, Massachusetts. The appointment was two months away, and Gina took it, knowing she was lucky to get one so soon. She was also relieved to learn that her health insurance would cover the cost.

In preparation for the exam, Gina was asked to complete several health and behavioral questionnaires about Katie's development. The endless questions made her feel more like Katie was being vetted for head of the CIA.

"How old was your child when she said her first word?

Rolled over?

Pointed?

Uttered a sentence?"

For Gina, who can barely remember what she had for breakfast each day, the task was insurmountable on her own. She turned to her husband for help.

"Mike, do you remember when Katie said her first word?"

"Well, I remember the Patriots were playing the Steelers and she said something just before Bledsoe threw that pick with two minutes, and thirty-five seconds left in the half. But I can't for the life of me remember when it was."

The actual examination took place over three afternoons. After the final session, the doctor walked Katie to the waiting room, where he found Gina pacing back and forth.

"So what is it? Will she grow out of it? Can she lead a normal life?"

"Mrs. Gallagher, we administered many tests. We'll analyze the results and get back to you within a few weeks."

A few weeks? Gina thought. She could barely last another minute, let alone two more weeks.

The wait was brutal even for Gina's mailman. ("Mrs. Gallagher, I have to tell you again. Please wait until the truck comes to a complete stop!") On the fifteenth day, Gina got what she was looking for—a big envelope from the doctor. She ripped it open and furiously scanned the report, desperately looking for an answer to what was wrong with her little girl.

"Katherine presented as an attractive, pleasant young girl who was casually attired and well groomed."

She has me to thank for that, Gina thought, beaming with pride.

The rest wasn't so pleasant—at least the parts Gina could under-

What Is a Neuropsychological Evaluation?

Impress your friends at your next cocktail party with this knowledge from LeeAnn Karg, MEd:

Neuropsychological evaluations focus on identifying and treating the functional deficits that can be created by structural damage, disease, and/or neurodevelopmental delays in specific areas or lobes of the brain. Neuropsychological evaluations can include but are not limited to the following areas:

✔ Intelligence   ✔ Memory

✔ Communication   ✔ Social interaction

✔ Movement   ✔ Emotional development

✔ Sensory processing   ✔ Executive functioning

For more information, visit kargacademy.com.

stand. "Katherine exhibited a high degree of systems reflective of a high-functioning Asperger's disorder."

Gina had never heard of Asperger's, but as she read on, she didn't want to learn any more about it. It said:

> A few people with Asperger's syndrome are very successful, and until recently were not diagnosed with anything, but were seen as brilliant, eccentric, absentminded, socially inept, and physically awkward. An Asperger's child may have a wonderful vocabulary and even demonstrate **hyperlexia,** but may not truly understand the nuances of language and may have difficulty with **language pragmatics**. Motor **dyspraxia** may be reflected in a tendency to be clumsy.

Dear God! Does anyone speak English anymore? Gina wondered.

Completely confused, she ran to her computer and discovered all she needed to know when she read, "Asperger's syndrome is high-functioning autism."

"Oh my God! My baby is autistic!" She wasn't even sure what it would all mean, but she knew it was bad.

Since it's never been her practice to wait until her husband comes home from work to break bad news ("Mike, when you come home, you might notice a slight dent in the garage door"), Gina picked up the phone and called him.

"I got Katie's test results," she said, sniffling.

"What do they say? Tell me!" he pleaded.

"She's got Asp—Asperger's," Gina replied, staring down at the report to make sure she had it right.

"She's got ass what?"

"Asperger's," she cried. "It's a type of autism. Our little girl has autism, Mike. It's never gonna go away."

Understanding Early Signs of Autism and Asperger's

At first, Gina didn't realize that Katie was exhibiting early signs of Asperger's. LeeAnn Karg has highlighted just a few of these signs below:

Pervasive developmental disorders (PDDs), otherwise known as autism spectrum disorders (ASDs), is a category of disorders involving significant developmental delays in language, movement, social skills, sensory processing, imagination/play, and behavior. Asperger's syndrome is often regarded as the mildest form in this category, with children demonstrating higher levels of language and intellectual development and more interest in social/peer interaction and activities. Early signs of pervasive developmental disorders can include the following:

LANGUAGE:
- ✔ Early language development followed by a sudden loss or lack of progress
- ✔ Inability to understand or use emotional expression in verbal or nonverbal communication
- ✔ Difficulty initiating, maintaining, and ending conversations
- ✔ Obsessive use of vocabulary and context well advanced for age

Patty's Story: The Perfect Family—Hair Today, Gone Tomorrow

Unlike Gina, who had dreams of athletic and academic grandeur for her future children, Patty's expectations were much simpler. She wanted three children. Each would possess the single physical attribute that had escaped Patty for much of her life, making her feel quite different from other children. ("What do you mean my hair is too curly for a Toni Tennille haircut, Mom? Everybody else has one!")

Understanding the Early Signs (continued)

SOCIAL SKILLS:

✔ Active avoidance of eye contact and interaction with familiar and unfamiliar people

✔ Inability to understand or engage in interactive communication or play (sharing objects or taking turns)

✔ Unusual attachment to or obsession with certain objects or topics

SENSORY PROCESSING:

✔ Active avoidance and resistance to imposed physical contact

✔ Unusual preference or aversion for smells/tastes/textures

✔ Unusual walking preferences involving specific areas of the foot (balancing or "perching" on toes, sides of feet, or heels)

✔ Delayed motor development, especially for balance and fine-motor tasks

BEHAVIOR:

✔ Unusual repetitive actions (hand flapping, spinning, bouncing), increasing in speed and intensity in response to internal stress or external/environmental activity level

✔ Significant distress around changes in routines

Yes, more than anything, Patty Terrasi dreamed of bringing three straight-haired children into the world.

She was so intent on realizing this dream that she searched endlessly for the "perfect" mate.

"Mom and Dad, I finally met someone!"

"That's wonderful, Patty. Does he come from a nice family?" asked our mother.

"Does he have a good job?" asked our father.

"Is he blind?" asked Gina.

"I'm not sure, but he has the straightest hair."

At age twenty-eight, Patty married Michael, the hair—err, man—of her dreams, and a year and a half later they welcomed their first child: a happy, healthy, straight-haired baby girl named Julianne. Patty fell in love with "Jules" and reached a grueling decision to stay home and raise her. ("No more wearing nylons? I'll do it, Michael. I'll stay home.")

Two years later, Patty was ecstatic to welcome her second child into the world, a seven-pound baby girl they named Jennifer Marie.

"Now Jules will have a baby sister to love, Michael," Patty enthused to her husband.

"But I thought you couldn't stand your sister growing up?"

From the moment Jennifer was born, Patty couldn't help but compare her two daughters.

"I don't get it, Michael. Jules had such light hair and pink skin. This baby is darker and looks like a coconut. And what's with that scraggly patch of hair?"

But by the time they took her home, baby Jennifer had blossomed into a beautiful, blue-eyed, straight-haired baby. Patty's plan for her "perfect" family was falling into place. ("Michael, just one more straight-haired kid and our family will be complete.")

From her first night home, it was clear that baby Jennifer was unique.

"Michael, wake up! Something's wrong with Jennifer!"

"Huh? What? What is it? What's wrong?" asked Michael, bolting out of bed.

"She slept through the night. No baby does that. Something's wrong."

But for the first few weeks and months of Jennifer's life, things could not have been any better. At about ten months, Jennifer developed separation anxiety. At first, Patty was flattered by the attention ("She likes me! She really likes me!"), but eventually Patty realized she couldn't leave Jennifer's side for a minute without causing an outburst.

"Here, Gene, hold Jenn while I sink this eight ball in the corner pocket."

"WAAAAAHHHHH!"

"You see? This is why I'm in no hurry to have kids, Pat. Now take your kid back and hand me my beer."

As both Jules and Jennifer grew older, they became increasingly different. Jules was a tomboy, and Jennifer the quintessential girly girl, constantly wearing dresses with matching jewelry and shoes. Their differences, however, didn't keep them from spending time together.

"Hey Jenn, do you want to play dollhouse after school?"

"Sure, Jules. I can't wait."

Jennifer was definitely the more sensitive of the two. If things didn't go her way, she would carry on for hours.

"Jenns, what's wrong? You've been in your room all day."

"Julie said I'm not beautiful. WAAAAAHHHHHH!"

Jennifer's sensitivity also made her very sweet and loving, particularly toward her younger brother, Michael (a straight-haired baby boy born four years after her), whom she showered with affection.

"Um, Jenn, it's ninety-eight degrees. Do you think you could get out of your little brother's face?"

"Okay, Mommy. But if it's cooler tomorrow, then can I get in his face?"

As early as age four, Jennifer showed she had a caring and sensitive heart rare in a child her age.

"Jennifer, honey, why did you smash your piggy bank?"

"Because, Mommy, I want to put the money in the box at church to help the poor people."

By the time Jennifer reached age eight, her sensitivity had deepened, often leading to full-blown **mood swings.**

"Jenn, why have you been crying all day? What's wrong?"

"I miss Nana Emily. I can't stop thinking about her."

"But Jenns, she's been in heaven for four years."

When Jennifer wasn't sad, she was agitated, walking around the house looking for someone to bother. Usually, it was her younger brother.

And whenever Patty tried to intervene, Jennifer would become more agitated and out of control.

"Jennifer, please leave your little brother alone."

"I'm running away. I hate you!"

DOCTOR, DOCTOR GIVE ME THE NEWS

When her family returned home from their Disney vacation, Patty immediately called her pediatrician and made an appointment.

"Something's wrong with my daughter. She's depressed and irritable. I'm afraid someone may have harmed her."

After examining Jennifer and conducting a series of blood tests, the pediatrician turned to Patty and said, "Mrs. Konjoian, I don't see anything medically wrong with your daughter. I suggest you take her to a psychologist." Patty couldn't believe it. *Who's crazy enough to take an eight-year-old to a shrink?* she silently wondered.

Answer? Patty and Michael.

Within a week, they were sitting in front of a psychologist, re-counting all the things they had observed with Jennifer—the sadness, **agitation,** and quick mood changes. At the end of that first visit, the doctor said, "With the severity and suddenness of the mood swings, it's possible Jennifer could have bipolar disorder."

"Have what?" asked Patty and her husband in unison.

"Bipolar disorder. You may know it as manic depression. I suggest you take her to a **neurologist** at Children's and get her checked out."

Patty and Michael were stunned. Immediately, they went home and searched the Internet for answers. They were saddened to find that there wasn't much information about bipolar disorder in children. *"Bipolar disorder is a mental illness characterized by periods of* **mania** *followed by periods of* **depression.** *Some signs of bipolar might include* **grandiosity,** *racing or suicidal thoughts, and* **hypersexuality."**

"Michael, I think that shrink is nuts. Jenn doesn't have any of these signs. She's just a child. This doctor doesn't know what she's talking about."

Nonetheless, Patty called Children's Hospital in Boston and was told she would have to wait six weeks for an appointment. The wait seemed like an eternity, particularly since Jennifer's emotional state was worsening. Her bad days were far outnumbering the good, and her aggression was escalating. She was also becoming increasingly sad, with no interest in things around her.

"Jenn, the neighborhood kids are all outside playing. Why don't you go and play with them?"

"No, Mommy, I don't feel like it. I'm just going to lie down."

When she wasn't sad, she was agitated, going out of her way to provoke her little brother.

"Mommy, Jenn won't leave me alone. She's scaring me, Mommy. Hide me!"

A "BREAK" IN THE ACTION

Jennifer's behavior was changing in other ways, as Patty noticed one evening when she went by Jennifer's room and saw Jenn lying on her bed and talking to herself. "Jenn, are you okay? Who are you talking to?"

"Mom, come here. I'm having a dream. I see Nana Emily," Jennifer announced in a strange, squeaky voice, referring to our grandmother who died when Jennifer was four.

"Where?" Patty asked, looking around the bed for a picture of Jenn's great-grandmother.

"Here in heaven."

"Huh?" Patty asked, sure she was hearing things.

"In heaven. She's holding me, Mom. I'm a baby and she's holding me in her arms."

"What is she saying?" Patty asked.

"She's saying, 'What a beautiful baby.'"

"What are *you* doing?"

When Should Your Child See a Therapist?
(Condensed from kargacademy.com)

As a parent, you know your child better than anyone else. If you feel your child needs help coping with a difficult life event, trust your instincts. Warning signs of childhood depression can include any *sudden and significant change* in normal activity patterns or interest levels involving:

- ✔ Academic achievement and/or participation
- ✔ Attention and memory
- ✔ Social interaction
- ✔ Self-esteem
- ✔ Mood
- ✔ Sleep patterns
- ✔ Appetite and/or weight
- ✔ Substance abuse
- ✔ Self-injurious behavior

"I'm coming down, Mom."

"Coming down from where, Jenn?"

"From heaven."

"How far down are you going?" Patty asked, concerned that Jenn might be paying a visit to that "other place."

"Wait! I'm going up again!"

"What do you see, Jenn?" Patty asked, fascinated and frightened by this elevator ride to heaven.

"I see Jesus. He's right there."

"Is he saying anything to you?"

"No, but I can see God, too. He's wearing a white robe with gold ties in the front and sandals."

"What's he saying?"

"Jenn, honey, what's he saying?"

And just like that, Jenn had fallen asleep. Fearful that Jennifer might be having a premonition about death, Patty raced to the phone and called the psychologist (whose number had been promoted to #2 on the speed dial, behind 911).

"She's having visions?" the psychologist asked. "Oh dear. Call Children's and tell them about this. It'll probably get your appointment moved up."

That's exactly what it did. "Can you bring her in tomorrow, Mrs. Konjoian?"

The next day, Patty and Michael took Jennifer to the ER at Children's. The **social worker** needed to learn more about the family's medical history.

"Mrs. Konjoian, let's start with you."

" . . . and my mother's cousin had a nervous breakdown, and my third cousin twice removed had anxiety . . ."

"Okay, Mrs. Konjoian, you can stop there. I think I have enough to go on."

Patty's husband just stared at her in disbelief.

After she finished answering the questions, Patty told the social worker about Jennifer's vision.

"The other night, my daughter had a beautiful dream about heaven and my grandmother. Have you heard anything like that before?"

"Yes we have, Mrs. Konjoian. We call them **psychotic episodes**."

"Oh," a dejected Patty said, thinking her name for it was so much more pleasant.

They then ran a series of diagnostic tests on Jennifer—all of which came back negative. "Mrs. Konjoian, we haven't found anything. We suggest you take your daughter to a **psychiatrist**."

Imperfect Trivia Question:
Was Dr. Frasier Crane on *Frasier* a psychologist or a psychiatrist?

If you answered psychiatrist, you are right and are probably watching entirely too much television.

Patty was getting frustrated. "Can't anyone freakin' tell me what's wrong with my kid?"

A week later, Patty and Michael were sitting in front of a psychiatrist, anxiously waiting to hear the fate of their daughter. Jennifer's

---

What's the Difference Between a Psychologist and a Psychiatrist?

It might seem like a simple question, but the truth is, many parents, including the two of us, weren't quite sure. LeeAnn Karg, MEd, offers this explanation:

Psychiatrists are medical doctors (MDs) who focus on the benefits and limitations of specific medications in treating disorders.

Psychologists are specialists (PhDs or PsyDs) who focus on teaching their patients to identify and resolve negative thought and behavior patterns through cognitive and behavioral intervention.

behavior was becoming more unpredictable, and Patty feared for her daughter's safety.

"Jennifer Marie, open this bathroom door right now."

"No! I'm gonna take all the medicines in here and kill myself."

Patty felt like something evil was overtaking her daughter, and she needed to know how to stop it.

"What's wrong with my baby?" Patty asked the psychiatrist, clutching Michael's hand.

"Your daughter's mood swings have come on suddenly. She needs to have a **CT scan** immediately."

Patty and Michael burst into tears, thinking the worst. "Oh no, it's a brain tumor." For the first time, Patty thought she might lose Jenn. "My God, Michael! What if there's something wrong with her? What would we ever do without her?"

The results of the CT scan came back negative, as did those of the subsequent **EEG** and **MRI** the doctored ordered. Patty felt a mixture of relief and sadness. Relief that it wasn't a tumor. Sadness because she knew it probably would be a mental illness. It had to be— Jennifer's behavior was too erratic. Even Jennifer's appearance, which used to give her pride, was proof that something was terribly wrong.

"Jenn, when's the last time you washed your hair?"

"I don't remember, Mommy."

The condition of her room was another sign of Jenn's disordered life. What was once a neat and orderly room had towels, clothes, and books strewn all over the floor. It broke Patty's heart, but she decided to pick her battles.

"Jenn, Mommy wants to tuck you in. Can you do me a favor and help me find your bed?"

The hardest part for Patty was dealing with Jenn's unpredictable moods. Patty would lie awake at night worrying. *Will she harm herself? Or her little brother?* There were times Patty thought she could, and she knew deep down that she had to get Jennifer out of the house. Several times Patty called 911 and brought Jenn to the emergency room, only to wait for hours and come home with more questions and worries.

It was the same pattern. On the way to the hospital, Jennifer would rage, but when the nursing staff questioned her, she was calm and polite.

"Jennifer, are you doing okay? Your mom says you're upset."

"I'm doing well, thank you," she would answer, flashing her most beautiful smile.

In fact, she was so polite that the hospital staff would look at Patty as though she were the one with the psychological problems, elevating Patty's anxiety.

"I swear, she just threatened to kill me."

"Mrs. Konjoian, I'm sorry. We can't admit her."

One day, Patty was sure Jennifer's behavior would land her in the hospital.

"Hello, 911? I'd like to report an emergency. My daughter has locked herself in our bathroom and threatened to jump out the window. I'm afraid she will harm herself. Can we check her into the hospital?"

"I'm sorry, we can't. She's not in imminent danger."

Patty was stunned. "What do I have to do? Wait until she goes splat before you take her?"

HOUSE OF HORRORS

Patty's house, which used to be calm, was like a war zone. Every day, Patty would gather "the troops" (Mikey and Jules) and give them strict instructions. "Okay, guys, here's the deal. Don't look at her. Don't breathe on her. Don't talk to her."

This is no way for them to live, Patty thought.

One night after a battle with her brother and sister, Jenn became so agitated that Patty had to wrestle her to the kitchen floor. They sat on the cold tile for what felt like hours with Patty's arms wrapped around Jennifer. Mikey entered the kitchen with a pillow and a blanket. He covered Jennifer with the blanket and placed the pillow behind his mother's back. "Here, Mommy. This will help your bad back."

In that instant, Patty was sick with worry. *What is this doing to him and Jules? Is this what they'll remember from their childhoods?* Patty's childhood had been so happy and normal. Didn't her kids deserve the same?

Types of Mood Swings with Bipolar Disorder

According to the National Institutes of Mental Health (NIMH), there are four types of mood episodes in bipolar disorder, each of which has a unique set of symptoms:

1. **HYPERMANIA:** The manic phase of bipolar disorder involves severe mood swings from hyperactivity, racing thoughts and speech, insomnia, heightened creativity, and feelings of euphoria, power, invincibility, and grandiosity to extreme anger, irritability, aggression, reckless "instant gratification" behaviors with little regard for consequences, poor judgment, delusions, and hallucinations.

2. **HYPOMANIA:** Hypomania is a less severe form of mania. People in a hypomanic state feel euphoric, energetic, and productive, but they are able to carry on with their day-to-day lives, and they never lose touch with reality. Hypomania can still result in bad decisions, and it often escalates to full-blown mania or is followed by a major depressive episode.

3. **DEPRESSION:** In addition to those of regular depression, symptoms of bipolar depression include irritability; guilt; unpredictable mood swings; feelings of restlessness or agitation; slow thoughts, movements, and speech; excessive sleep; weight gain; a much higher tendency to lose contact with reality through a true psychotic depression; and a much higher tendency for a major disruption in work and social functioning.

4. **MIXED EPISODES:** A mixed episode of bipolar disorder features symptoms of both mania or hypomania and depression. This combination of high energy and low mood makes for a particularly high risk of suicide.

But the fact was, all their lives were anything but normal. Jennifer was suffering, Mikey and Jules lived in fear, and Patty was constantly barking at her husband, "Michael, I need you to come home from work now!"

Patty didn't realize how bad things were until one evening when her husband was away at a conference. Jennifer had been agitated all day and was babbling in a squeaky, high-pitched voice. "Mom! She's freakin' me out! Why is she talking like that?" asked Jules.

Then Patty and Jules watched as Jennifer calmly placed a plastic bag over her head. Immediately, Jules rushed over to her and took it off. "Are you crazy, Jennifer? You'll kill yourself!"

Patty immediately called Jenn's psychologist.

"Your daughter put a bag on her head? You can bring her in to the hospital."

Patty felt like she had won the lottery. *Congratulations, Mrs. Konjoian. Your daughter is so crazy right now, you've just won an all-expenses-paid trip to a psychiatric hospital.*

PREPARING THE FAMILY

After Patty was told that Jennifer would be admitted, Patty and Michael made arrangements for Jules and Mikey to stay with Michael's parents. The next day, while all three kids were at school, Patty somberly packed a bag for each of them.

When school ended, Patty watched Jennifer get off the bus. She looked so innocent and sweet. *What happened to my little girl?* Patty wondered.

When Jennifer went to her room, Patty quickly rounded up Mikey and Jules to tell them about the plans.

"Dad and I are going to take Jennifer to the hospital today, and the two of you are going to stay with Grandma and Papa. Okay?"

"Is she coming back soon, Mom?" Mikey asked, his beautiful long eyelashes holding back tears.

"No, Mikey, she's probably gonna have to stay there for a while."

"But she's gonna come back, right, Mom? She's still gonna be my sister?"

"Yes, of course she will. She just needs to go somewhere where she can get help," Patty responded, crouching down to his level and holding him tightly.

Jules stood with her arms crossed, staring at the floor. Patty knew she was trying to be strong despite her fear and anger. Whenever Jenn lost control, Jules was the first to criticize her, but in that instant Patty knew how much Jules loved her sister.

"Jules, we have to do this. You know your sister is sick and we have to get her better."

Jules nodded and wiped away the tears that were falling down her cheeks. When Michael came to get them, Patty hugged them good-bye. She couldn't bear to watch them leave. It was just too much.

When Michael returned home, they were ready to tell Jennifer.

"Where did Jules and Mikey go?" Jenn innocently asked.

When she saw Patty and Michael exchange worried looks, Jennifer instantly knew what was wrong.

"Nooooo! Nooooo!" she wailed. "I'm not going to the hospital again! I don't need a stupid hospital!"

"But Jenn, honey, you need help," Michael assured her.

"Yeah, Jenn, we're doing this because we love you," Patty added.

Jennifer turned to run, and Michael and Patty each grabbed one of her arms and dragged her to the car.

"I hate you, Mom! How can you do this to me? You're the worst mother ever! I hate you! I wish I was never born."

They pulled her into the car, and Patty sat in the back, restraining Jennifer's flying elbows as they set out on their scary journey to a nearby hospital. "I'm gonna jump out of this car! I hate you! You're ruining my life."

Jennifer has always been very petite and thin, but on this day, she had the strength of a professional wrestler.

Michael hit the gas. And as they peeled out of the driveway, Patty couldn't help but wonder what the neighbors in her quiet cul-de-sac were thinking. *I probably just skyrocketed to the Department of Children and Family Services' parent hit list,* she thought.

THE ER (NOT THE ONE WITH GEORGE CLOONEY)

When they arrived at a hospital known for its work with mental illness, Patty gave the intake coordinator Jennifer's medical history. Within a few hours, they were instructed to go to Massachusetts General Hospital (MGH). Patty was happy because she had heard that MGH was on the cutting edge of diagnosing childhood bipolar disorder. *Finally, Jenn is going to get the help she needs!* Patty thought.

When they told the intake coordinator they'd had to restrain Jennifer during the ride, Jennifer got a trip in an ambulance to MGH. During the whole ride, Patty felt numb, as though she was watching a movie play out in front of her.

What had happened to her simple life plan?

When they arrived at MGH, Patty had to give a new intake coordinator all of Jenn's information. Then, after hours of waiting in triage (a fancy name for a long wait), Michael and Patty received bad news. "Mrs. Konjoian, your pediatrician is not affiliated with the hospital. Your daughter can't stay here."

"Where are you going to take her?"

"We don't know. We have to find a hospital with an available bed for her."

Twelve bad cups of coffee, two shift changes, and six candy bars later, Patty and Michael finally got the news.

"Mr. and Mrs. Konjoian, we found a bed for your daughter. It's in Westwood."

"But that's over an hour away from us," protested Patty.

An hour later at Westwood, an attendant took Jenn away, and Patty and Michael sat down and provided a third intake coordinator with Jenn's medical history. They were then asked to fill out paperwork, and were instantly overwhelmed.

"Pat, this is unbelievable. There's more paper here than when we bought our house," Michael remarked.

"You know what this is about, right?"

"Not really," replied Michael. "I don't know anything anymore."

"With these papers, we're signing away our parental rights. We can't take her home until they let us."

"Oh my God, Patty. Are you sure we're doing the right thing?" Michael asked.

"Michael, we have to do this. She can't continue at home. She's getting worse. What if she kills herself? Michael, I don't want to lose her."

With a heavy heart, Michael signed his name.

When they were finished, they were escorted down the dark, dreary hall, where they ran into Jennifer. "Don't leave me!" she shouted while being pulled toward her room.

Patty's heart was shattered with fear and uncertainty. Leaving Jen-

Thoughts on Early Childhood Bipolar Disorder

(Condensed from kargacademy.com)

According to the National Institutes of Mental Health, early-onset bipolar disorder can begin well before adolescence. When considering symptoms, it is important to remember that bipolar mood swings do not involve normal changes in mood or energy. Nor do they involve appropriate emotional responses to intense life occurrences.

Bipolar symptoms tend to be unusually extreme and prolonged. Depressive or manic episodes in early-onset bipolar disorder also differ from normal childhood mood patterns with symptoms often severe enough to warrant in-patient hospitalization, evaluation, and treatment.

SYMPTOMS OF MANIA CAN INCLUDE:
Mood Changes
✔ Persistent and frenzied and/or hysterical feelings of euphoria
✔ Delusions of grandeur, extravagance, authority, and/or influence
✔ Irrational or unreasonable anxiety, irritability, or anger

nifer was the hardest decision she had ever had to make, but deep down a part of her knew that to bring her baby back, she had to let her go.

Thoughts on Early Childhood (continued)

Behavioral Changes
- ✔ Extended episodes of insomnia, or unusually high levels of energy
- ✔ Excessive impulsivity, or racing thoughts
- ✔ Difficulty concentrating
- ✔ Uninhibited, irresponsible, and inappropriate speech, thought, or activity patterns
- ✔ Being sexually overcharged
- ✔ Engaging in risky, thrill-seeking behaviors

SYMPTOMS OF DEPRESSION CAN INCLUDE:

Mood Changes
- ✔ Persistent and excessive sorrow, melancholy, and/or misery
- ✔ Loss of interest in previously favored activities
- ✔ Feelings of guilt and despair

Behavioral Changes
- ✔ Complaints of extended and/or unresponsive pain or illness
- ✔ Significant changes in appetite, weight, or energy level
- ✔ Unusual insomnia despite exhaustion
- ✔ Recurring thoughts of death or suicide

CHAPTER 3

From Tissues to Facing the Issues

Coming to Grips with Your Child's Disability and Your Own Imperfections

For many parents, learning that their child has a disability is the start of a long and painful process. It's a period of mourning; a time to grieve the loss of the perfect dream you had planned for your children. It doesn't matter whether your child is affected by **AD/HD** or **OCD, anorexia** or **dyslexia,** depression or aggression; you will have to go through a long and painful grieving process and set out on a frightening and unknown path.

The Sister Who's Afraid of Failure Faces Her Biggest Challenge

For Gina, the grieving process began when she first got Katie's Asperger's diagnosis. The experts could define *Asperger's* any way they wanted, but to Gina, it meant one thing only—failure. And failure was something Gina feared more than anything (even more than fixing hair).

You see, from a young age, Gina experienced success in almost everything—whether on the sporting field or in the academic arena—and she worked herself senseless to achieve it.

"Dad! Please come outside and hit grounders to me so I can practice my fielding. Please! Please! Please!"

"Mom, can you buy me some more workbooks? I want to improve my math skills."

Our parents were amazed; they'd never experienced this before. "Wow, Vi," our father said. "Patty was nothing like this. It's hard to believe they're related."

Gina was so used to success that she became paralyzed with a fear of failure and went out of her way to avoid situations that could lead to failure, even in her adult life.

"Gina, are you going to put your name in for that promotion?"

Grieving for the Loss of the Perfect Child
(Condensed from kargacademy.com)

In 2004, there were more than 9 million children in the United States with physical, development, behavioral, or emotional disabilities requiring services, according to the U.S. Department of Health and Human Services. Numerous studies have been conducted that review the grieving process the entire family experiences due to the loss of the "perfect child." Here are some highlights:

✔ The grieving process for families of disabled children can last just as long as the grieving process for families with children who have died.

✔ The negative emotions experienced as part of this grieving process are significant in both intensity and duration, and can include sadness, anger, resentment, shock, denial, anxiety, guilt, shame, depression, disappointment, confusion, stress, cynicism, frustration, helplessness, self-doubt, humiliation, and any combination thereof.

✔ Every person progresses through their own personal stages of grief in their own order and time.

✔ Negative emotions that are not addressed can lead to alienation, avoidance, withdrawal, and isolation for the family members.

"I don't think so. It involves a lot of public speaking, and I'm not good at that."

But this Asperger's was something Gina couldn't avoid. It was there every day. She saw it in Katie's schoolwork ("Honey, your ballpark estimates aren't anywhere near the ballpark"); she saw it on the soccer field ("Katie Lynn! Pay attention! Stop trying to catch butterflies in the soccer net!"). But mostly she saw it in the looks of pity she got from other parents, who loved to compare their children.

"Which solar system cutout is your kid's?"

"Oh, it's that one right there—with the shark bite on Jupiter."

THE BLAME GAME

Gina really couldn't blame them for feeling sorry for her; she felt sorry for herself. However, she had no problem throwing around blame, particularly with the people she loved most.

"Mom and Dad, why did you have me? You had a boy and a girl. You should have stopped there."

"Well, it's not like we planned it."

She made sure to blame her husband. "You were the one who wanted kids first. I was content just playing golf. My handicap was trending toward a ten."

But more than anything, she blamed herself—for so many reasons, most of which defied logic.

"It's punishment because in second grade I made fun of that girl with the Dutch shoes."

"I should have gone to the prom when the boy from the resource room asked me."

"It's because I had that epidural."

NOWHERE TO TURN

Eventually, Gina got so tired of the blame that she decided to take a more positive approach. "Mike, this is adversity. And some of the most successful people in life have to overcome adversity. We can beat this. We just have to become more knowledgeable." So she went to the local bookstore and bought every book she could find about Asperger's. "Knowledge is power," she said. But as the started reading books from "experts," she felt more and more powerless. All they seemed to focus on was the bad stuff, which let her anxiety and imagination run wild.

"Mike, I just know Katie's going to be drug addicted by six, pregnant by eight, and incarcerated by ten."

"And I just know you're going to be divorced by thirty-eight if you keep reading these books."

Gina was so preoccupied and worried about Katie that she often forgot that her other daughter, Emily, four years younger than Katie, needed her, too.

"Mommy, will you play with me?"

"I can't, Emmy. I have to do Katie's **vision therapy** exercises with her."

"Can I do them, too?"

"No, honey, you don't have to. You're fine."

Besides her work, Gina's entire focus was on Katie. Her days were only as good as Katie's, which were getting increasingly challenging. By the time Katie reached third grade, her differences were becoming very apparent to the other children.

"They were choosing kids in gym class and no one wanted me on their team. They say I stink."

"Mom, my one friend was out sick today. I played by myself at recess."

The more Katie suffered, the more angry and bitter Gina became. "How come other people don't have to deal with this? Why me?"

Eventually, Gina became very depressed. All she seemed to do was cry. And no one understood why. Not her husband. "Gene, you've gotta stop crying. You went through three boxes of Kleenex this week."

Not our father, who has always been very easygoing. "Gina, that's life. Just stop worrying and enjoy her."

Not our mother, who has never been easygoing. "Saint Anthony! Stop crying; you're going to make me cry! Do you think I like to see my daughter like this? I'm so worried about you!"

Not Patty, her sister and best friend, who just handled things differently. "Believe me, Gene, I know how you feel. I feel the same way with Jennifer. But you've got to pull it together. You're not helping Katie by being like this."

And she certainly couldn't take comfort from friends who didn't have kids with disabilities. Whenever they tried to make her feel better, she ended up feeling worse.

"Trust me, Gina, I understand your pain about Katie's disability. When Ethan got that cavity, I was devastated."

One Saturday, after watching Katie struggle on the soccer field, Gina broke down to her husband. "Why can't she be like them, Mike?" she said, watching all the children engaged in the game. "I should never have had kids."

"Don't say that, Gene. Katie's great. You're just too hard on her because you were such a good athlete. Not everyone's like you. You need to pray to accept her."

Gina felt so terrible for her thoughts that after the game, she took Mike's advice and drove herself straight to church for confession.

She knelt down in front of the priest, and with tears rolling down her face, poured out her soul. "Father, forgive me, for I have sinned. I have this daughter with autism and I just can't accept it. I don't know why she can't be like everybody else. I feel like my daughter's a failure. And I'm a failure."

The priest put his hand on Gina's praying hands and softly said, "Your daughter is your cross to bear in life. Now go say four Our Fathers, three Hail Marys, and two Glory Bes."

That day, the priest affirmed what Gina already knew. She was alone.

NEIGHBORLY ADVICE

The day she received the call about the snowflake essay, Gina had reached the breaking point. She really *did* want to die. Oh, she never thought about killing herself (she was too chicken to do that). But she would have been content with an accident, carbon monoxide poisoning, or a fast, terminal illness. Anything to make the pain of dealing with Katie's disability go away.

Feeling completely shattered, and realizing she probably would not be getting the quick death she hoped for, Gina placed a call to her neighbor Jane. Jane is a friend of Gina's unlike any other—a seventy-something retired teacher, counselor, and psychiatric nurse, and the mother of one of Gina's closest friends. Gina felt an instant connection to Jane because of her charming Southern drawl, kind eyes, and gentle spirit. In many ways, Jane is the perfect friend.

"Pat, I finally found a friend who has the time and the patience to actually listen to my problems. And because of her psychiatric nursing background, nothing I say scares her."

"Thank God. Now I don't have to listen to you."

Gina knew Jane would be there when she needed her; she always was. What she didn't know was how much Jane would help her.

"Jane, I've got a problem," Gina blurted out. "I just got this call from the school and I don't know what to do."

Jane heard the sadness and desperation in Gina's voice and knew her neighbor needed help. (The torrent of tears running down Gina's driveway was probably a clue, too.)

"Gina, why don't I come over," she said in her soothing voice.

When Gina opened the door and saw Jane, she broke down. Instinctively, Jane hugged her. "Oh my. Let's sit down. Tell me what's goin' on," Jane said, quietly ushering Gina into the house.

In a nanosecond, Gina blurted out all she was feeling. "I got this call. And Katie's a unabomber. And I don't know what's going on in her head. And I cry all the time. And Mike says I've got to stop. And the Our Fathers and Hail Marys didn't help."

Jane just sat there quietly and listened, passing Gina tissue after tissue.

When Gina had gone through the entire box, Jane said, "Well, I can see why you're so upset. This Asperger's must be overwhelming for you all to deal with."

"It is! It is!" Gina said, getting ready for Jane to tell her to suck it up or to mop up the pile of water under her.

"Of course it is, and you're the mother of the house and everyone is depending on you."

"Yes, they are. And I feel so alone and so guilty and so angry that other people don't have to go through this. All I do is cry. I have no idea what to do."

"Well, you are just terribly overloaded, Gina. And it's absolutely no wonder that you are, given all you're dealing with."

"Really?" Gina said, almost inaudibly.

"Oh my goodness, yes! So why don't you tell me more about what's been so awful for you?"

For the next hour, Gina continued pouring her heart out as Jane quietly listened. When Gina finally stopped, Jane said, "I'm gettin' a good picture of what you're livin' with. So would you be up to lookin' at things you could do to help some of these situations?"

"Okay," Gina said, not realizing that Jane had done something no one else could do—she'd stopped the floodgates of tears.

"Well, I can call Katie's psychologist and get an emergency appointment."

"Good. What else? What can we do to help her at school?"

"I've been thinking about looking at other schools."

"Good. What can you do to help yourself deal with your feelings?" Jane asked.

"Well, my sister and I were talking about writing a book about this. I could do that."

"Gina, I think it's a great idea to write down everything you're talkin' to me about."

They sat there for another hour, brainstorming ways to help both Katie and Gina.

Jane may not have realized it (and still may not), but on that gray day, she helped light a path that would ultimately change Gina's life, her values, and her outlook on both her daughters' futures.

Yes, on that dark day, Jane Lynn gave Gina Gallagher something Gina thought she had lost forever.

She gave her hope.

Patty's Reality: The Sister Who's Afraid of Success Makes a Startling Admission

To understand how Patty dealt with Jennifer's situation, you must understand Patty. Unlike Gina, who is extremely emotional and driven, Patty is levelheaded and laid-back. "I don't know why you're always pushing yourself, Gene. I like being average. It comes with no pressure."

So when the day came that she had to admit Jennifer to the hospital, Patty didn't cry or agonize over her decision. She moved forward, accepting Jennifer's sickness as something in her life that she had to face. Gina was amazed.

Jane's Thoughts on How She Helped Gina

How did I help Gina? I asked her to talk. I listened to her. I asked her many questions. I did not give her advice or lectures. I validated her anger, fears, and frustrations. I felt honest compassion for her. I did not feel "sorry" for her. I did not get upset over her dilemma or judge her. I was not impatient. I believed deep down she knew exactly what she needed to do, and my only job was to let her talk until she could come up with her own solutions.

You could say that I was a safe person for Gina.

Who Is a Safe Person?
A safe person is someone who . . .

✔ Allows you to be confused and crazy—even off the wall—and doesn't automatically want to "fix" you
✔ Listens to you, hears you, and encourages you to keep talking until you can begin to hear yourself
✔ Is clear, direct, and honest with you
✔ Has no personal agendas or ulterior motives
✔ Listens to you for as long as it takes for you to find your own solutions

"You haven't cried, Pat. Are you kidding me?"

"Well, Gene, I think you've cried enough for both of us."

Don't get us wrong; Patty hated the thought of having Jenn in the hospital. After all, Jennifer had never really been away from home, except for an occasional sleepover with friends or family.

And though Patty may not have cried, she felt plenty of guilt for actually finding the house peaceful. In the short time Jennifer had been gone, Patty's house had become more "normal" for Jules and Mikey.

"Mommy, it's been two whole days, and you haven't called 911 once."

To maintain that level of normalcy, Patty arranged for Michael and her to alternate nightly visits to the hospital.

When it was her night to visit, Patty couldn't wait to see Jenn, and

---

Jane's Thoughts (continued)

✔ Is compassionate and interested in your welfare (no pity, please!)
✔ Validates your feelings and experiences
✔ Is neither judgmental nor impatient
✔ Believes in you
✔ Accepts you—just the way you are

Where Can You Find a "Safe Person"?

They could be anywhere . . . in your neighborhood, at work, among your dear old friends. Just begin looking around. But keep two things in mind:

1. Sometimes the people we love the most—close friends and family—are not the safest people we can talk to during a crisis. They often care about us so much that they find it difficult to be clearheaded about our situation.

2. If you can't find a safe *person*, you may want to find a support group or a therapist/counselor to talk to.

she knew that Jenn missed her. In many ways, Jennifer felt like a prisoner, and a visit from Patty was something she looked forward to (a true testament to Jennifer's fragile mental state).

The hospital was a depressing place to visit. The walls were painted a dingy, somber gray and there were always kids screaming. Jennifer was heavily sedated, and much of Patty's time with her was spent just holding Jennifer while she slept. Patty's goal was to get Jenn diagnosed, medicated, and brought home as quickly as possible. Yet, another part of her worried about disrupting the newfound peace at home.

"Michael, I miss her, but I'm so afraid for her to come home."

DON'T CRY FOR ME, ARGENTINA

What was most surprising about Jennifer's situation was Patty's strength. She never cried, though there were plenty of others who shed tears on her behalf, including our mother. "Saint Theresa! My baby granddaughter is in a mental hospital. Why did this happen?"

Some might have thought Patty was cold, but her apparent lack of emotion was her way of coping. It was almost as though she was on autopilot, quietly trying to be there for Jenn and to make things as normal as possible for Jules and Mikey. She knew that if she fell apart, her husband and kids would do the same.

Patty's friends couldn't believe how strong she was, particularly one friend who came over to pick up Jules one day. "Patty, I'm sorry about Jenn. I will keep her in my prayers."

"I'd appreciate that. But Jennifer has plenty of support from family and friends. Please pray for all those kids who haven't got anyone to pray for them. Jennifer will get better."

Throughout Jennifer's first hospitalization (and two subsequent ones), Patty remained strong. It wasn't until the exit interview with Jennifer's doctor after Jennifer's third hospitalization that Patty began to feel the gravity of her daughter's situation.

"So, Doctor. Are you prepared to be the one to confirm that Jennifer does have bipolar disorder?"

Even though deep down Patty knew what she was dealing with, she was stunned when the doctor looked her square in the eye and said, "Yes, Mrs. Konjoian. I believe your daughter has bipolar disorder."

In that brief moment, Patty felt as if her heart had stopped beating. This was reality—her little girl had a serious mental illness that would never go away. An illness that conjured up images of crazy people in straightjackets.

When they sent Jennifer home with lithium and a mood stabilizer, Patty realized that her daughter's life—and her life—would never be the same.

To Medicate or Not to Medicate?

There's no shortage of controversial subjects in America today. There's the burning Roe vs. Wade dispute, the age-old Republican vs. Democrat battle, and, of course, the always divisive paper vs. plastic debate. But there's another controversial topic that's drawing battle lines all over the world—medication. It seems that everyone has a strong opinion about it.

As passive women who hate choosing sides (we both drive our cars through forks in the road), we are not in any way advocating medication. We can tell you, however, that our children have both been on medication. What started off with harmless Vitaballs and Flintstones chewables has escalated into powerful drugs to help our children function on a daily basis.

But the decision to medicate was not an easy one for us, nor is it for any parent. One only has to look at the side effects: headache, nausea, sleeplessness, frequent urination, weight gain.

The fact is, the subject of medication can generate more outrage and guilt than a Lifetime, Television for Women marathon. We've met parents who feel guilty for putting their kids on meds, for not putting their kids on meds—heck, even for taking their kids' meds.

THE FLOODGATES OPEN

Within a few weeks of her being home after her third hospitalization, Jennifer's medication started to kick in, and she quickly started to improve. Patty, however, was growing increasingly sad. One night after everyone had gone to bed, Patty sat in the dark and watched home movies. As she saw images of baby Jennifer crawling, blowing out her birthday cake candles, and prancing around the house in her Dorothy dress and ruby slippers, Patty got down on her knees and cried like a baby.

Was Jennifer bipolar then? Why didn't I pick up on the signs? she wondered.

A few days later, Patty was sitting alone in the living room with tearstained cheeks when Michael came in to talk with her.

Using his affectionate nickname for her, he said, "Patrick, is everything okay?"

"Michael, please just leave me alone. I don't feel like talking."

"I don't understand you. Why are you crying now? Jenn has been better for weeks."

"I don't know, Michael," Patty sadly responded. "I don't know why I feel this way. I don't know anything anymore."

Michael was hurt, but the truth was, Patty really didn't want to talk to anyone. Without even realizing it, she had started withdrawing from the people around her, failing to return calls and get together with her friends.

She also had no interest in the things she used to love. "No, Gene, I don't want to come over your house for Frosty Friday. I'm kinda tired."

Unlike Gina, who cries to our mother when she has a hangnail, Patty didn't say anything to anyone, especially our mother. But our mother knew her daughter and was worried sick. "Gina, your sister hasn't called me in two days. Something is wrong."

"I know, Mom. She was a no-show at Margarita Monday, too."

FIGHTING BACK

It wasn't until one sunny day that Patty woke up and decided she needed to do something about her sadness. She started by talking to

Jennifer's psychiatrist. He told Patty she was "moderately depressed" and prescribed an antidepressant to help her get back on her feet. He then encouraged Patty to find her own therapist.

Within a few weeks, Patty started to feel better.

Patty took the medication for a little less than four months. It had gotten her through a difficult period of time, and she was starting to feel stronger and ready to face the road ahead. She felt like she finally had the strength, courage, and support to learn to cope with Jenn's struggles and continue on with her life.

"Yes, Gene. Count me in. I'm coming over for Sombrero Saturday."

Medication for Mommy

The decision for a parent or other caregiver to take medication is a difficult one. It certainly was for Patty. In the beginning, she fought it, thinking, *I can handle this on my own.* To her, taking medication felt like admitting weakness—that she no longer had control of her emotions. She eventually realized that in order to help her family, she needed to get stronger. The medication helped lessen her stress and depression. While medication isn't for everyone, it certainly helped Patty get back on track. When things got better, she went off the medication and reverted to the home remedy that was introduced to us by our grandmother.

"Pat, do you want white or red wine?"

"I don't like to play favorites, Gene. I'll have a glass of each."

Coming Out of Our Messy Closets

Nothing in life is to be feared.
It is only to be understood.

—MARIE CURIE

Coming Out of
Our Messy Closets

CHAPTER 4

I Could Tell You, but Then I'd Have to Kill You

Telling Others About
Your Child's Disability

When you live on a perfection-preoccupied planet, the last thing you want to do is stand out and be different. Often this means desperately trying to fit in even when you're not necessarily comfortable doing it.

We, of course, are no exception. From the time we were young girls, we've always strived to be like everybody else.

"Patty, why are you wearing those skintight Jordache jeans? You can barely walk in them. How are you gonna roller-skate?"

"I know, Ma, but everybody else wears them. Now do me a favor and lift me into the car."

Even as adults, we've been known to occasionally pretend we are "perfectly normal" parents. But anyone who knows us knows our parenting is far from perfect. Or normal. That's pretty obvious from the second you meet us.

"Hi. Welcome to our neighborhood. I'm Gina, and this is my husband, Mike. We have two girls."

"Yeah, we know. We hear you yelling at them."

So you can imagine how difficult it was to face the reality that we weren't just imperfect *parents,* but parents of imperfect *children.* What would people on our perfection-preoccupied planet think about that? Would they pity us? Make fun of us? Or worse, talk about us?

"That's one polluted gene pool. One sister has a kid with autism and the other sister has one with bipolar disorder."

"Yes, but I suppose it could be worse. They could be Octomoms."

Our worries about what other people thought left us with a difficult dilemma; one that a lot of parents like us face. Should we come clean about our kids' disabilities or pretend everything was "normal," even when normal was a distant dream?

"Patty, is everything okay? I saw Jennifer clinging to your front bumper when you were backing out of your driveway."

"Uh, yeah. Everything's great. Jenn just loves to hang with me."

The question of whether to disclose your child's disability is particularly difficult when your child has an **"invisible disability,"** or one that is not readily recognizable—like **AD/HD,** bipolar disorder, dyslexia, **nonverbal learning disorder,** autism, or epilepsy. Because your kid may look like everybody else's, any unusual speech or behavior patterns stand out as even more socially unacceptable.

"Little Bobby, can you do Mommy a favor and try not to point with your middle finger?"

So is it better to put the diagnosis out in the open or to say nothing and simply let people think our kids are rude?

Or stupid?

Or poorly behaved?

Or just plain weird?

At one of our speaking appearances, a mother posed this very question.

"My son's six and has Asperger's. I'm afraid if I tell people about his disability, they'll get to know his 'label' before they get to know him. Does that ever worry you—that people will prejudge your daughters by their labels?"

We thought the best answer came from the mother of an eighteen-year-old girl with autism who said, "People know your child is different—and are probably talking about him. I've found it's better to get the disability out in the open. That way you can educate others about it."

Dancing Around the Issues

Our friend Darcy, mother of Jessica, a six-year-old girl with pervasive developmental disorder, wrestled with the same question when she enrolled Jessica in ballet school for the second time. Yes, ballet school, the place where even the strongest of special needs parents fold like origami (more on that later).

It was a "delicate" step for Darcy, especially since Jessica's first ballet experience, at age two, ended painfully. Through the bulletproof ballet glass, Darcy helplessly watched Jessica run to the corner of the room and scream at the top of her lungs while the other ballerinas pliéd around her.

"Never again!" vowed a horrified Darcy.

But four years later, when Jessica asked Darcy if she could join ballet again, Darcy gave in, rationalizing *Okay, that was when she was a baby. She's six now.*

Fearing there might be Not Wanted posters of Jessica at the previous studio, she enrolled Jessica at her local YMCA, where ballet was a little more relaxed, at least for the mothers. ("You mean you don't have a window to watch? Sign me up!")

On the way to the first Y class, Darcy pondered a difficult question: *Should I tell her teacher about Jessica's PDD, or is that unfair to Jessica?* But when Jessica pranced into the class with the other ballerinas, Darcy reasoned, *Maybe I'll just wait and see how she does first.*

For the next fifteen minutes, Darcy anxiously waited with the other parents. When the ballerinas filed out for a break, the dainty teacher sashayed over to Darcy.

All at once, Darcy was hit with panic about the "production" that was sure to come.

"Are you Jessica's mom?" the teacher asked, smiling pleasantly at Darcy.

"Yes," Darcy admitted.

"I just wanted to tell you, Jessica is doing great," the teacher said, giving Darcy two thumbs up.

"She has autism," Darcy blurted out before she even realized what the teacher had said.

"I guessed as much," the teacher said with a smile. Unfazed, she sashayed her way back into the room.

Eating Her Words

Often, parents of special needs children don't encounter people who "get it" like Jessica's dance teacher did. Yes, every so often, we encounter people who unfairly judge us—and our kids.

"Did you hear the way that **Tourette's** boy was talking to his parents? If that were my kid, I'd wash his mouth out with soap."

When that happens, it's hard not to take it personally and be excessively guarded about our children. Even Gina has been known to occasionally (okay, frequently) be overprotective of Katie, who has a very noticeable quirk of picking up objects and rapidly flapping them in front of her face. Katie does this so often that it's barely noticeable to her family and close friends (well, most of the time).

"Uh, Katie, do you think you could flap a piece of paper instead of that steak knife?"

"Yes, Aunt Patty."

But kids and adults who aren't familiar with Katie's quirks sometimes ridicule her, which has caused Gina to become defensive. Sometimes to a fault.

"Whadya mean some kid threw a ball at you? I want a name."

"But Mom, we were playing dodgeball."

Gina's protectiveness toward Katie was very apparent one day when our family went to see our niece perform in a community play. Katie, a lover of theater, was sitting with her cousins, deeply involved in the second scene and flapping the program in front of her face. Her cousins, used to this behavior and some of Katie's quirkier habits, were completely unfazed.

Unfortunately, three cranky older women sitting in front of Katie weren't as tolerant.

"Knock it off, kid!" one of them turned around and said.

"That's annoying!" said another to a stunned Katie.

"How rude!" said the third "golden girl."

Katie's protective older cousin, Jules, was incensed, whispering to Gina and Mike, "Those mean ladies yelled at Katie. I just want to punch their fat heads."

Mike was fuming. He told Gina, "I'd like to tell those old bags where to go."

"Calm down! I'll handle those blue hairs at intermission," Gina said to her husband, ignoring his full head of gray hair. Of course, before they had Katie, Gina and Mike would have probably been annoyed if a child was behaving like Katie. But this was their daughter; they knew she couldn't help it, and how much Katie's flapping bothered her. They were furious that these women humiliated Katie.

When intermission finally arrived, Gina stormed off to find them, with her posse (Patty, Mike, and all the kids) trailing behind.

When Gina spotted one of the women out front, she didn't hold back.

"Excuse me. My daughter was sitting behind you inside. You told her she was rude," Gina said, her voice cracking like that of a boy going through puberty.

"Excuse me?" the woman asked, staring blankly at Gina.

"Well let me tell you, Granny! My daughter has a form of autism and a neurological need to flap that program!" Gina shouted.

"Oh," she said, with a confused look on her face.

"So before you start flapping your gums, you should stop and think that maybe the child might have autism or something she can't help!"

"I see," she responded with a blank look on her face.

"Yeah, well, we're writing a book for people like you! It's called *Shut Up About Your Perfect Kid.*"

"Yeah, *Shut Up About Your Perfect Kid,*" echoed Patty, the book's coauthor, slowly rolling up her sleeves behind Gina.

"Please accept our apology and sympathy," the woman politely responded.

"Sympathy? I don't need your sympathy! My daughter is a blessing, lady!"

"Yeah, a blessing!" said Patty, getting up in the woman's face.

Feeling satisfied (and a bit nauseous), Gina raced off, with her posse following in support.

"Wow, Gene! I'm so impressed!" Patty said, running to catch up and congratulate her little sister.

"Yeah, Aunt Gina, that was, like, great," said Jules. "One problem, though. That wasn't one of the ladies!"

A More Effective Solution Is in the Cards

In our imperfect travels, we've met some resourceful mothers who use a highly effective and creative method of responding to critical looks and responses from strangers.

"You know what I do when people give me and my daughter dirty looks? I hand them my card."

You can buy business cards like the following at autismgear .com:

"I apologize if my child was disturbing you. Autism is a neurological disability affecting about 1 in every 150 children born today. **Behavior that may on the surface seem rude is my child's ONLY way of dealing with the world.** If this is the first time autism has touched your life, I hope you will be patient and understanding."

"To learn more about autism, please visit www. autismgear.com and click on Links."

TEXT COPYRIGHT © 2005 AUTISM GEAR.

Jill, a wonderful mother from Quincy, Massachusetts, has made her own card, which she has her autistic child hand out (see page 69).

Helpful Resources for Autism Awareness

There's good news and bad news for parents and caregivers of autistic children. The bad news is that there will always be people who judge you and your child. The good news is that there's no shortage of helpful resources to create awareness and educate others. Some of the sites we have found helpful include:

> "Ask me about my autism.
> (I'm nonverbal,
> so I may not answer.)"

AUTISM GEAR (www.autismgear.com). This site is equipped with autism cards in a variety of languages. When you hand people one of these cards, they'll see that you mean business.

DO 2 LEARN (www.do2learn.com). This helpful site features games, songs, and information on special needs. You'll also find more communication cards.

BUTTONS AND MORE (www.buttonsandmore.com). You'll look cute as a button when you wear buttons and other merchandise designed to show support and create autism awareness.

CHILD-AUTISM-PARENT-CAFÉ.COM (www.child-autism-parent-cafe.com). Uncover helpful information, resources, and strategies to educate yourself and others on autism.

OMAC (www.omacconsulting.blogspot.com). This informative website provides information on the organization and management of an autism classroom.

LUCAS WORKS (www.lucasworks.org). Showcase your autism pride with a variety of items, including shirts, coffee mugs, aprons, and totes.

AUTISM SOCIETY OF AMERICA (www.autismsociety.org). Learn what you can do to help increase autism awareness.

BELLAONLINE (http://autismspectrumdisorders.bellaonline.com). Gain insight, support, and advice from mothers of children with autism.

Gina's Strategy for Dealing with Katie's Disability: TMI

[AUTHORS' DISCLAIMER: By now you've read enough of this book to know we are not in any way experts on parenting children with disabilities. Our goal is simply to share strategies that have worked for each of us, in the event it may help those in a similar situation. If you're different from us (i.e., you are bright or of the perfect persuasion), we advise you not to try the following strategies at home.]

Throughout her life, Gina has consistently been an open book, often telling people more than they need to know about her life.

"Gina, that's a great shirt you have on."

"Thanks. T.J. Maxx. Ten bucks."

So it's not surprising that she's employed a simple and direct strategy for dealing with difficult situations—by openly sharing her troubles and insecurities with anyone who will listen.

"I can't believe I didn't get any work this week. My freelance writing business is dying. I just know it!"

"So ma'am, are you saying you don't want me to supersize your fries?"

Some may disagree with Gina's strategy, but she strongly believes it has earned her the respect of friends and family alike.

"Pat, I didn't realize I had so many friends."

"Of course you do. People love to be around you. You make them feel so much better about their lives."

So when she learned about Katie's Asperger's, Gina felt compelled to constantly educate others about her daughter's "differences"—even when Katie looked and behaved just like everyone else.

"And I want a kitchen set and a Powerpuff Girls video."

"Have you been a good girl this year?"

"Excuse me, Mr. Claus. If I may just interject. (Push over, honey, and make room for Mommy on Santa's lap.) As I was saying, Santa, don't be fooled by her lack of eye contact. She's not lying. She's been a very good girl. She just has this disability called Asperger's."

If Gina had had her way, she would have glued a disclaimer on Katie's back.

Warning!

This child has been diagnosed with a disability known as Asperger's syndrome. It means she learns and eats differently. If she doesn't look you in the eye, it's because of her Asperger's and not because she is stealing from you. Please be advised, she did not get this from her mother's family. In all likelihood, it came from her father's side. Thank you.

HAVING KATIE'S CAKE AND EATING IT, TOO

Without even realizing it, Gina was quickly taking her Asperger's educational series nearly everywhere she went, including to kiddie birthday parties. Gina found these events to be a feeding ground for parents who loved to talk (okay, brag) about the accomplishments of their children. ("Trask bowled an eighty-six without even using the bumper guards.") It was painful to listen to them talk about their kids, because Katie struggled at everything.

"Now, which one is your daughter?"

"Oh, she's the little blonde flapping the tail on the donkey."

Gina found herself dreading birthday parties even more than her yearly physicals. ("Are you sure I gained ten pounds, Doctor? I recently started wearing a padded bra.") Katie, however, loved attending the parties, even though she rarely participated in the activities.

Instead, she played along the periphery, despite Gina's constant efforts to draw her in.

"Honey, why don't you play the video games with the other kids?"

"I don't want to, Mommy. The noise hurts my ears."

"Okay, let's go line up for the piñata."

"But Mommy, I don't like candy."

"Your sister and I do."

The most awkward activity was the serving of cake and ice cream, when all the parents and children gathered together. While other kids were staring at the cake, excitedly pointing to the piece they wanted, Katie sat quietly, staring into space.

"Katie, do you want chocolate or vanilla ice cream?" the party mother would ask.

"No, thank you. I'll just have saltines."

Feeling the need to save her daughter (and herself) from embarrassment, Gina would often corner the party mother and privately launch into her speech.

"She has this form of autism and is sensitive to tastes and textures. So there's a perfectly good reason why she doesn't eat cake. I, on the other hand, would love a piece. Or maybe two."

Gina thought this strategy was helping others understand Katie. And, with some parents, it worked beautifully, as they openly shared their own tales of imperfection:

"Believe me, I understand. My brother has a son with autism."

"I have AD/HD myself."

"I understand. My daughter's on an IEP. She has dyslexia."

"I used to teach special ed."

Gina wanted to hug them for their understanding. But she also realized that for every one or two people who understood, there were just as many who never would. People who loved nothing more than reveling in the imperfections of others. Gina was once like that herself, and on occasion, still is. ("Did you hear that Mary Jones left her husband for the FedEx man? She said he's the whole package.") She even took great pleasure in hearing about the struggles of other "imperfect" children and their parents.

"Do you see that mother over there?" Kathy, a fellow ballet mother, asked Gina years ago, pointing to a well-dressed, attractive woman closely watching her daughter perform through the window.

"What about her?" Gina asked Kathy, instantly disliking the other woman for being so well put together (the antithesis of Gina, who is always coming apart).

"Her son's crazy. He's in a mental hospital," said Kathy.

"Really?" Gina said, feeling satisfaction that this woman was far from perfect.

"Look at her. She's like a zombie. You can tell she's medicated," Kathy continued.

"Sheesh, if she's on drugs, no wonder her kid is so messed up," Gina added, raising her large, imperfect nose high in the air.

Gina didn't know it, but years later that "medicated" woman would become one of her dearest friends and most valued advisers.

"So Lis, do you think I should go on Paxil or Zoloft?"

WHAT GOES AROUND, COMES AROUND

When Katie really started struggling, it didn't take long for people to start talking about her "issues." Gina expected this from strangers, but not from people she knew, particularly friends whom she had taken the time to educate about Katie.

But Gina had misjudged how understanding people would be about Katie. She openly talked to Leslie, the mother of one of the kids in the neighborhood.

"Leslie, as you'll see in the manual I prepared, Katie has Asperger's, and it's really just a different way of relating to people. This bar chart shows she's in the ninety-ninth percentile for verbal-related tasks. There's no question she's bright. She's just in her own little world sometimes and has poor eye contact."

"Hey, Gina, everybody's got something," Leslie replied, putting Gina instantly at ease. "Trust me, Brittany's got her issues," she said, referring to her own daughter, who was the same age as Katie.

Hallelujah! Gina thought. She'd finally met a neighbor who understood—someone who would not judge her or Katie. It was particularly comforting because this woman's children were all "developing typically." (*Maybe parents of perfect kids will understand after all*, Gina thought.)

But one day, when the neighborhood girls came knocking on her door, Gina was awakened to the painful reality.

"Gina, we were over at Brittany's," said the youngest girl, running out of breath. "And Brittany started saying bad things about Katie and her mother told us all 'not to pay any attention to Katie because Katie is just slow.'"

"Mom, what does 'slow' mean?" asked a worried Katie.

"Nothing you need to worry about, honey," Gina said. "Trust me, you're far from slow," she said, rubbing Katie's back and mustering her sweetest smile, even though she felt like she'd been sucker punched.

After the kids left, a dejected Gina collapsed on the couch and wondered if that was how people saw her baby. In all honesty, Gina had never thought of Kate as slow. Quirky? Yes. Different? Yes. A strange eater? Absolutely (French fries made her sick). But *slow*? Never. Gina knew Katie was bright, but she was sick that some people would never take the time to see past her differences. Was this what Katie was going to have to face for the rest of her life?

Gina wasn't quite sure *she* could face it.

Patty's Approach to Coming Clean: Start Talking

While Gina was an open book about Katie's struggles, Patty was a vault, choosing not to utter a word to anyone about Jenn's diagnosis. Who could blame her? She was dealing with a mental illness. It was hard enough for *her* to understand; how could she expect others to? Sure, she'd learned enough about bipolar disorder to know it was a chemical imbalance in the brain, but other people wouldn't see it that way.

They'd see Jenn as crazy.

Or dangerous.

Or crazy and dangerous.

How could they not? People with mental illness weren't exactly talked about in a positive way. You only had to turn on the television or pick up a newspaper to prove that.

"Bipolar Woman Kills Husband and Two Kids."

Patty had never noticed it before, but since Jenn's diagnosis, she was becoming increasingly sensitive to how people with mental illness were portrayed. And she didn't like it.

"You know, Gene, I'm so sick of watching TV shows that portray bipolar people so negatively. We need to come up with a show of our own."

"I agree, Pat. How about a feel-good show, *Touched by a Bipolar Angel*? Or a soap opera—*The Bipolar and the Beautiful*?"

Fully aware of this mental illness stigma, Patty felt that the best way to deal with Jennifer's disability was to keep it quiet. She and Michael decided to tell only immediate family members. Patty's mother-in-law, Vera, assured Patty she was doing the right thing by remaining silent. Like our parents, Vera grew up in a generation that didn't talk about their problems, particularly those involving mental illness. Heck, the same is true of our generation. When we were growing up, we never saw the kids around the neighborhood with disabilities or mental illness, though there were certainly some signs they existed.

"Mommy, how come our neighbor gets to ride in that little bus? I wanna go on it."

"Don't say that, Gina. She's got problems."

Like a lot of children, we were taught not to talk about or stare at people with differences. It would make them "uncomfortable." So we often pretended they weren't even there.

During a discussion with a support group in Concord, Massachusetts, a lovely woman, Liz, shared her thoughts about this.

"I remember when my daughter was young and in her wheelchair," Liz began. "We were in a store and a little girl came in with her mother. The girl looked at my daughter and pointed straight at her and asked, 'Mommy, what's wrong with her?' Immediately, the mother shushed her daughter and turned her away from mine. I walked over to the mother and told her that her daughter *should* ask questions if she needed information, and that by not talking about disabilities, she was making them shameful. My daughter had nothing to be ashamed of."

LICENSE TO SPILL

Patty's mother-in-law had only Jennifer's best interest at heart. ("Patty, I'm worried people will treat her differently if they know about her struggles. You don't want her to have to live with this for the rest of her life.")

Patty and Michael knew she had a point, but they quickly became frustrated because they just weren't getting the support they needed to help Jennifer. Sure, they read books—like *The Bipolar Child*, the bipolar bible. (Well, *Patty* read it. Like Gina's husband, Patty's husband isn't much of a reader. "Can we get that book on cable?")

Although the books helped Patty understand more about bipolar disorder, she felt that something was missing. She needed to know she wasn't alone—that others shared the same struggles, fears, and anxieties. ("So you padlock your aspirin, too?")

Patty started seeing her own therapist and discussed this need during one of her many sessions.

"I understand that Jennifer's illness is common and a neurological brain disorder, but I'm worried that if people find out about it, they won't let their kids play with her. The last thing I want to do is ruin her privacy. I'm her mother; I'm supposed to protect her."

The therapist looked at Patty and gave her advice that would change Patty's life.

"Patty," she said. "Every time you talk about bipolar disorder, you help break the stigma."

An Article of Hope

Patty felt instant relief. Maybe it *was* okay to talk about it. Maybe her little sister, "the bullhorn," had it right after all.

Not long after Patty received the advice from the therapist, she stumbled upon an article in her local newspaper written by Karen, the mother of an adult son with schizophrenia. In the article, Karen shared her pride at how her son was successfully living with schizophrenia after two failed suicide attempts.

After reading the article, Patty did something she hadn't done since her teen years. She penned a fan letter—not to David Cassidy this time, but to this courageous mother, applauding her for sharing her son's story in such a public way.

Karen immediately responded, "Thank you, but I have NAMI to thank for that."

"Who's he?" Patty asked, proving yet again that she really isn't that bright.

"It's not a person. It's an organization—the National Alliance on Mental Illness. They provide advocacy and support for families affected by mental illness. You should join and come to our support group. I'll send you some information."

Patty was deeply moved when she read the signature on Karen's e-mail, which said, "Karen, proud mother of Timmy." She couldn't suppress her excitement that someone actually understood what her family was going through. "Oh, Michael," she sang out to her husband. "I need you to watch the kids next Monday night."

"Where are you running away to this time?"

"I'm not running away *Monday*," she answered, a bit perturbed that after more than a decade of marriage he still didn't know her. "I'm going to a support group to help Jennifer. And by the way, I'm

Stomping Out Stigma with NAMI

Throughout our imperfect travels, we've had the privilege of speaking to parents, grandparents, and professionals affiliated with the National Alliance on Mental Illness. Founded in 1979, NAMI is a nonprofit organization that provides support, education, advocacy, and research to improve the lives of individuals and families affected by mental illness. NAMI's Stigmabusters is a network of dedicated advocates across the country and around the world who seek to fight inaccurate and hurtful representations of mental illness. For more information on NAMI and Stigmabusters or to join a local chapter, visit nami.org.

running away tonight. I need to get out of this house. You're all driving me crazy."

Reading Between the Lines

When we began telling people about our daughter's disabilities, we weren't quite sure of the reactions we would get. Sometimes people were compassionate and sympathetic and asked thoughtful questions, such as:

"When did you find out she had autism?"

"Is the school system supportive?"

"What are some of the signs of bipolar disorder? Sometimes I wonder if my son has it."

"Do you believe in the theory that immunizations cause autism?"

"What should I say when I see someone struggling with a child with a disability?"

They genuinely wanted to be educated. Others, we felt, weren't as sincere, but were just feigning interest. We and other parents have learned to read between the lines. For example:

WHEN THEY SAY . . .	THEY MEAN . . .
"You poor thing."	"Whew! Thank God my kid isn't like hers."
"I'm here if you need help."	"Oh God, I hope she doesn't call me."
"That's wonderful that medication helps you cope with things."	"Drug problem."
"I think it's great you're seeing a therapist."	"She's crazy as a loon."
"So your sister also has a child with a disability?"	"That's one polluted gene pool."
"I love that you have your daughter playing soccer. We're happy to have her on the team."	"If the coach puts her kid in this game, I'm gonna scream."

Top Ten Best Responses to Unsolicited Rude Comments

In addition to meeting people who pretend to care, we've met our share of folks who just say whatever is on their minds, without even thinking. We have, however, learned to give it right back to them.

10. "Give me your bipolar kid for a week and I'll whip him into shape."

    RESPONSE: "Great. My husband and I have really been looking forward to some quality alone time. When do you want us to drop him off?"

9. "I realize your child has sensory issues, but don't you think she's way too sensitive?"

    RESPONSE: "I'd ask her, but she might cry."

8. "Your daughter has autism? Is she like the Rain Man? Can we take her to Vegas and have her win us money?"

    RESPONSE: "Only if there's a Go Fish table."

7. "Aren't you worried about putting your bipolar daughter on medication?"

    RESPONSE: "No, right now, I'm more worried about her jumping out the window."

6. "I just don't know how you do it."

    RESPONSE: "You mean I could choose not to do it?"

5. "I don't think your son is autistic. He's just stubborn."

    RESPONSE: "Great, thanks, Doctor. That will be really helpful with our denial phase."

4. "Your son's hearing is perfect. There's no way he could have **central auditory processing disorder.**"

    RESPONSE: "I can't believe what I'm hearing."

3. "I don't know why you think your son has AD/HD. He's very focused in my class."

   RESPONSE: "Yeah, that's kinda the purpose of the medication he's on. But if you want to see him in his true form, come by tonight at eight. He should be plenty wound up by then."

2. "How did you get the school system to pay for two out-of-district placements?"

   RESPONSE: "My husband promised to have a vasectomy."

Tips for Positive Responses to Negative Comments

What are you supposed to do when people make rude remarks about your child? LeeAnn Karg, MEd, offers her insights:

✔ **Offer knowledge.** Most unhelpful comments are made because people are misinformed about your child's disability.

✔ **Be informed.** Providing positive, informed answers to real questions from real people will encourage awareness.

✔ **Be prepared.** Develop and practice a set of standard responses that can be used in different circumstances.

✔ **Have an escape plan.** Create some sort of signal (text, code, gesture, expression) to alert your partner or friend when you need to escape a particularly difficult situation.

✔ **Just ignore it.** Intentionally hurtful comments simply don't deserve a response; and sometimes a deliberate change of topic will send the best message.

✔ **Laugh it off.** Use humor to defuse situations if you can. Laughter can be a gentle and effective way to point out differing points of view.

✔ **Accept imperfection.** Some people have neither the capacity nor the compassion to be tolerant and understanding. Accept that there will be times when you will be surprised, hurt, and even offended by harsh or ignorant reactions. Let it go!

1. "If your AD/HD son was my child, he'd be different."

RESPONSE: "If my son was your child, *you'd* be different."

Check Your Pity at the Door

Of all the responses we've received from parents, none have bothered us more than the comments that express pity, and the sad puppy-dog faces that often accompany them.

When Gina was in her "Why me?" stage, she fed right into it.

"My daughter has autism," she would sob.

"Oh, you poor, poor thing. I feel so bad for you, Gina! Your life must be so terrible."

"Yes! That's why I'm wearing all black."

Now, when people express these feelings, Gina has a completely different response.

Tips for Positive Responses (continued)

✔ **Be patient.** Put things in perspective. Everyone is guilty of speaking without thinking at some point in their lives.

✔ **Be honest.** A quiet, honest explanation about how and why a comment may have hurt your feelings is usually the best preventative medicine, especially when you're talking to someone you feel comfortable with.

✔ **Educate the kids.** Children often say whatever is on their minds. Their honest and open questions can be a good opportunity to help educate everyone in the vicinity about your child's disability.

✔ **Focus on perception, not opinion.** Use every opportunity to create an informed, aware support system for your child by changing the perceptions of the people in your community through what you say and how you say it.

✔ **Relax.** Try to stay calm. Negative emotional responses only increase the negative stigma and stereotype, not the awareness.

"I'm telling you, Pat. I'd like to beat the tar out of that lady!"

"Why? What did she do that's so bad?"

"She told me she was sorry about Katie."

A Lesson for Teacher

One evening, Gina was sharing her dislike of "pity mongers" with her high school friend Rosalie, the mother of a beautiful four-year-old daughter, Hope, with Down syndrome. Rosalie, who like Gina disdains pity, told her a great story involving her older daughter, Tessa, who was age eight at the time.

Rosalie was picking up Tessa at school. Tessa jumped in the car and excitedly announced, "Mommy, we had a new substitute teacher today. She was so pretty and nice, and she acted like my friend. She asked me all kinds of questions about my family."

"What did you tell her?" Rosalie asked.

"I told her I have a twin sister, Sarah, in another class and another sister, Ellie, in first grade. Then I told her I have a sister in preschool named Hope who has Down syndrome."

"What did she say?" Rosalie asked.

"She said, 'I'm sorry.'"

"She did?" Rosalie asked, disappointed.

"But then I told her Hope can walk . . . and Hope can sing . . . and Hope knows all her ABCs."

"What did she say when you told her that?"

"Well, she kinda acted surprised."

"Really?" Rosalie asked.

"Yeah. In my head I kept thinking she didn't know anything about Down syndrome. I wanted to tell her not to be sorry for Hope. Would it have been all right for me to do that, Mommy?"

"Yes, honey, it would, but I think you already did in your own sweet way."

All We Are Saying Is Give People a Chance

With the remarks people sometimes make about our kids, it's easy to think they are rude and insensitive. We now believe that it's simply because they don't know how to talk to us about our kids. They're afraid to say the wrong thing. We, too, have been guilty of saying the wrong thing when placed in uncomfortable situations.

"Gina, thank you so much for coming to my mom's wake."

"Are you kidding? I wouldn't miss this for the world."

We both believe that our sense of humor and openness have made people feel more comfortable about talking to us about our kids. We've even discovered that our willingness to share has made other people feel comfortable sharing with us. This reality hit Gina one day when she was waiting in the long deli line at her local supermarket when a woman came barreling around the corner with her shopping cart and shouted out, "Hey, Gina! Guess what? I'm bipolar!"

We firmly believe that when we talk openly about our kids' disabilities, we take away the shame, which is one of the many reasons we never shut up.

Teaching an Old Dog (Patty) a New Trick

Our understanding of how best to treat persons with disabilities continues to evolve. For example, early in our speaking career, a lovely woman with a service dog attended our presentation. Patty, seeing the dog and not being so bright, immediately went up to the dog and started petting him. She was just about to play fetch with him when the young woman kindly informed Patty that you should not pet a service dog without the owner's permission. It was something Patty had never learned. Now she knows to ask and to put away her Frisbee.

CHAPTER 5

Sharing Imperfect Family Secrets

Telling Family Members About Your Child's Disability

When we were growing up, we were forced to share a bedroom, in addition to wearing the same goofy matching outfits. ("Ma, why do I still have to dress like her? I'm eighteen.") With a seven-year age gap and different interests, we had very little in common. We did, however, agree on one major thing: We couldn't stand each other.

It's ironic that as adults, we've become the best of friends, sharing the same sense of humor and hobbies. ("So Gene, you definitely want to run away from home with me?")

We've always been there for each other and for each other's kids, as Patty demonstrated by giving Gina an incredible gift when Katie was just three months old.

"Gene, I know you have to go back to work and are worrying about who's gonna take care of Katie. I was thinking I'd like to take her a few days a week. My girls would love it. And I don't want you to pay me."

When our kids were diagnosed with their disabilities, we grew even closer. With Katie as her oldest child, Gina had no one to compare Katie to and often relied on Patty's experience with her daughters.

"Hey Pat, I'm really worried about Katie. She never comes out of her room or spends time with us. All she does is sleep."

"That's not Asperger's. That's an annoying teenager. She sounds pretty normal to me."

And whenever Jennifer and Patty are in crisis, Gina is always the first to step up and support her sister.

"Gene, Jenn's really been acting up, and the other kids keep fighting. Would you mind coming to get Mikey?"

"No problem. I'll be there in an hour."

We didn't realize how fortunate we were to have this relationship until we started meeting parents of children with disabilities who reminded us:

"You're so lucky you can rely on each other for support. I don't even talk to my sister anymore. She thinks her kids are so perfect. She has no idea how hard my life is."

"If I ordered a book, could you anonymously ship it to my brother and his wife? I'm so sick of them putting down my kids and bragging about theirs."

During one of our speaking engagements, we met a caring woman who was saddened by the isolation she was feeling with her younger brother. In this case, she didn't have a child with a disability; *he* did.

"He never comes to family events anymore," she told us. "I love my brother and miss him. He's withdrawing from us. What can I do?"

The group offered some helpful insights:

"Do you ask him how his kids are doing?"

"Did you consider having family events at his house? Sometimes our kids are more comfortable in their own homes."

"Are you careful not to talk about the accomplishments of your children in a way that might make him feel bad?"

"Have you read books about his child's disability?"

"Maybe you could attend a seminar with him on his child's disability."

Parental Pride

When we speak to parent groups, we're also reminded of another blessing we've taken for granted—the support of our parents.

"You're so lucky your parents support you. Mine just don't understand bipolar disorder. They think my son needs a good spanking."

"I never see my parents anymore. It's just too hard. They have no idea how to handle my kids."

"I wish my mom and dad were still here. They'd help me through this. I miss them so much."

We're the first to admit that our parents are not perfect (whether *they* realize this is a discussion for another day or book). They have, however, always wanted only the best for all of their children, which is why it was so hard for them to watch us struggle with our children's disabilities.

It certainly wasn't anything they saw coming. In fact, when Gina told our father about Katie's Asperger's diagnosis, he was shocked. Because Gina lived closest to them, our parents spent a great deal of time with Katie, and our newly retired father had grown particularly close to her.

"Hi, Mom. Where's Dad?"

"Oh, hi, Gene. He's at a tea party under the kitchen table with Katie."

The day Gina told them about Katie's diagnosis, our father was convinced she was wrong.

"Mom and Dad, Katie has a form of autism."

"Gina, are you sure? She's so smart. Just last week, your mother and I got lost and Katie directed us home. I just can't get over that they think there's something wrong with her."

"Dad, it's true!" Gina cried. "This is serious. She'll probably never get married or have kids, or leave home."

Our mother, a type A worrier, reacted a little differently. "Saint Anthony! My beautiful baby has a form of autism! What exactly is autism?"

When Patty told them about Jenn's diagnosis, they were equally surprised.

"Are you sure she's not just acting up to get attention because she's in her sister's shadow?"

"You mean Jan Brady syndrome?" Patty asked. "I wish it were that easy, but this is real."

Our parents would have liked to believe that Jennifer's problem was behavioral or, even better, the result of some parental mistake on the part of Patty and Michael. They loved to point those out.

"Patty Ann, you buy your kids too many gifts for Christmas. Do you know what we got when we were kids? Tangerines."

A parental problem could be fixed. But a mental illness? That would stay with Jennifer for the rest of her life. Even worse, our parents, who had practical advice for every situation ("Gina, put baby oil on your countertops to give them a healthy sheen") didn't know anything about dealing with a mental illness.

When Patty told them about Jenn's violent moments ("I'm afraid she's gonna hurt Mikey"), they almost didn't believe her.

"How could that sweet girl be doing those things, Patty?"

In their eyes, Jenn was their sweetest grandchild. She was always the first to say thank you, the first to help someone in need, and the first to come running whenever our parents visited. ("Nana and Grampy are here!") She was particularly close to our mother, sharing the same interests, which were somehow lost on the two of us.

"Nana, is that a new soap dish in the bathroom? I love it. It really brings out the misty taupe in your curtains."

"You noticed! Your mother and aunt walked right by it. I don't know what's wrong with those two."

Wake-up Call

It took a desperate phone call from Patty for them to fully grasp the depths of Jenn's struggles.

"Mom and Dad, I need you to come to my house right away," said an eerily calm Patty. "Jennifer is really bad and Michael is out of town."

"Saint Anthony! We're on our way!" our mother replied.

When our parents arrived at Patty's house, Jennifer was frantically pacing back and forth in the living room. When she spotted our parents, she screamed, "What are they doing here? I told you I'm not going to the hospital!"

Then she ran upstairs to the bathroom and slammed the door screaming, "If you try to take me to the hospital, I'll jump out the window!" Our mother was frantic. "Tony, do something! She could kill herself!"

Without any thought, our father raced up the stairs and slammed his seventy-year-old body into the door, breaking the lock. He found Jennifer in a ball in the corner and went right over to her, picking her up and holding her in a tight bear hug.

"Let me go, Grampy!" Jennifer screamed, kicking away. "Please don't take me to the hospital! I can't go there, Grampy. No!" she cried.

Our mother raced in to help. "Jennifer, please! We love you! Don't do this to your mother," she pleaded. "Do you think I like seeing you this way?"

"Mom, please, go downstairs," a calm Patty commanded, knowing our mother's anxiety was not good for her health—or for Jennifer's fragile state.

"Why can't you all just leave me alone?" Jennifer screamed as Patty and our father each got on one side of her and carried her down the stairs and out of the house to Patty's car.

On the way out the door, Patty spotted her two other children, who were silently taking everything in.

"Jules! Take care of your brother!" Patty told her eldest child.

"My poor baby!" my mother cried, fully realizing what Patty had been enduring.

"Mom, just sit in the back with Dad and hold on to her!" Patty ordered as she and our father forced Jennifer into the car.

"I'm not going to that stupid hospital! I'm gonna jump out of this car and kill myself! I hate you, Mom!"

At that, our parents, who had sandwiched Jenn between them, tightened their grip on Jenn's bony arms, while Jennifer cried out, "Don't make me go! I can't do it."

After about ten minutes, Jennifer started to calm down, resting her head on her grandmother's shoulder.

"That's better. It's gonna be all right, Jennifer, honey. Your mom loves you so much. She's only trying to help you," our mother said, brushing Jennifer's hair away from her red eyes.

Hours later, when Michael relieved them at the hospital, our parents drove home in silence—both too exhausted and stunned to say anything. When they got home, our mother phoned Gina. "Gina, it was awful! You think you have it hard with Katie, but this was far worse. I feel so terrible; I had no idea things were so bad. Your poor sister is suffering."

Following Our Lead

When Patty joined her support group and began talking more openly about Jennifer's struggles, our parents slowly began to follow her lead. Our father, usually a man of few words, surprised us with how much talking he did in public about the kids' disabilities.

"Hey Gina, did you know that Johnston girl you used to chum around with has a kid with autism?"

"How do you know, Dad?"

Tips for Special Grandparenting

Many grandparents are finding that traditional grandparenting roles and rules simply cannot meet the challenges of special needs grandchildren, and are discovering new ways to become amazing sources of support and strength for their children and their grandchildren. LeeAnn Karg, MEd, stresses these key points to remember in successful special grandparenting:

✔ **Unity.** Always follow the parents' lead. Consistency is the foundation of every routine, schedule, and program for your grandchild. Deviating from that consistency will only create confusion and anxiety in your grandchild and frustration for his or her parents.

✔ **Information.** Read every evaluation thoroughly. Ask questions if you need clarity. Read books, go online, visit the library, do whatever you need to do to research every aspect of your grandchild's disability. You can't help if you don't know.

✔ **Awareness.** Make supporting your children and grandchildren a community affair. Community awareness leads to community tolerance and community acceptance: everyone wins!

"My barber told me."

Our mother was the same way. "Patty, did you know Patty Duke has bipolar disorder? And Jane Pauley, too? I love her hair, by the way."

Before we knew it, they were telling friends and members of our extended family, who were surprisingly open with them as well:

"Well, Vi, you know my grandson has ADD."

"My granddaughter was diagnosed with bipolar disorder last year."

"My husband's sister is dyslexic. But they didn't know it back then."

Our parents never knew any of it, and were instantly comforted to know they weren't alone. Even to this day, they're constantly collecting information for us:

Tips for Special Grandparenting (continued)

✔ **Acceptance.** Do *not* speculate about what might have caused your grandchild's condition. Blame, guilt, and shame are negative emotions that will only cause pain; they will not change your grandchild's disability.

✔ **Patience.** Slow down. Plan on spending time with your grandchild. You and your unconditional love are very much needed. Find the pace that your grandchild needs to feel safe. Make the connection.

✔ **Respite.** Raising a child with a disability is a twenty-four-hour-a-day, seven-day-a-week commitment. There are no vacations or sick days. Sometimes the greatest gift you can give your *children* is relaxation time.

✔ **Compassion.** Realize that the stress of raising a child with a disability may cause family members to be more sensitive than they would otherwise be. We know there are no easy answers or quick fixes to our particular issues and stressors. Sometimes we just need to vent—and we need you to just listen!

"Gina Frances, I cut out this article about a support group that meets in the town over from you."

"Patty, NBC has a special report on bipolar disorder. Don't forget to watch it."

Before long, our mother, who loves to inform—okay, nag—us about health-related issues ("Gina, you need grains to stay regular") now had a whole new topic to talk to us about.

"Patty, is Jennifer getting enough sleep? I just read that bipolar kids need their sleep. Make sure you give her a warm glass of milk before she goes to bed."

Our parents even became bragging grandparents.

"This is my granddaughter Katie. She's eleven and has autism, and she's so smart."

"And this is her older cousin, Jennifer. She has bipolar disorder. It's very common today and is difficult at times, but she's so strong. We're so proud of her."

"Ma and Dad, stop it or someone will write *Shut Up About Your Imperfect Grandchild!*"

Before we even realized it, our parents had joined The Movement of Imperfection, openly bragging about their grandchildren to anyone who would listen.

Are You Talking to Us?

Our parents are also constantly expressing their pride to us, which is somewhat surprising, since when we were growing up, they tended to dwell on the things we needed to improve (they sure had a lot to choose from).

"Gina Frances, your posture is terrible. Every night we want you to stack encyclopedias on your head and walk around the house."

"Okay, I'll do it, but I'm only going as high as the letter L."

Today, our parents attend all our Massachusetts-based speaking events, sitting at the back of the room and giving us hand signals to tell us when we need to speak up (or fix our hair).

"I'm so proud of you girls. I can't believe how you can just get up there and speak," our father often tells us, beaming with pride.

"Well, Dad, we're speaking about a subject we know well—imperfection," Gina replied.

"Gina does have a point, Tony," affirmed our mother.

"Yeah, thank God you didn't send us to charm school like you wanted to, Dad. People love our imperfections," added Patty.

Even Patty's mother-in-law, Vera, who was initially reticent to open up about Jenn's struggles, stood behind our efforts with the book. "I'm just so proud of what you girls are doing. It's so important," she repeatedly told us after attending one of our talks in her hometown.

A Divided Family

We would have loved it if all our family members reacted the way Vera and our parents did, but the fact is, many of them didn't. Some were, and still are, highly critical of us for openly discussing our children's disabilities.

"We believe some things should be kept private," one close family member told Gina. "It's nobody's business."

You can imagine how this person took the news that we were not only telling people about our kids' struggles but also writing our book and going on an extensive media tour to talk about our kids.

Even when stories about our book and The Movement of Imperfection were printed in their local newspapers, these family members never acknowledged that they had read them. In fact, when Gina's husband asked one if she planned to read the book, she responded, "No, why would I want to read that?"

If a book was written about their kid's disability, we'd want to read it and learn more about it, Gina and Mike thought.

What surprised us most was that these family members had always shown Katie so much love. Why then would they not want to read a book about the child they adored? Were they ashamed of her?

We hoped they would eventually understand our perspective, but for whatever reason, they simply couldn't. Initially, we took this personally, but then we realized that sometimes people have to work through their own issues to be able to accept those of others. Maybe they found it too painful. Maybe they weren't strong enough to deal with Katie's pain. Or maybe they were caught up in the perfection-palooza.

Whatever the reason, it made us appreciate the people in our lives, including our parents, who were willing to open their eyes to a different perspective. And if anyone knows how hard that is to do, it's us. Heck, we've struggled with change in general.

"Pat, I figured it out. I've had the same hairstyle since 1980. I think it's because I fear change."

"I hear ya, Gene. I hate changing sheets. I think it's because I'm a terrible housekeeper."

But when you have a child with a disability, you simply have no choice. Change is a part of our everyday life. We never know what each day will bring, or what crazy direction life will take us in. ("Wow, I didn't expect to be back at the pharmacy today. I was just here yesterday.")

We realized that if we wanted to do what's best for *all* our children, we had to put aside our own fears, beliefs, and expectations, and stop worrying about what people think. Unfortunately, we've met many parents who haven't been able to do that. Like Betty, a friend of a family member whose son, Ryan, has severe AD/HD. Over the years, Ryan struggled academically, and Betty did what she could to help him—having him tested and putting him on medication to help him stay focused. But as he grew older, Ryan's struggles intensified, and Betty grew increasingly helpless, though Gina tried to offer support.

"I don't know what to do, Gina. Ryan's flunking out of high school, and the school says they can't help him. I'm so stressed."

"You should go to a support group," Gina suggested. "You'll meet other parents who may be able to guide you."

"Oh, I can't go to one of those meetings. What if someone saw me? They'd know something was wrong with Ryan."

We've also met parents who chose not to advocate for other reasons.

"Thanks for the referral, Gina and Patty. I really appreciate your help. But I just can't afford to spend three thousand dollars on a neuropsych exam. We just spent a fortune on our new landscaping. We were the only house in the neighborhood that didn't have mulch. It was so embarrassing."

The truth is, most of us don't enjoy the change and uncertainty in our lives. And if given a choice, we'd prefer to spend money on retail therapy than on family therapy. But if we don't get assistance and advocate for our children, no one else will.

And where will *that* leave them?

"Hey Gene, I was looking at my check register. My last ten transactions were all to therapists."

"You mean you actually balance your checkbook?"

CHAPTER 6

Mommy's Got Some 'Splaining to Do

Breaking the Imperfect News to Your Child

Ask any parent and they will tell you—children like to ask lots and lots of questions. It starts early in their toddler years with queries like "Juice, Mama?" and continues right through the grade-school years. "What makes an ocean wave wave, Mommy?"

We must admit that over the years, we've both become very adept at answering our children's questions with quick-thinking responses like the always effective "Go ask your father." Or in this modern era of technology, "How do I know? Google it!"

But there was one question we just didn't know how to answer. One that left the two of us, nonstop talkers, speechless.

"What's wrong with me, Mom?"

It's a question every parent of a special needs child must ponder, even if their child doesn't ask it. Should you pretend your children are perfectly fine? Or be honest and tell them they are facing a life of difficulty? A life that will always have them battling for acceptance?

Gina's Approach: Give It to Katie Straight

Because she had told nearly everyone she encountered about Katie's disability, it seemed logical that Gina would eventually tell Katie herself. After all, the last thing Gina needed was for Katie to hear it from the butcher, the mailman, or any of the thousand other strangers Gina told.

But telling Katie was much more complicated than that; Gina

feared it might break her spirit. You see, from the time she was little, Katie has always had a very positive opinion of herself and her abilities, even when others (i.e., her mother) might not have shared the same viewpoint.

"Mom, don't you think my coloring is really good?"

"Uh, yeah, you've definitely improved. I like how you don't let the lines stop you from being creative."

It was only when people pointed out Katie's differences that she felt badly about herself. Plus, the last thing Gina wanted was for Katie to feel the sadness and grief *she* had felt over learning about the disability. (What would that do to the family Kleenex budget?)

"You're not different, honey. You're just like everybody else," she would tell Katie again and again. But Katie was smart enough not to believe her mother. "It's not true, Mom. I'm different. Kids think I'm weird. They make fun of the way I flap my hands."

Taking a page out of our mother's book, Gina replied, "They're just jealous 'cause you're so beautiful. Look at your blond hair and blue eyes. And I must say, you have the prettiest clothes."

When Gina finally got the Asperger's diagnosis, she decided to tell Katie, figuring that Katie would feel better knowing there was a neurological reason she was doing some of the things she did. "So you see, honey, there's a reason you can't stop flapping your hands. It's not your fault. It's called stimming, and it's part of your Asperger's."

Gina's greatest challenge was trying to explain Asperger's in a way Katie could understand, especially since Gina barely understood it herself. She was waiting for the right opportunity, which came one evening when she was tucking Katie in and Katie asked, "Mom, do you think I'm stupid?" At that, Gina laid down beside her daughter on Katie's Powerpuff Girls comforter, looked Katie straight in the eye, and answered, "Oh honey, you're not stupid. You've got to believe that."

"Yes, I am, Mom. I'm weird, too. Everyone thinks so. I can't understand math, and sometimes my brain tells me to say things that just don't make sense," she cried.

"Like what?" Gina asked.

"Well, today I was really nervous and I told all the kids I had a tail."

"Honey, you're not weird. Your brain just works differently from other people's and sometimes makes you say things without thinking."

"I hate my brain. Why does it have to be that way?" Katie cried.

Gina could barely respond; she had asked herself the same question over and over again. *Why me? Why does my daughter have to*

About Hand Flapping and Stimming
(Condensed from kargacademy.com)

Gina had a hard time understanding why Katie was constantly flapping her hands. LeeAnn Karg, MEd, explains:

Katie's hand flapping was a form of self-stimulation, or "stimming," which can be defined as any nonfunctional behavior involving repetitive or rhythmic action that is an unconscious or purposeful response to anxiety, stress, or boredom. Examples of *normal* stimming might include gum chewing, toe tapping, nail biting, or cracking knuckles.

Examples of *abnormal* stimming might be:

✔ Repetitive rhythmic movement patterns (hand flapping, body rocking, spinning or flipping of objects)
✔ Repetitive vocal sequences (humming, mouth or throat noises)
✔ Imposed sensory input behaviors (atypical body postures, teeth grinding, smelling, tasting, staring)

In children with PDDs, stimming also serves as an effective way to reduce or increase the amount of stimulus from their environment to achieve a more comfortable level of brain activity. Self-stimulatory behavior is a problem when the repetitive actions are considered socially unacceptable in nature, or socially stigmatizing, or if they preclude normal academic or social functioning. Fortunately, once the behavior is understood, there are a number of socially appropriate or acceptable behaviors that can replace it.

suffer? How come other people don't have to deal with this? But she couldn't say all that to Katie. She was the mother, and everyone knew a mother was supposed to make her kids feel better.

"I know, honey. It isn't fair. You're such a good kid. I think God gave this to you because he knows you can handle it."

"I *can't* handle it. And I don't want it. Why couldn't he give it to someone else?"

"Because he knows how strong you are. Look at you. Every time things get tough or you get knocked down, you get right back up again. You're the strongest girl I know. I would never have been able to go through what you've gone through as a kid. You get teased and bullied and you get up for school the next day ready to try again. I've learned so much from watching you. You have so much heart."

And she really did, as she demonstrated when she said, "Thank you, Mommy. I love you. I feel much better already."

"I love you, too," Gina responded, thinking that Katie had no idea how much she meant it or how much their little talk was meant to comfort Gina as much as Katie. Which is why, before she closed the door, Gina felt compelled to ask, "Katie, just so I'm clear, you know you don't have a tail, right?"

"Yes, Mom. I know I don't have a tail. Now can you get out of here?"

A BRILLIANT TRAIN OF THOUGHT FROM A NOT-SO-BRIGHT SOURCE—PATTY

Because Patty helped care for Katie as an infant, she and Katie have always had a particularly close relationship. As Katie's godmother, Patty has continually been one of her biggest supporters. In her mind, Katie is the ultimate underdog, and there's nothing Patty loves more than rooting for the underdog, probably because she's always been one herself.

"Thanks for coming to my basketball game, Mom and Dad. Sorry I didn't play again."

"That's okay, Patty. At least we don't have to wash your uniform."

Patty admires Katie's resilience and laid-back approach to life. "You just gotta love her, Gene. She told me getting all A's is boring."

And she's always the first to believe in Katie when others (mostly her mother) have their doubts.

"Pat, I'm a nervous wreck about Katie's first Communion with all her sensitivities. Do you know if it's a sin if a kid spits out the wafer?"

"Gene, don't worry; she'll be fine. She always lands on her feet when you least expect it."

Patty was right. Despite Gina's anxiety, Katie accepted the Communion wafer just like all the other kids.

"I did it, Mom! Now can you help me get this awful cracker thing off the roof of my mouth before I throw up!"

I THINK I CAN!

One day, when Katie was struggling with feeling different at school, Patty came to visit and handed Katie a book, *The Little Engine That Could*. "Gene, I saw this book in the store and had to get it for Katie. She reminds me of that engine. She's got so much heart."

The inscription Patty wrote said:

Katie,

Don't ever quit. Stay true to the person you are.
I love you, my godchild.

Auntie Patty

Gina thanked Patty and put the book on Katie's bookshelf, forgetting about it. Then one evening when Katie was feeling sad about being different, Gina spotted the book and thought, *That's it! The Little Engine That Could!* She pulled out the book, climbed into bed next to Katie, and began reading to her. When she finished, she put the book down and rolled over to face her daughter.

"So you see, honey, you are that little train," Gina said, brushing Katie's blond hair away from her bright blue eyes.

"This one?" Katie asked, pointing to the cute blue train.

"Yes, honey, that's you."

"But that train was so slow," she protested.

"Yes, honey, but it was the only one that had heart. And I may be prejudiced, but I think you are much cuter than those other trains."

"*Mom . . .*"

Steaming ahead with this brilliant analogy, Gina continued, "And, as you can see, there's nothing wrong with you. You got to the same place as everyone else; you just had a bumpier ride. Sure, you had to carry a heavy load and make it up that awful hill, and then you had to deal with that clown jumping up and down and distracting you—"

"Okay, Mom, I'm that train. Now can I just go to bed? You're making my head hurt!"

Gina read the book to Katie every night. She wasn't sure how much Katie understood her message until five years later, when Gina walked into Katie's room to say good night and spotted the familiar book on Katie's bed.

"Katie, why is *The Little Engine That Could* out? Did you read it tonight?"

"Uh, duh, Mom," she said in her sarcastic teen tone. "I read that book all the time. Every time I have a bad day and I worry about being different."

Gina couldn't have been more proud. *No wonder I got that #1 Mom necklace for my birthday. I really am the number one mom,* she thought. Then she picked up the phone to call Patty, the number one aunt, to share the news.

KATIE GETS THE SCOOP

In addition to sharing *The Little Engine That Could,* Gina was constantly trying to explain Katie's disabilities in ways Katie could understand.

"Katie, being different isn't bad. It's actually good. Think of everyone else as the same. Like . . . like . . . vanilla ice cream."

"But I don't really like ice cream that much," Katie said, once again causing Gina to suspect she wasn't Katie's biological mother.

"I know, but just follow me. Vanilla is the same—no chocolate, no nuts, no sprinkles. You are not vanilla or the same as everyone else. You're more like . . ."

"Rainbow sherbet," Katie completed. "I really like rainbow sherbet."

"Yes! Exactly!" Gina said, beaming with pride and thinking Katie couldn't have picked a better flavor to describe herself.

"What ice cream are you, Mommy?" Katie asked.

Gina thought about it. "Hmm, let's see. I'm definitely not vanilla. Too smooth. I'm more bumpy. Like rocky road! Yeah, rocky road."

Gina could tell Katie liked her analogy, especially when she asked, "Mommy, what kind of ice cream is Emmy?" (her little sister).

"Oh, she's cookie dough."

"Mom, how about Aunt Patty?"

"Oh, definitely something with nuts!"

Patty's Strategy for Telling Jenn: No Day at the Beach

Patty really didn't have a choice in talking openly about Jennifer's disability. Jennifer knew there was something wrong with her (the hospital visits were certainly good indications) and was often apologetic. "Mom, I'm sorry I acted that way. I don't know why I get so angry."

When Patty finally got the bipolar diagnosis, she was relieved to finally know the reason for Jenn's struggles. On the one hand, it was validation she wasn't a terrible mother. On the other, this was a serious illness that would be difficult to understand or explain, especially to Jennifer. Patty knew she had to tell Jennifer, but she wasn't sure how to go about it.

She found her opportunity a few days after Jennifer was released from the hospital, when Patty's family was on their annual Cape Cod vacation.

One evening, Patty and Jenn were walking along the quiet beach when Patty stopped, put her arm around Jenn's slight shoulders, and said, "Jenn, I'm so glad you're out of the hospital. I missed you so much."

"I don't know why you did. I make everyone unhappy. I don't mean to; it just happens. Sometimes I can't control it."

"Well, Jenn, you can't help it. The doctors told us they think you have bipolar disorder."

"I heard you and Dad talking about it, but I don't know what it means."

"It means you have a chemical imbalance in your brain. The good news is that with your medication you can lead a normal life as long as you stay on it."

"But there's nothing normal about my life, Mom. I'm the only one in our family who has this. How come Jules and Mikey don't have it?"

"I don't know," Patty answered honestly.

"Sometimes I feel like I just don't fit in with this family. At the hospital they kept telling me I was a 'model patient.' I knew that some of the other kids were either yelling or disrespectful, so I was different from them and didn't really fit in there, either. I just don't know where all of this came from or where I belong."

"I don't know, Jenn, but we do have a cousin on Nana's side who has it. It's in our family."

"But that doesn't answer my question, Mom. Why do I have it? Why me?"

Like Gina, Patty tried her best to answer.

"You were chosen because God knows you're strong enough to handle it. Look at how well you're doing. Two days ago, you were in a hospital and now you're here, doing great. I'm so proud of you. Do you think any of your friends would handle what you've been through as well as you did? I don't think so."

"Mom, can we go back now? I'm really tired, and I don't want to talk about this anymore," Jenn said as she slowly walked away from Patty toward the car.

My poor baby, Patty thought, watching Jenn walk away from her. *She looks so thin and fragile. She's been through so much.* The worst part was, Patty had no idea what was ahead.

JENN'S QUESTIONING CONTINUES

As Jennifer got older, she began to inquire more about her illness with her therapist and Patty. By the time she reached age fourteen, her questions were getting increasingly challenging for Patty, who would have preferred to use a lifeline and phone a friend to get the right answers.

"Mom, how do the doctors know I have bipolar disorder? Are they absolutely sure? Because it seems like they diagnosed me too quickly."

"Well, Jenn, you met the criteria—the depression, the mania, the visions—and you responded to bipolar medications."

"Why do you have to disclose my illness on the school forms? I never act out at school."

"Jennifer, it's important that the school have your history so they can understand your needs."

"Will I have to be on medication for the rest of my life? I don't like the way I feel on it. What happens if I stop taking it?"

"Bipolar disorder is a chemical imbalance, Jenn. Your medication helps you stay stable—so you don't have the highs and lows. When you're an adult you'll have to decide for yourself if you'll take it. But if it helps you, I hope you will, because you've seen how sad you get when you're off it."

I'm Not Okay, but That's Okay

It was our decision to tell Jennifer and Katie—whether they chose to tell their friends was up to them. That is, until we put our not-so-brilliant heads together and conceived the idea of writing a book. Before we could proceed, we needed to know they were okay with the idea. So we asked them.

"Katie, is it okay if I write a book about your journey with Asperger's?"

"Sure. Does this mean we'll be rich and I'll have a swimming pool?"

Since then, Katie has been extremely open about her disability to her friends and family, often telling jokes about it.

"Hey Mom, I have a joke for you."

"Okay, honey. What is it?"

"What do you get when you sit on a hamburger?"

"I don't know. What?"

"An Asperger."

She's so proud of this joke that whenever we travel for speaking engagements, she asks us to tell the joke and report back to her.

"Hi, honey, it's Mom. We just finished our talk in Montana."

"Did you tell my joke?"

"We sure did, and the whole room roared."

"Hey Dad! Guess what? They love me in Montana! I'm famous!" Katie exclaimed.

Katie also openly talks about her Asperger's around the house to educate us on her quirks and idiosyncrasies.

"Mom! Please fix the microwave! I can't stand it when the clock isn't set!"

Tips for Success at Home
(Condensed from kargacademy.com)

Katie finds home to be her safe place, which is really important to children with disabilities. LeeAnn Karg, MEd, offers these tips for creating success and comfort at home:

✔ **Create predictable schedules.** Develop a structured, predictable daily schedule simple enough to be adapted to any situation or setting. Then commit to *always* following that routine, no matter where you are or who you're with. Remember that any sudden change to the schedule, even for "fun" activities, will create stress and anxiety.

✔ **Structure everything.** Break down every activity into small, simple steps. Approach every activity one step at a time. Practice every new activity or skill privately before trying it in a social setting.

✔ **Get prepared.** Don't plan any change in schedule or new activity without allowing at least one full week for preparation time. Make sure you have pictures of anyone or anyplace you're going to visit. Get floor plans of any buildings, maps of any amusement parks or zoos, samples of any sights, sounds, and scents you might encounter. Leave nothing to chance; let nothing be a surprise.

Tips for Success at Home (continued)

✔ **Simplify your speech.** Give logical, concrete explanations and directions, and reduce the amount of information you are providing to your child indirectly to any increases in stimulation from the environment.

✔ **Pay attention.** Be aware of sensory input from the environment: noise, temperature, smell, lighting, textures, people, animals, etc.

✔ **Employ coping strategies.** Teach specific coping strategies to your child for each anxiety-provoking event or thought and every possible instance of sensory overload. Practice those coping skills every day.

✔ **Be concrete.** Be logical, organized, clear, concise, and concrete in all communication with your child. State every direction and expectation clearly and precisely, and follow them up with visual cues and timed verbal reminders.

✔ **Understand cause and effect.** Teach your child specific cause-and-effect relationships to help them cope with the unpredictability of social interaction. Learn about social competence and how to teach it.

✔ **Organize.** Teach your child specific organizational and time management skills for specific tasks at school and at home.

✔ **Use strengths.** Make use of your child's strengths to help with weaknesses. Verbal explanations can clarify visual material just as well as visual demonstrations can enhance verbal instructions.

✔ **Reflect.** Teach your child how to recognize and use nonverbal communication and show them how to practice in the mirror. Teach your child to recognize specific physical and facial reactions from their audience to determine whether they are communicating effectively. Practice and role-play social interaction in group activities.

"All right, but what's the big deal, Katie?"

"Mom, I can't explain it. It's an Aspie thing."

Katie has also helped educate her family on when she needs quiet time. "Mom, I have to go to my room for a few hours. Being around you peeps all day wears me out."

Gina is so used to Katie's being open about her disability that she often forgets that many other children and their families aren't.

"Katie, I really like that Adam kid at school. What's his disability?"

"I don't know, Mom. What, do you think we sit around and talk about what's wrong with each other? Duh!"

Special Surprise

We have met a lot of parents like us who have chosen to openly discuss their children's issues with them, including Stacy, the mother of twelve-year-old John.

"John, you have bipolar disorder, AD/HD, and some learning issues," she repeatedly told him from the time he was eight.

The news didn't seem to affect John, until one day when he came home from school and saw a book on the dishwasher.

"Mom, what's that?" he asked.

"Oh, I got it today when I went to hear these two special needs mothers speak about their kids. I figured I'd get one for us."

"Are you saying I have *special needs*? You never told me that!" a distressed John cried.

"What do you mean? I told you about your learning issues, AD/HD, and bipolar disorder. It's why you're on an IEP."

"Yeah, but I didn't know that meant I have special needs. When were you gonna tell me?" John cried, devastated.

The Word Is Out

As open as we've been about our kids' disabilities, we've met our share of parents who, for whatever reason, choose not to tell their kids. But as our friend Alice, the mother of a ten-year-old son with nonverbal learning disability, shared with us, that's no guarantee they won't find out through the "imperfect" grapevine.

Alice has always been very open with her son Carl about his disability. Her friend Liz, also the mother of a ten-year-old with the same disability, has taken the opposite approach in telling her daughter, Lacy. Lacy actually had no idea about her disability until one day when she was on a playdate with Carl.

"Got teased again today," Carl casually announced as they walked around the block.

"How come?" Lacy asked, giving him a concerned look.

" 'Cause I act weird when kids are around sometimes. I get really nervous. My mom says it's because of my nonverbal," Carl answered.

"I do that, too," said Lacy.

"That's 'cause you have nonverbal, too," Carl replied.

"I have what?" Lacy asked, stopping in her tracks.

"Nonverbal learning disability. You don't know?"

"No. I don't even know what that is," she replied, confused.

"It's a different way of thinking. That's what my mom says."

"Are you sure I have it?"

"Oh yeah, your mom told my mom, and my mom told me."

Upon hearing this, Lacy went running toward the house. When she opened the door, she hollered out, "Mom! How come you never told me I have . . . what's it called again?" she asked, turning to Carl.

"Nonverbal learning disability," he answered quite proudly, folding his hands on his stomach.

Liz turned to look at Alice as a flushed Alice announced, "Well, Carl, I think we'll be going now. We've probably overstayed our welcome."

Jennifer's Philosophy

Unlike Katie, Jenn was a little more reluctant to openly talk about her disability. She may have wanted to learn more about it herself, but she didn't want her friends to know. She was, however, always willing to reach out to others with disabilities, most notably Katie. When Katie was experiencing difficulty with bullying, all of Patty's children were sympathetic, but it was Jenn who was the most bothered by it. "Mom, I can't sleep. I can't stop thinking about Katie. Can we call her tomorrow and invite her to sleep over?"

Recommended Children's Books on Disabilities

One of the biggest challenges parents of children with disabilities face is finding ways to explain the disability to their children. We and other parents have found some wonderful books designed to help facilitate that communication. These include the following:

All Cats Have Asperger Syndrome (Asperger's syndrome)
by Kathy Hoopmann

Brandon and the Bipolar Bear (bipolar disorder/mental illness)
by Tracy Anglada, illustrated by Jennifer Taylor and Toby Ferguson

Susan Laughs (physical handicaps)
by Jeanne Willis and Tony Ross

Eukee the Jumpy Jumpy Elephant (AD/HD)
by Clifford L. Corman, MD, and Esther Trevino, illustrated by Richard A. DiMatteo

Mommy, I Feel Funny! A Child's Experience with Epilepsy (epilepsy)
by Danielle M. Rocheford, illustrated by Chris Herrick

Leo the Late Bloomer (developmental delays)
by Robert Kraus, illustrated by Jose Aruego

Otto Learns about His Medicine: A Story about Medication for Children with AD/HD (AD/HD)
by Matthew R. Galvin, illustrated by Sandra Ferraro

What It's Like to Be Me (physical handicaps)
edited by Helen Exley

What-to-Do Guides for Kids
by Dawn Huebner, illustrated by Bonnie Matthews

This series of books offers support for children with a wide range of challenges. Books include:

And whenever Katie's little sister, Emily, who suffers from anxiety and learning issues (more on that later) is upset, Jennifer is the first to comfort her, "Emmy, you worry a lot, huh? I do, too. We're a lot alike."

Jenn wasn't as quick to talk about her struggles with her friends. In fact, she didn't tell most of them about her mother's book. But a few of her friends surprised her by buying the book and asking for her autograph.

"Hey Jenn, I read your mom's book. It's awesome. I'm so proud of you!"

When the opportunity presented itself for us to speak in Patty's hometown, Patty wasn't sure it was a good idea. ("Gene, I'd love to do this, but I have to check with Jennifer first. It might be too close to home. The last thing I want to do is make her life harder.")

But, as she's done so many times in her life, Jennifer surprised her mother.

Recommended Children's Books (continued)

What to Do When You Worry Too Much:
  A Kid's Guide to Overcoming Anxiety

What to Do When Your Brain Gets Stuck:
  A Kid's Guide to Overcoming OCD

What to Do When Your Temper Flares:
  A Kid's Guide to Overcoming Problems with Anger

What to Do When You Dread Your Bed:
  A Kid's Guide to Overcoming Problems with Sleep

What to Do When You Grumble Too Much:
  A Kid's Guide to Overcoming Negativity

What to Do When Bad Habits Take Hold:
  A Kid's Guide to Overcoming Nail Biting and More

"No, Mom, I want you to speak. You and Aunt Gina are doing a good thing."

Jennifer not only allowed us to speak, but she also attended the event. It meant so much to Patty.

When Jennifer got older and entered high school, her need for privacy increased. "Mom, please take that 'My bipolar kid loves me and hates me' bumper sticker off your car. It's, like, so embarrassing."

Though Jennifer was growing more and more worried about kids at school finding out about her illness, she had no problem sharing her struggles with other kids in similar situations.

"Jenn, I had the saddest phone call today from a mother whose daughter has bipolar disorder. The mother said her daughter is depressed because she doesn't have any friends."

"Can I call her daughter, Mom? I'd like to talk to her."

"Sure, Jenn. I'll ask her mom," Patty responded, not at all surprised. Jennifer always loved to help others.

A Surprise Speaking Appearance

One day, Jennifer gave Patty a wonderful surprise when she asked, "Mom, can I come to your speaking event tonight?"

Patty was shocked and thrilled. Her other two children were always eager to attend events, but Jennifer went through a period where she showed little or no interest.

At the event, Jennifer sat in the back of the room and was attentive the entire time. At one point, Patty introduced Jenn to the crowd. The mother of a bipolar child turned around to face her and said, "I can't stop looking at you, Jennifer. It gives me hope that my daughter might be okay."

On the way home, Jennifer surprised Patty again when she asked, "Mom, do you think I could get up and talk sometime and share my experience?"

"Jennifer, Aunt Gina and I would love that. People really need to hear from you, and about how well you're doing."

Patty drove home with a feeling of elation.

The Movement of Imperfəction Starts Rolling

When we began our speaking tour, we were amazed at the number of children with disabilities who rallied around our message. One of the children was Anthony, a bright thirteen-year-old with AD/HD. Ever since he was diagnosed, Anthony had had difficulty accepting his disability. Whenever a commercial for AD/HD medication came on, he would run out of the room, ashamed. His parents weren't even allowed to talk about it.

While writing our book, we asked Anthony's parents, Cheryl and Tony, if they'd be willing to share some stories.

"We could fill your book with Anthony stories, but we don't think he'd let us; he's very private. We'll ask him, though."

Anthony surprised them with his response. "You mean I'm gonna be in a book? Oh yeah, you can tell my stories."

Cheryl and Tony were even more surprised one day when Anthony came home from school and announced, "Hey Mom, did you know John Smith has AD/HD, too?"

"How do you know that?" Cheryl asked, shocked that he was talking openly about this.

"He told me. He says that his parents don't believe him."

"Anthony, I can't believe you're talking to him. I thought you weren't friends with him. And why are you all of a sudden so open about your AD/HD?"

"That's easy, Mom. It's because of the book. I realized that I'm not alone and that I have nothing to be ashamed of."

We love to hear these stories of how children openly share their disabilities with other children and are still accepted. It's truly what The Movement of Imperfəction is all about.

Gina also loves it when kids know about Katie's disability and don't treat her any differently. She experienced this at Katie's tenth birthday party. While Gina was cutting the cake, Katie's friend Annie excitedly announced, "I get the first piece!" Then, realizing she was not the birthday girl, she corrected herself: "I mean, after Katie."

Smiling, Gina looked at her and said, "Annie, you know Katie doesn't like cake, right? It's part of her Asperger's."

"Oh yeah, I forgot. She's, like, so weird, but so cool."

A friend of Patty's shared this humorous story about how her son told his friend about his disability. Her son and his friend were walking down the hall at school when her son stopped his friend and blurted out, "I have AD/HD."

His friend continued walking down the hall and casually said, "Really? I have Comcast."

PART 3

Back to School Blues

Treat people as if they were
what they ought to be, and
you help them to become what
they are capable of being.

—GOETHE

CHAPTER 7

Team Meetings and Other Lessons in Dealing with the School

Insights (and Absurdities)

We all have goals for our lives that, for one reason or another, we've yet to achieve. The two of us certainly have them. Patty, for example, has long aspired to lose twenty pounds, which sadly has yet to pan out. "Gene, do you realize I've been on a diet since 1978?"

And Gina has continually strived to become more organized, to no avail. "Pat, I was gonna sign up for that organization class, but I still can't find the registration form."

There is, however, one goal we both actually have achieved. One that neither of us in our wildest dreams thought we would ever have the time or the energy to accomplish.

We both have gone back to school.

Sure, it would be great if it were for advanced degrees at institutions of higher learning, but we've actually gone back to institutions of "shorter" learning—our children's schools.

It's true. For the past several years, we've been getting hands-on practical experience dealing with our children's schools. And we're not alone. In a given year, parents of children with disabilities or special needs log more hours at their children's schools than the custodial staff. Here are just some of the many reasons we've been known to visit:

✔ To set a positive tone for the school year by sucking up to the teacher. ("Nice to meet you, Mrs. Fox. My Emily is so excited to be in your class. She picked out these apple earrings for you.")

✔ To participate in the cultural phenomenon known as the *team meeting*. (Note: In an informal survey we conducted, nine out of ten parents indicated they would prefer a colonoscopy to a team meeting, though both are pains in the a$&!)

✔ To bring in our children's medication. ("I know there's a no drug policy at school, but if I could just give my daughter her fifty milligrams of Ritalin, I'll be on my way.")

✔ To visit with the principal to conduct damage control for discipline-related events. ("Trust me, Mr. Belding, Bobby is very remorseful about telling Mrs. Jones she has a beard. He has AD/HD and sometimes blurts things out without thinking.")

✔ To drive them to school when they miss the bus, as they sometimes do for one reason or another. ("Sorry I missed the bus again, Mom. I was practicing my funny faces in the mirror!")

✔ To give back to the community by selflessly volunteering our time to aid our children's teachers. We're actually there to spy, but that's our story and we're sticking to it. ("Why, Mrs. Krabappel, I'd be happy to clean your desk.")

✔ To drop off things our special children are sometimes prone to forget. ("Mom, I was in a hurry and forgot my pants. Can you bring them in?")

✔ To rectify mistakes we forgetful parents occasionally make. ("Mom! You got the days mixed up again! Today is school picture day, *not* crazy hair day! You gotta come fix me!")

✔ And in extreme cases, to egg the school for refusing to provide the services our children need, or for not seeing our kids' true potential. (We joke, of course. Everyone knows stink bombs work much better.)

The Team Meeting: No More Pencils, No More Books, No More Teachers' Covert Looks

For many parents, including Gina, the orientation to our "special" education begins with the team meeting. In theory, a team meeting is a very good idea; it brings together educators and parents to help them work together to solve a child's challenges. When Gina first heard the word *team*, she felt instantly at ease. *Okay, this is nothing to worry about. It's a team, and I've been on plenty of teams in my life. It's about camaraderie—a group of dedicated people working together toward a common goal.* Plus, Gina truly liked Katie's teachers and many of the professionals at the school. It was clear to her that they cared about Katie and were doing the best they could to help her along. That's why she was so caught off guard when the team meeting started. Just seeing so many of them there lined up together made her feel as though they were "teaming up" against her.

Unfortunately, that's how many parents of special needs children feel in these meetings—like the school district team members are ganging up on us or not listening to us. ("Why do they call us part of the team when they don't seem to listen to anything we say about our kids?")

KILL 'EM (WITH KINDNESS)

Oh, team meetings certainly don't start out badly—at least the ones Gina's been to haven't. Usually, they start out on a positive note, with the team members working hard to let Gina know she's a welcome addition. Yes, from the moment they (all fifty-five of them) file into the room, they go out of their way to be gracious and welcoming:

"Hi, Mrs. Gallagher. Welcome! I'm the special ed teacher."

"I'm the speech therapist."

"I'm the occupational therapist."

"I'm the guidance counselor."

"I'm the adjustment counselor."

"I'm the lunch lady."

"I'm the night custodian."

Gina's always surprised to find so many of them in attendance each year. ("Wow, I love how involved everyone is. Most of my friends tell me the crossing guards don't come to their team meetings.")

At her first few team meetings, Gina was very impressed with the cohesiveness and politeness of the group.

"That's so nice of them to sit together on the other side of the table and leave me alone with all this extra legroom."

She liked them even more when they started throwing around compliments about her daughter.

"Katie is just so cute. I love her!" her classroom teacher said.

"Yeah, and she has the best clothes," commented the speech teacher.

"I know. Did you see that outfit she had on with the matching headband yesterday?" asked the lunch lady.

"And I never have to mop under her desk," remarked the custodian. Often, Gina found herself blushing. "Well, I do try my best with her."

LESSONS LEARNED IN TEAM MEETINGS

Though the topics sometimes vary, Gina and many other parents have noticed a few commonalities about Individual Education Plan (IEP) team meetings:

✔ **They can be depressing.** There's nothing worse than sitting there and listening to teacher after teacher go over what's wrong with your kid. And if it's not hard enough to listen to it, you have to see it when they start producing evidence. "We asked Katie to draw a self-portrait. At this stage in a child's development, we look for the children to put body parts in the right places. As you'll see in Exhibit A, Katie drew the arms coming out of her head."

Exhibit A

When they tell you these things about your child, it's hard not to get defensive. ("Well, I can see why she did that. We come from a long line of big-headed people. I, for example, had the biggest graduation cap in my high school's history.")

✔ **Team members like to sit together.** We're not sure if their mutual love of apples has bonded them or if they're taking this team concept a little too far. Either way, it can be very intimidating when you see them all lined up next to one another. It makes many parents feel like they are testifying in front of Congress. "Okay, Mr. Speaker. I'll admit it. Sometimes I just throw away box tops."

The two following diagrams demonstrate our point: Figure A represents the typical team meeting seating plan, with Figure B representing our proposed "parent" plan.

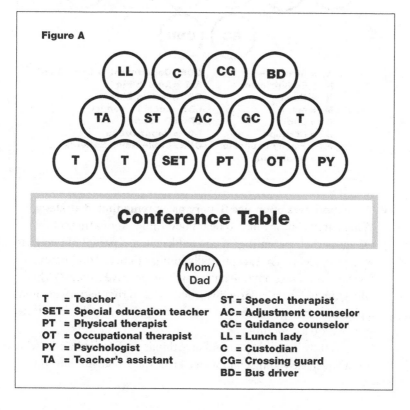

Figure A

Conference Table

Mom/ Dad

T = Teacher
SET = Special education teacher
PT = Physical therapist
OT = Occupational therapist
PY = Psychologist
TA = Teacher's assistant

ST = Speech therapist
AC = Adjustment counselor
GC = Guidance counselor
LL = Lunch lady
C = Custodian
CG = Crossing guard
BD = Bus driver

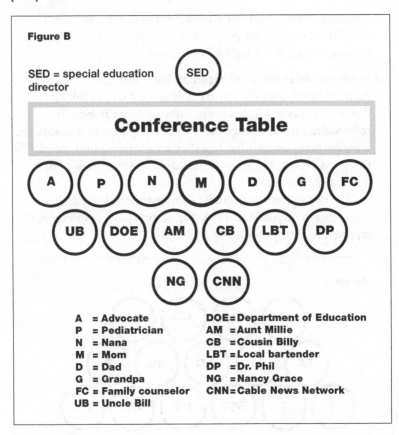

Figure B

SED = special education
director

Conference Table

A P N M D G FC

UB DOE AM CB LBT DP

NG CNN

A = Advocate
P = Pediatrician
N = Nana
M = Mom
D = Dad
G = Grandpa
FC = Family counselor
UB = Uncle Bill

DOE = Department of Education
AM = Aunt Millie
CB = Cousin Billy
LBT = Local bartender
DP = Dr. Phil
NG = Nancy Grace
CNN = Cable News Network

✔ **Team members often use flattery as a premeditated strategy.**
What parent doesn't like to hear good things about their child?
Or about their parenting? If you're like Gina, a parent of two girls
who struggle, you're exceptionally hungry to hear good news.
("Dear God! Does anyone have anything positive to say?") That's
why Gina was particularly disturbed to learn that flattery is often
a planned strategy on the part of teachers to ensure that meetings
start out on a good note.

Certainly it was easy to find nice things to say about Katie, who
was a sweet, easygoing child with a killer wardrobe. But how do

teachers manage to follow this strategy with kids who are not as sweet or as eager to please? Kids who might have learning styles that are especially resistant to standard teaching strategies? Or who are just plain sneaky. "Nice to meet you, Mrs. Madoff. Your son Bernie has taken a real interest in learning about the pyramids."

✔ **Team members often use their own language.** Gina witnessed this in the initial evaluation team meeting when she couldn't understand the words teachers were using to describe Katie's test results. Many parents describe the feeling of listening to teachers speak in these meetings as being transplanted in a foreign country. Sometimes you want to say to the teachers "Speak in English." Gina found the occupational therapy terms to be the hardest to comprehend. And to help those who may feel intimidated by these fancy terms, we've put together this brief guide.

The "Street" Guide to Occupational Therapy Terms

YOUR CHILD'S DIFFICULTY	WHAT IT IS	"STREET" TRANSLATION
Reduction in Dynamic Postural and Proximal Stability	Maintaining balance during active trunk or limb movement	Your child may never be a tightrope walker in the circus.
Bilateral Motor Integration	Using both sides of the body at the same time cooperatively and smoothly	Your child will never be an Olympian in skipping or in the butterfly.
Sensory Motor Function	Organizing sensory information (sight, smell, hearing, taste, touch, balance) from the body and the environment to plan and execute movement	Your child may be poor at dodgeball, but may enjoy watching reruns of Lost in Space.

The "Street" Guide to Occupational Therapy Terms
(continued)

YOUR CHILD'S DIFFICULTY	WHAT IT IS	"STREET" TRANSLATION
Visual Motor Integration	Demonstrating eye/hand/foot coordination	Your child may never win *Dancing with the Stars*.
Visual Perceptual Conception	Taking in, organizing, and interpreting visual information	You don't want your child doing your taxes or your bookkeeping. They may get the numbers mixed up, leading to a painful audit.
Occular Motor Integration	The ability for the eyes to work together in a smooth and coordinated fashion	You want to always wear your seat belt (and possibly a helmet) when your child starts driving.

✔ **Team members are masters at nonverbal communication.** Anyone who has been to a team meeting knows that teachers have an unwritten, unspoken way of getting messages across to one another.

"Mrs. Gallagher, our evaluation shows that Emily may have difficulty picking up nonverbal communication."

"Oh, well, she must get that from me. For example, I've noticed that whenever I ask a question, you guys give each other strange looks, and I can't for the life of me figure out what you're saying."

✔ **Kleenex are always plentiful at team meetings.** Gina has never been to a team meeting where there wasn't an ample supply on hand. Somewhere in both her daughters' school files must be an annotation, "Mother is like Old Faithful." This explains why each team member usually plunks down a box of Kleenex in front of Gina. Gina has noticed that over the years, budget pressures have greatly reduced the quality of the Kleenex she has been offered. "Sheesh, Pat. They used to give me Puffs Plus. Now I get some generic kind that hurts my nose. Next thing you know, they'll be giving out paper towels."

✔ **Team meetings are not very "green."** Today, our society has become increasingly concerned about reducing paper and energy consumption. The team meeting is in direct contrast to this philosophy. Parents who attend them are often sent home with reams of reports, evaluations, and explanations of their rights. In fact, studies estimate that approximately 6 billion trees could be saved if these meetings were eliminated.*

*Source: Gina and Patty made it up, but we think you get the point.

See a Team Meeting in Action

To demonstrate how team meetings can seem overwhelming to parents, we've created a brief video. To see it, just visit YouTube.com and type in "Shut Up About Your Perfect Kid! The Team Meeting." If you like what you see, forward the link to your friends and family members. (**Authors' Note:** If you're an acting coach and want to sign us up for lessons, please e-mail us at info@shutupabout.com.) Film critics need not respond.

STREET TIPS FOR PREPARING FOR A TEAM MEETING

The most successful team meetings are the ones where parents and teachers come together for the benefit of a child. So what can you do to make the experience more successful, more productive, and less stressful? We asked parents and teachers to share their thoughts.

Tips from Parents to Teachers

✔ Call us or send an e-mail before the meeting to tell us what to expect and who will attend.

✔ Sit next to us; we don't have fleas. Sitting all together across from us makes us feel like you're not on our side, or that we're contestants on *America's Top Bad Parent.*

✔ Show compassion—not pity. Imagine how you would feel if you had to hear difficult things about someone you loved. Choose your words carefully.

✔ Use language parents understand and try to explain complex terms.

✔ If you want to compliment the child, make sure you do so on relevant topics. While every parent loves to hear their child has the most colorful backpack, it isn't really helpful when it comes to educational matters. Telling them that their child decodes words well is.

✔ Follow up with parents after the meeting with an e-mail or a phone call and ask them if they have any questions or concerns.

Tips from Teachers to Parents

We spoke with teachers, who enlightened us on how parents can better prepare for team meetings.

✔ Be on time. Showing up late is just taking away valuable time from your child.

✔ If you bring your spouse or partner, don't fight in front of us.

✔ Don't talk about yourself—you're there to talk about your child. If you feel the need to talk about yourself, sign up for Facebook or Twitter.

✔ Do your homework by preparing questions to ask beforehand.

✔ Don't be afraid to ask questions or to have the teachers explain things to you.

✔ Turn off your cell phone.
✔ Arrange for child care for younger children.
✔ Don't chew gum (they may make you put it on your nose and stand in the corner).

Tips for Parents on Preparing for a Team Meeting from LeeAnn Karg, MEd
(Condensed from kargacademy.com)

✔ Bring in a special education advocate or a disability specialist to provide expertise on every aspect of your child's disability as it pertains to state and federal education law. You can't expect a school district to respect your child's civil rights if you don't know what they are. (Think of your advocate as your translator when the teachers start speaking their own weird language.) You can find an advocate through your local parent information and training centers, state child advocacy groups, or national disability organizations. You can also check the Wrightslaw "Yellow Pages for Kids with Disabilities" for your state at wrightslaw.com.

✔ You have the right to receive copies of any district evaluation two days before an IEP or evaluation team meeting. Read and research all tests and test results *before* the meeting. Type up any questions you have and make copies to hand out to every IEP team member. Insist that a copy of your questions be included in the team meeting notes. Then follow up the IEP meeting with an e-mail to all the team members summarizing their answers to your questions. This is really the only way to document your concerns.

✔ Create an "evaluation narrative" for quick and easy reference and comparison. Chart the date, evaluator (with their credential), name of the test, scores (with percentiles and age/grade functioning levels), interpretations, and recommendations of each of the evaluations your child has had.

✔ Ask how each evaluation, therapy, and/or teaching strategy suggested by the district has been researched and proven to help your child achieve their educational and/or social goals.

✔ Type up any questions you have for the team *before* you get to the IEP meeting. Make a copy for every team member. Make sure you ask your questions, and write down who answered them and what was said. Again, insist that your questions be included in the team meeting notes, and follow up the IEP meeting with an e-mail to all the team members documenting their answers to your questions. Save all e-mail correspondence!

✔ You have the right to audio record the entire meeting as long as you give prior notice of your intent. (Remember, you're no Linda Tripp if you ask for permission.)

✔ *You* are your child's first and foremost line of defense. Preparation will always be your best offense. Knowledge will always be your best defense.

✔ "To err is human." Check and double-check *any* information *anyone* tries to give you.

✔ You have the right to stop anyone at any time to ask questions. You also have the right to insist on getting your answers immediately, not at the end of the meeting.

✔ Bring someone to write down *all* of your concerns as the meeting is happening so you can devote all of your attention to what is being said.

✔ Bring in a picture of your child and put it on the table to remind everyone that they are talking about a living child, not just a test subject. Make sure it's a cute one.

For more tips from LeeAnn on getting your child the services they need, see page 249 in our Resources section.

Tip from Gina

Wear waterproof mascara. Unless you want the teachers to think you're a Goth parent.

Tip from Our Mother

To eliminate puffy eyes from crying at team meetings, lie down for an hour with cucumber slices on your eyes. In about an hour, get up and vacuum your curtains.

A Few Bad Apples Don't Spoil the Whole Bunch

Though we've poked a bit (or a ton) of fun at teachers, we have met our share of wonderful teachers and administrators who really do want what's best for our children. Both of us have been fortunate to find teachers who have honestly wanted to learn more about our daughters' disabilities and work with us to develop new strategies and tactics to help our kids succeed. These teachers continually listen to our concerns and the needs of our children and work tirelessly to meet them. And no one knows that more than our children, who can pick out the teachers who truly care. Gina's daughter Emily said it best when she described one of her teachers: "Mom, Mrs. Mauro really cares about me." It's wonderful teachers like these who give us hope and strength, and keep us out of rehab.

To these teachers, we say, This apple is for you!

CHAPTER 8

The Individual Education Plan—a Blueprint for Confusion

How to Read Between the Confusing Lines

No discussion of special education would be complete without a conversation about the Individual Education Plan (or IEP as it's known on the street). An IEP is a legal document that provides a list of goals and objectives that detail the level of specialized instruction needed for students with disabilities to participate in the state curriculum as fully as their nondisabled peers. It also includes the **instructional modifications, environmental accommodations,** and any therapy services required for students with disabilities to achieve their IEP goals and objectives in the least restrictive educational environment possible.

Gina has become very versed in the Individual Education Plan. Undoubtedly, she's come a long way from that initial evaluation meeting when she sobbed to her husband about "IUDs."

When Gina had Katie's initial evaluation meeting in kindergarten, she really had no idea what an IEP was, nor what role she would play in helping to create it. So she just sat "on the bench" as the team started filling it out without her. She was drifting off when the team leader called her into the game, asking, "Mrs. Gallagher, what's your vision for Katie?"

"Well, I'd like her to be happy," Gina responded.

"Okay, what else?" By the looks the team members exchanged with one another, it was clear that Gina had given the wrong answer.

"Well, I'd like her to clean her room every now and again. And to stop leaving the light on in her closet."

Setting the Bar Low

One thing that has always mystified Gina about IEPs is the benchmarks the teachers set for achieving goals and how they arrive at them.

"Excuse me, but can you put me on an IEP so that I can understand IEPs?"

What Is an IEP Vision Statement?
(Condensed from kargacademy.com)

The purpose of the IEP vision statement is to direct the focus of the IEP team on your child and your child's potential. This is your only chance to detail the progress you expect to see as a result of the implementation of the IEP. It is important that your vision statement include challenging but achievable expectations. For example:

"The entire team would like to see [child's name], through the successful direct instruction, remediation, support, and services included in this IEP, achieve growth in all areas by demonstrating significant improvement in the following areas:

✔ The academic skills necessary to be an independent, motivated, and competent learner
✔ Age-appropriate self-monitoring and self-regulation skills
✔ The ability to identify, comprehend, and perform age- and gender-appropriate social rules (including independent self-care) that meet the expectations of his or her preferred peer groups
✔ The ability to recognize, identify, and perform the nonverbal communicators necessary to expand his or her social language skills

Here are some examples of benchmarks Gina has had on her children's IEPs:

✔ Given school supplies, Katie will place them where they belong, leaving them there so she can find them when needed in eight out of ten opportunities.

✔ Given a writing prompt, Katie will complete the initial steps of writing using graphic organizers and lists to address this prompt independently in five out of ten opportunities.

We both find these benchmarks a little disturbing. Isn't this setting the bar too low? Shouldn't we be striving for ten out of ten opportunities? How will this affect our kids later in life?

"Hi, dear! How was your day?"

"It was wonderful, love. How was your day?"

"Well, I changed five diapers in ten opportunities."

"I wondered what that smell was."

It would probably hurt them in their careers as well.

"Mr. Ford, I'm really sorry I missed putting in the brake lines on a few of the cars on the assembly line. On a happy note, I did remember to put them on six out of ten cars."

The occupational therapy goals are the strangest to read. Often, the therapist sets these very specific goals without explaining how they will help our children.

✔ Emily will be able to throw and catch a tennis ball in four out of five trials, demonstrating improved arm control using appropriate force modulation and accuracy.

The team was so intent on this goal that Gina didn't have the heart to tell them that Emily probably would never make it on the tennis tour. She didn't even have a racket. It seemed like a waste of time.

Katie's occupational therapy goals were just as strange:

✔ Katie will demonstrate improved **midline crossing** while using classroom materials in four out of five trials.

Gina couldn't wait for Katie to finally master this skill. "I'll celebrate by getting one of those bragging bumper stickers on my car 'My child crossed the midline 4 out of 5 times at Kane School.'"

Understand the Goals

The most important thing you can do in helping to get your child the services they need is to become knowledgeable. And that starts by asking questions. Ask the teachers to explain the goals they are setting and why they are important to the child's development.

An Organized Parent Is a Less Stressed Parent

One of the greatest challenges for parents of children on IEPs involves keeping track of your child's evaluations, paperwork, and communications with the school. The paperwork can mount quickly, as it did in Gina's house.

"Mike, I think we need to move before we outgrow our house."

"Don't tell me we're having another kid!"

"No, not another kid. We need more filing space for the IEP paperwork."

Keeping all your child's IEP paperwork organized is arguably one of the most tedious (and difficult) tasks ever known to parenting. But if you have *what* you need, *when* you need it, you can truly advocate for your child.

To make this easier, many parents have used organizers that allow them to manage information and track their child's progress. One option we like is the My IEP ToolKit: The Complete Organizer for Your Child's Individualized Education Plan. For more information, visit organized4kids.com.

Progress Reports

When Gina was a kid, she couldn't wait for report cards to come. It was her favorite time of the year—to show her parents the results of her hard work and to make Patty and our brother, Bob (who didn't take education as seriously), look bad.

"Mom! Mom! I got my report card today!" she'd announce while excitedly jumping off the bus.

"Really? That's strange. Patty and Bob said nothing about theirs."

Gina couldn't wait for our father to get home so she could share the news with him.

"Dad! I got my report card!" she'd yell out when he came in the door.

"Gina Frances, how come all A's and no A pluses? I think I'll have to ground you," our father would joke, beaming with pride.

Today, report cards offer no excitement or surprise factor for Gina. She always knows where her daughters need improvement because the school either tells her in the meeting or calls her with bad news (see next chapter for details).

The general report cards her daughters receive along with the typically developing children tell her absolutely nothing. That's because the measurement criteria they use is vague. It usually looks something like this:

A = Advanced (so Gina was told; her kids have never brought one home)
M = Mastered (ditto)
PW = Presently working (Gina has seen a lot of these)
NS = Not meeting the standards (ditto)

In fact, her daughters' report cards would probably spend the year in their backpacks if it weren't for Gina's "nosy" neighbor (mother of two neurotypicals) reminding her.

"Gene, I forgot to ask you. How did Emily do on her report card?"

"What report card? I must have missed it. When did it come out? Yesterday?"

"Hello, Gene—it was last month."

It's not that Gina isn't proud of her daughters; it's just that these report cards really don't help her gauge their progress. Even the IEP report cards she receives don't provide much information. But that doesn't stop her from bragging right along with all the other parents.

"Arthur Jr. got all A's on his report card. They're talking about moving him up to the next level."

"Emily caught a tennis ball in eighty percent of trials. They're talking about moving her up, too—to kicking balls."

A Few Remarks About Report Card Remarks

If the grades are difficult to decipher, the comments the teachers provide are even worse. When she was a young girl, Gina loved to read the comments her teachers wrote about her. She even memorized some.

"I wish all my students were like Gina. She's a bright girl who is always eager to learn more. She's a delight to have in my class."

For a while, she couldn't read the comments on her daughters' report cards without getting depressed. But now she's learned to find the humor in them (pouring a drink beforehand helps). The humor is from the teachers' vain attempts at trying to say something positive. But Gina and other parents have quickly learned how to read between the lines.

For example:

When they write:
"Emily is a sweet, pretty girl who is kind to her classmates."

They mean:
"Oh God, this kid is struggling so badly. Quick! Let's change the subject."

When they write:
"Katie is a pleasant young woman who is an active participant in class."

They mean:
"This kid can't stop fidgeting."

When they write:
"Bonnie always gives her best effort to understand the material."

They mean:
"This poor kid just doesn't get it."

When they write:
"Joseph is a sweet boy with an appetite for learning."

They mean:
"Lunch is the only subject this kid is good at."

New Proposed Report Card

We think the problem isn't so much with our children as with the report cards, which are supposed to indicate the skills our children have obtained for future success. But most of us parents think our children have already mastered many of those. So we propose adding a few more categories to the report card. By these standards, our children would be on the honor roll every year.

Courage: A+
Resilience: A+
Character: A+
Creativity: A+
Perseverance: A+
Stamina: A+
Energy: A+
Loyalty: A+
Honesty: A+
Compassion: A+

A sample comment on our report cards might look like this:

Katie is a joy to have in class. Her courage, resilience, and compassion have made her a positive role model for all the children.

She always strives to do her very best, despite the difficulties she sometimes faces. The hard work, perseverance, and stamina she shows on a daily basis should be a great aid in helping her overcome her difficulties and reaching her full potential. She is truly a gift to the world as are her charming mother and aunt.

CHAPTER 9

Reality (or the School) Calling

Dealing with Those Embarrassing Calls from the School

Throughout our lives, we have learned simple principles we know to be true. The sun will always rise in the east and set in the west. Earth will always rotate on its axis. And no matter how much we hope, our children will never think to clean their rooms on their own. ("Mom, I actually like my room messy. It's cozier this way.")

But now that we're parents, we have stumbled across another truth—a simple one that really applies to parents of all children, including perfect ones:

No good can come from a school call.

Our anxiety is instant when we see the school's name lit up on caller ID. (It's even worse than seeing your credit card company's name.)

Here are just a few examples of calls we and other parents have received over the years:

"Your son keeps sticking up his middle finger when pointing."

"Mrs. Konjoian, this is the school nurse. Is Jennifer getting enough sleep? The only reason I ask is because she's sleeping in my office."

"Your daughter stuffed five tissues up her nose, and we were only able to get two out. Can you come get her?"

"Jessica says she is a cat and is hissing at the principal."

"Mrs. Gallagher, your daughter's skirt is way too short and she's up on the rock-climbing wall."

"We caught Amanda eating grass on the playground. You might want to take her to the doctor to make sure she doesn't get sick."

"Your second-grader is exhibiting ganglike activity."

"Your son was surfing on his desk. I'm just curious if you thought about having him tested for AD/HD."

Some teachers are very aware of our nervousness when getting calls, so they're quick to preface the calls with "Nothing's wrong." This, however, is usually followed by a "but" and some piece of bad news.

"Mrs. Gallagher, nothing's wrong with Katie, *but* she did pass out while dissecting a chicken wing."

"Nothing's wrong, *but* I just wanted to let you know Annie failed the eye test for the fifth year in a row."

"Nothing's wrong, *but* we can't seem to find your child."

Of course, if given the chance to receive bad news by phone or in person, most parents would welcome the call. Our friend Diane, mother of Nate, an eleven-year-old with Tourette's syndrome and AD/HD, knows this all too well. One day, she was volunteering at her son's school when he approached her.

"Mom, can I have a ride home?" Nate asked.

"Nate, don't you have to bring in the school flag first?" Diane asked her son, who had been assigned the special privilege of flag duty after school.

At that, the school principal appeared and asked, "Nathaniel, didn't you tell your mother about 'the incident'?"

"Which one?" responded an innocent Nate.

"There's more than one?" asked a horrified Diane, silently reminding herself to stop at the liquor store on the way home.

"Well, last week, your Nathaniel was seen playing tug-of-war with the school flag and using it as a Superman cape. His flag duties have been suspended until further notice."

It took all of Diane's strength not to laugh in the principal's face. She knew how important it was to respect the flag, but she couldn't stop visualizing her son and his friend (also with AD/HD) running around with the flag cape. She couldn't help but think, *I wish this had been a phone call. I could be laughing my tail off and he'd never know.*

Call Me Positive

Although we know bad news school calls are sometimes necessary, we think every school should implement a good news call policy where teachers call to express positive news:

"Just wanted to tell you how smart your child is."

"Your daughter is such an angel. You should really have more kids."

"FYI, we just promoted your child to the next grade because he is gifted."

"This is the school nurse. I don't know what you're feeding Little Bobby, but he sure does look healthy. Keep up the good work."

The Writing Is on the Wall

We met the mother of a child with autism who received an unexpected call from the school principal. He said, "Mrs. Mathews, your son Billy wrote on the bathroom wall in permanent marker."

Concerned that the principal was unfairly accusing her son, Mrs. Mathews responded, "How do you know it was my Billy?"

"Well," the principal said, "he signed his name and put your phone number underneath it."

If this school implemented our "positive policy," the principal may have said, "Mrs. Mathews, I'm calling to let you know your son Billy wrote on the bathroom wall, but his penmanship has never looked better."

Or in the case of that embarrassing call Gina received, "Mrs. Gallagher, your daughter's skirt is way too short and she's up on the rock-climbing wall, but boy is her underwear clean."

Ooh! Ooh! Pick Me, Teacher!

Parents don't receive calls just for the things their children do; sometimes it's simply for things their children say. Karen, the mother of Ben, a boy with AD/HD, received an interesting call from his teacher one day.

Ben's class was studying the Internet. "What do we use the Internet for in class?" his teacher asked.

Ben shot his hand up like a stock market surge. "I know, I know. Pick me!"

"Yes, Benjamin," the teacher responded.

"We use the Internet to help us with homework and to look up pornography."

Communication Is Key

When you have a child with a disability, it's critical to stay in constant contact with the teacher to communicate updates about your child. Unfortunately, given the nature of the school day, it's often very difficult to reach a teacher. In fact, most of us would have an easier time connecting to the Oval Office than trying to catch a teacher during the school day. ("Mrs. Gallagher, I'll be available from 10:59 to 11:00 if you want to call me back.")

There are, of course, other means for staying in contact with our children's teachers. One is the parent/teacher conference, where a teacher has dedicated an evening or an afternoon to meeting with parents for a limited amount of time. In Gina's daughters' schools, ten minutes was allowed per parent. To enforce this time limit, teachers often set egg timers or used other methods to politely tell parents their time was up.

"Mrs. Gallagher, my microwave popcorn is done. That means we have to stop."

Any parent of a child with special needs knows that ten minutes is simply not enough time to review the educational progress of your child. "Mrs. Gallagher, don't bother coming to the parent-teacher meeting. We've decided to set aside a long weekend for you. If that's not enough, we'll block off the month of August."

LeeAnn Karg's Tips for Putting the "Parent" Back in Parent-Teacher Conferences
(Condensed from kargacademy.com)

Many parents feel that their role at parent-teacher conferences is that of listener rather than participant. It doesn't have to be that way. As a parent, you are an equal and essential part of the equation and therefore should be able to actively participate in your child's conference. These tips will help you:

✔ **Be on time.** The teacher has to schedule conferences one right after the other to make time for every student. Being late only wastes *your* time!

✔ **Be united.** Whenever possible, both parents should attend. Showing up together demonstrates your united commitment to your child's education.

✔ **Be positive.** Share any positive comments from your child about the teacher, class, or classroom to set a positive tone for the meeting.

✔ **Plan ahead.** E-mail any concerns to the teacher in advance if you want a thorough response.

✔ **Do your homework.** Make sure you've talked with your child to see if there are any particular concerns about school. Look over recent assignments and tests so you know what your child has been studying and how your child has been performing in class.

✔ **Bring the report card.** Most schools plan parent-teacher conferences after the first progress reports or report cards are sent home. Make sure you review your child's progress to see if there are any areas where your child may be struggling or other concerns you would like to discuss.

Important Note for Teacher

While preparing for a parent-teacher conference, Lauren, the mother of an eleven-year-old with AD/HD, went to her son and asked for his feedback.

"David, hon, I'm meeting with your teacher tomorrow night about some of the problems you're having at school. You know, with blurting things out? Is there anything special you'd like me to tell her?"

LeeAnn Karg's Tips (continued)

✔ **Bring a list.** Make a written list of your top questions and concerns. Give a copy to the teacher, with all of your contact information included. Ask that any unaddressed items or concerns be responded to by e-mail if you run out of time.

✔ **Bring an action plan.** Prioritize your concerns and the steps that you feel need to be taken to ensure that your child reaches his or her educational potential for that school year. Bring a brief, structured action plan with you for discussion, and bring a copy for the teacher. Make sure you leave the meeting secure in knowing the next step that will be taken to help your child succeed.

✔ **Respect the next parent.** Schedule a follow-up meeting to address more lengthy concerns if you run out of conference time.

✔ **Thank the teacher.** Teachers don't get paid any more for the additional time, attention, or effort they put into our kids. They are truly underpaid and underappreciated for what they do.

✔ **Follow up with your child.** Your parent-teacher conference offers a wonderful opportunity to praise and express your appreciation for the positive accomplishments and effort your child has been making *and* to discuss any areas that may need improvement. Use this opportunity to create short- and long-term goals, reinforcements, and expectations.

A thoughtful child, David scratched his chin and said, "Oh yeah, there is one thing. When you're talking to her, can you kind of work into the conversation that . . . well . . . I hate her!"

Communication Books

Another method special needs parents often use to communicate with teachers is the communication notebook. These backpack notebooks allow parents and teachers to send notes back and forth.

Tina tried using one with her daughter Samantha, a child with autism, but many times it came home blank because there was nothing to report. Eager to see how it worked, Tina sent in her first note.

Tips for Effective School Communication and Protecting Your Child
(Condensed from kargacademy.com)

So what's the best way to communicate with your child's school? Disability specialist LeeAnn Karg, MEd, shares her insights on why documentation is vital in ensuring that your child gets the services they need.

Well-documented communication with your school district is essential for protecting the rights of your child. These simple steps will help to document and safeguard your efforts to communicate with your school district:

✔ **Keep a journal.** Document all informal communications with your school system, including taking extensive notes during all meetings and telephone calls.

✔ **Keep copies.** Use separate binders to store copies of *all* daily notes written to and from any teacher and *all* class work, homework, tests, and quizzes that are sent home, especially anything you are required to sign and return. Make weekly copies of your child's daily planner or communication notebook.

"Testing. 1, 2, 3, testing."

When she didn't receive a response she wrote, "Hello, can anyone hear me?"

Apparently, the teacher was not amused, because the notebook could not be found in the backpack after that.

One of the downsides of communication notebooks is that often our children don't like the idea of parents and teachers being in constant contact. For these reasons, many parents prefer using e-mail, which allows us to stealthily communicate with our children's teachers.

"Dear Ms. Bliss, Cassie has been a little irregular lately. Please note that if she makes frequent trips to the bathroom, it's because of the prune juice I gave her for breakfast."

Keeping It Positive

In all fairness, we must admit we've met our share of teachers who contact parents for positive reasons:

"Your son had a great day. He didn't bite anyone once."

Tips for Effective School Communication (continued)

✔ **Document everything in writing.** Use formal, signed letters and e-mails for all requests. Follow up every phone call and meeting with a written narrative. Document exactly what is said, by whom, and when.

✔ **Be professional.** Remember, education is a business. Approach all communications with a professional attitude and a businesslike demeanor. Give yourself some time to calm down and think through any response.

✔ **Stick to the facts.** Keep your communication short and to the point.

✔ **Acknowledge the positive.** Recognizing and praising any positive aspects of your child's educational experience will lend validity to your concerns about the negative aspects.

We've also met our share of teachers who truly love working with special needs kids:

"I couldn't see myself teaching any other kids."

"I just love their perspective on life. It's so unique."

"My job is hard, but I can't think of anything more rewarding."

"These kids are so pure and innocent. They just say the funniest things."

When we brought up the subject of bad news calls during one of our speaking engagements, a teacher got up and confessed, "You're right. I don't call for positive reasons. I'm gonna start doing that."

In the spirit of openness, we parents don't exactly call for good reasons, either. We're usually calling to report some problem to the teacher. And it's not like they have to deal with just one of us.

"Emma says some girl with brown hair gave her a dirty look in the lunchroom. Can you interview brown-haired girls in the school to find out who it might have been?"

"I think someone is stealing Andrew's milk money. Could you conduct an investigation?"

When you have an open, solid relationship with your children's teachers, everyone wins—especially your child.

Calling Signals in the Classroom

When Jennifer was transitioning to middle school, she was extremely anxious and feared making her disability public would cause her to stand out. To help Jennifer deal with the anxiety, early in the school

A "Tini" Gesture to Say Thanks

If you want to thank a teacher for their hard work, please refrain from giving them apples. A teacher once told us she had "appleobilia" (apple frames, apple mugs, apple pictures) all over her house. If you feel compelled to give them an apple, take the next step and turn it into a pie, or better yet, an appletini.

year, Patty collaborated with one of Jenn's teachers to devise a strategy to deal with Jennifer's worry about being called on in class. The strategy was as follows:

- ✔ On the days Jennifer was feeling well, she would place her assignment book faceup.
- ✔ On the days she was feeling stress or anxiety, Jenn would place the book facedown so the teacher wouldn't call on her.
- ✔ On the days when Jennifer forgot her assignment book, her mother would down a drink.

CHAPTER 10

A New School of Thought

How the Right Placement
Makes All the Difference

Decisiveness. It's one of the most important qualities of a good parent, and one that has managed to escape both of us. And we're not talking about the ability to make everyday decisions—we're talking about making decisions that affect our children's futures. Often, we have to make very difficult choices, and it's not uncommon for us to question them along the way.

For parents of imperfect children, the most important decisions we'll make for our children involve their education.

One Less Thing to Worry About

Patty and Jennifer were fortunate that Jennifer really didn't have learning disabilities to accompany her bipolar disorder. Over the years, we have met our share of parents whose children have both Asperger's and bipolar disorder. They often use the term *comorbid* to describe this dual diagnosis, though we had no idea when we first heard it.

"Are your daughters comorbid?"

"Oh yes. They're definitely killing us both."

When we realized that comorbidity was common, we were amazed.

"That's like Jennifer's mood swings with Katie's social issues."

"Or Katie's flapping with Jennifer's mania."

"Or your medication bills plus my medication bills."

As a result of not having learning issues, Jennifer did not require an IEP. Instead, Patty's school district put Jenn on a **504 plan** (the little brother of the IEP), which provides accommodations to help Jennifer deal with her anxiety. Some of the accommodations included allowing

Jennifer to take tests in a separate room from the class or excusing incomplete homework after a difficult day. Surprisingly, Jennifer never took advantage of any of them. She didn't want to stand out from the other kids and was, for the most part, a model student. It was when she got home that she fell apart.

Katie's Difficulties at School Intensify

Katie was the opposite of Jennifer. She was relaxed and happy at home; her problems were all at school, where she struggled with acceptance.

As she progressed through elementary school, her social difficulties intensified. Students were singling her out for her hand flapping, and girls were starting to form cliques, leaving Katie out. ("She can't be in our club. She's weird.")

Throughout her elementary school years, Katie was placed in an inclusion classroom, which allows special needs children to get the support and accommodations in the classroom with typically developing students. The team determined that an inclusion setting would be best for Katie.

"This way, she'll have typical role models, Mrs. Gallagher."

At the time, it seemed like a great idea to Gina. The last thing she wanted was for Katie to be put in a separate resource room, the room where special needs children in Gina's childhood elementary school were placed. Everyone knew that the kids in that room had learning difficulties, and they were constantly the butt of jokes.

But Gina eventually learned that inclusion would not keep Katie from being singled out. This painful reality hit her once during field day at Katie's school: a mini-Olympics that would have her class battling it out for all-important bragging rights. Katie was ecstatic.

"They're having field day on my birthday, Mom. It's gonna be so much fun!"

"Can I come? Can I, huh?" Gina asked excitedly.

"Sure!" she said. "And can you bring cupcakes? I'd rather eat hot dog rolls, but the kids really like cupcakes."

When Gina arrived at the field day festivities, Katie's class was in the middle of a grueling egg and spoon race. Her team had a big lead.

When it came time for Katie to run with the egg and spoon, Gina shouted, "Scramble, sweetie!" Then Gina watched in horror as Katie dropped the egg, bent over to pick it up, and, at a turtle-like pace, drifted over to the other lanes with no idea where she was headed. By the time she reached the pylon on the other side (which was not hers), the opposition had all passed her, setting off her teammates.

"She's making us lose!" shouted the daughter of one of Gina's neighbors—a girl who was supposed to be Katie's friend.

"Why did we have to get her on our team?" said a pretty girl wearing a "Life Is Good" T-shirt.

"She can't do anything right!" said another "friend."

When Katie reached the finish line, the last one to do so, her teammates walked away, shaking their heads. Then Gina watched her sweet little girl sit down on the ground and cry—on her birthday!

Frustrated and angry, Gina reached for Katie's hand and said, "Come on, honey. You don't need this. It's your birthday and we're going home!"

"No, Mom! I'm fine. I want to stay here with the kids," she said, getting up.

"But honey, the kids are being mean. And it's your birthday."

"But I want to stay," she said, wiping tears from her eyes.

Not willing to cause her any more disappointment, Gina gave her a kiss and walked away.

When she got in her car, Gina sobbed like a baby. *She stands out like a sore thumb! Why can't she be like everybody else? Is this what her life's gonna be like?*

By fourth grade, Katie's social struggles had worsened, particularly during unstructured time in the classroom or at recess.

"Katie, do you have to go to the bathroom?" her teacher would ask a wiggling Katie.

"No, it's fine."

When Gina asked Katie about this one evening, Katie told her, "Well, when I'm playing with my friends, I'm afraid to leave to go to the bathroom because they may not wanna play with me when I get back."

And if her friends were absent from school, Katie would stand alone at recess and cry. Her distress was taking its toll on Gina and the entire family.

"Gene, you've got to stop crying. Katie might see you."

"I know, Mike, but I can't help it! I just keep picturing her all alone at recess. It breaks my heart."

Lost at School

Gina had considered putting Katie in another school, but the school system kept reassuring her. "Mrs. Gallagher, we can handle her needs."

"Have you had kids like Katie?" Gina would frequently ask.

"Absolutely," they would repeatedly reassure her.

"And have they gone on to college?"

"Mrs. Gallagher, our goal here is to ensure that Katie will lead an independent and productive life."

Gina felt a pit in her stomach. Did this mean they thought Katie would be bagging groceries for the rest of her life? What if Gina wanted more for Katie? Like a college education? Gina had loved college and wanted both her daughters to enjoy that wonderful experience. And, more important, Gina didn't want her daughter to suffer anymore in the public school.

To prevent Katie from sticking out, Gina asked the school to put Katie in a classroom with other children with autism.

"What about the autism program? Kids won't tease her if she's like them."

"Mrs. Gallagher, she's too high-functioning for that program." Gina was beyond frustrated. She felt like there was no place for her daughter.

Taking Katie's Life Back

The day Gina got the snowflake essay, her neighbor Jane, a public school teacher for twenty years, asked Gina, "Why don't you put her in another school if she's having so much trouble in the public school?"

"Because the school system says inclusion is the right model for her. They say it will build her self-esteem."

"But Gina, every day she's in that school, she's reminded that she's different and that she'll never be as good as the other kids. What do you think that does to her self-esteem?"

"You're right, Jane. I never saw it that way. I just wanted her to be like everyone else and to find her place, the public school. Her teachers told me the public school was the best option for her."

With Jane's advice, Gina began looking at school alternatives for Katie. She discovered one located just a few miles from her house and our parents'—a small private school for kids with learning disabilities. The school, Willow Hill School, had a big red barn nestled in a beautiful rustic setting in Sudbury, Massachusetts. Gina fell in love with the school the moment she saw it. "It's beautiful. And it feels so safe and comfortable."

Gina applied to the school and got an interview. She brought Jane along to help her evaluate whether it was the right fit for Katie. It had everything Gina wanted for her daughter—a low student-to-teacher ratio, a new gym, a computer lab, a drama program, and, most important, other students with disabilities. It even had an outdoor education program. Gina couldn't wait to go home and tell Katie, though Katie didn't want to hear it.

"Mom, I don't want to go to a different school. I wanna go to the middle school with my friends."

Gina was forced to try a desperate though proven parenting strategy—positive extortion. "If you come for an interview, I'll buy you a new Tamagotchi."

"Deal, but I'm not going there!"

A week later, on the way to the interview, Katie continued to protest. "Why do I have to go to this stupid interview, Mom? I don't even want to go to that school. I want to be with my friends."

As Gina pulled into the parking lot, Katie surprised her by asking, "Mom, they have canoes?"

"Yes, they do all kinds of outdoor adventures, including canoeing."

"Cool!" Katie said, perking up.

Gina and Katie then went in for the interview. Gina was a nervous wreck when the admissions counselor asked Katie if she wanted to attend the school.

"No, not really," said Katie. "It's a nice school, but I don't want to leave my friends."

Gina was panicked and quickly tried to step in and explain. "What she means is, she'd be honored to attend your school. Right, Katie?" Gina said, giving Katie "the eye."

The admissions counselor was very kind. "Of course, Katie. A lot of kids are nervous about changing schools."

"That's what I told her," Gina said, smiling nervously.

The admissions counselor then asked Katie if she'd like a tour.

"She'd love one," Gina answered before Katie had the chance to say anything.

When Gina and Katie visited the science class, a teenage girl came immediately over to Katie. "Hi. Are you thinking about coming here?"

"Yeah," said Katie, surprising Gina by looking this girl straight in the eye, something Katie rarely did. "I'm just nervous, 'cause I'm afraid to leave my friends."

"You'll make friends here. The kids are really nice, though sometimes they can gossip a lot."

Katie laughed. "Okay, thanks."

"Good luck," the girl said. "I hope I see you back here."

"Me, too," Gina blurted out, ignoring Katie's embarrassed look.

On the way home, Katie surprised Gina when she said, "Mom, if you want me to go there, I will. It's pretty cool."

"I knew it! I knew you'd love it."

"Yeah, yeah. Now about that Tamagotchi you promised me . . ."

Gina's plan was falling into place, except for one last hurdle—she needed the school district to pay Katie's tuition. She knew it wouldn't be easy; she'd heard her share of horror stories about lengthy, expensive battles between school districts and parents.

In preparation, she contacted a lawyer and was about to send off a retainer check when someone advised her, "Talk to the district first."

Heeding this advice, Gina wrote an impassioned letter to the director of pupil services in her city, telling her about Katie's issues and why Willow Hill was better equipped to meet them. She thanked her for the support they had given Katie, but explained that Katie's social needs were too great for the school to manage. The director responded immediately and said, "You can discuss Katie's placement at your upcoming team meeting."

For Gina, that meant waiting. Every night before going to bed, she'd pore over the Willow Hill brochure. When she read about the high rate of students who went on to college and about the school's "everyone makes the team" sports policy, she became more and more excited. In her heart, she knew with 100 percent certainty Willow Hill was the right place for Katie, which made the waiting period all the more difficult.

"Oh God, please let her get into this school," Gina would pray at night.

To Gina, Willow Hill represented so much more than a school; it was her daughter's future, which up to this point had looked bleak.

One evening, Gina woke up in the middle of the night in a full panic. "What if she doesn't get in? What if she *does* get in, but I'm making the wrong decision?"

To calm herself, Gina turned on her iPod. Kelly Clarkson's "Breakaway" was the first song she heard. She had never really listened to the words until that moment.

Make a change, and break away.

As she listened to the song, Gina got the strongest feeling she had ever experienced in her life. She knew Katie would somehow get into Willow Hill.

Like clockwork, Katie's letter of acceptance from Willow Hill arrived in the mail the very next day. Gina was ecstatic, but scared because she still had to find a way to pay for it.

"Gene, I don't care. We're sending her one way or the other," Mike vowed.

"Mike, I don't know how we can do that," Gina, the family accountant, announced.

"What if we cut out the extras?"

"I don't think food and heat are extras, Mike."

A few days later, the school district called to arrange for Katie's annual placement team meeting. The meeting was scheduled for the following Friday. Prior to scheduling the meeting, we had planned a trip to Florida to visit our aunts. Leaving was the last thing Gina could think about. "Pat, if this doesn't work out, I may be too depressed to go with you."

When they arrived at the school for the meeting, Mike came over to Gina, grabbed her hand, and said, "Let's go get 'em for our little girl!"

The meeting began, and the IEP team went through Katie's needs and the proposed placement for the following year. They talked about the services offered at the middle school, and Gina's worst fears were realized. They were expecting Katie to continue on in their school system. Gina was shattered; her daughter would have to continue to suffer and be singled out.

But just as Gina was losing hope, the assistant director of pupil services turned to Gina and Mike and said, "Mr. and Mrs. Gallagher, I know you've been looking into schools, so why don't you tell us what you've found?"

With tears in her eyes, Gina shakily explained why she thought Willow Hill was the best placement for Katie. "They are better suited to her needs. They have a very low student-to-teacher ratio and a drama program that is incorporated into the curriculum." The inclusion specialist, who was there to talk about the benefits of the middle school, looked at Gina and said something Gina had waited seven years to hear—the honest truth. "Mrs. Gallagher, we don't have anything like that for her at our school."

The assistant director said, "So the team agrees that Willow Hill is the best placement for Katie?" The team members nodded in unison. And then the director put her hands on Gina's and said, "Mrs. Gallagher, you can relax. We'll send her to Willow Hill. You did a good job."

With tears in her eyes, Gina thanked her. "You just saved my daughter's life. God bless you!" Gina went around the room and hugged the teachers. They were all genuinely happy.

When Katie got home from school, Gina and Mike couldn't wait to tell her the news.

"Katie! Katie!" Mike yelled.

"What's wrong? I didn't do it, I swear!"

"Nothing's wrong."

"What is it?" she said a bit annoyed that they were interrupting her valuable after-school "Katie Time."

"You're going to Willow Hill."

"I am?" she asked, looking at them out of the sides of her eyes with a big smile slowly forming across her face.

"Yes! You are! And I promise, things are gonna get better for you," Gina vowed.

Mike swooped her up in a big bear hug as Gina and Katie's little sister, Emily, joined in. "No more suffering, honey," Gina said. Her eyes filled with tears as she rubbed Katie's back. "No more."

"All right. Now can you guys let me go?"

Later that evening, Gina sat on the airplane with Patty as they took off to Florida. Gina had never felt higher in her life. How could she not?

This was the day Gina had been waiting for since Katie was diagnosed several years before. This was the day Katie Gallagher was finally going to break away.

The Smartest Decision Gina Ever Made

When the day came for Katie to begin at Willow Hill, Gina's mind was racing with worry. *Oh God, what if I made the wrong decision? What if she doesn't like it? Then what will we do?*

When the short bus came to pick Katie up, Gina was in full panic mode. *What if it's too hard for her? What if she doesn't make any friends?* Katie, too, was nervous, asking the same questions. ("Mom, what if kids tease me here, too? I can't go through that again.")

At the end of Katie's first day, Gina waited for the bus in front of the house. When it rounded the corner, she raced down the street, nearly getting herself run over in the process.

Katie climbed out of the van with her shoulders slumped. She looked exhausted. *She doesn't like it! Oh no! What am I gonna do now?* Gina worried.

Gina was crushed, but she mustered the courage to ask Katie, "How was your day?"

[**Authors' Note:** Gina has since learned that with kids like Katie, it's better to ask a more direct and specific question, such as "Did you make any friends? Do you like your teachers? Am I gonna get any school calls?"]

"Good," she said.

"Just good?" Gina asked, deflated.

"Mom, I'm really tired," Katie said.

"So you didn't like it?"

"Are you kidding, Mom? I loved it. The teachers really understand me and the kids are so nice."

"You really loved it?" Gina asked, her eyes filling up.

"Yes, Mom. Now can you let me rest?"

Gina was thrilled. From there, it was smooth sailing. Katie's entire sixth-grade year went beautifully. And in December, Katie shocked Gina when she decided to try out for the school play.

"You want to do what?" asked Gina.

Gina was even more shocked when the drama teacher pulled her aside one day and said, "I'd like to give 'our girl' the lead of Alice in *You Can't Take It with You*. I've never given the lead to a sixth-grader before, but I know she can handle it."

Gina couldn't believe it. "My daughter? Katie Gallagher—with the blond hair and blue eyes, about this tall?" Gina asked, sure there was some mistake. Her shy Katie would never want to get up in front of a crowd and act. It had to be a case of mistaken identity.

"Yes, Mrs. Gallagher. *Your* daughter. She's quite talented," the wonderful drama teacher responded.

"Well, she does get that from me. I played several key roles in my elementary school plays. One year, I was a tree. It wasn't easy to stand still for that full hour."

On opening night of the play, Gina and Mike were nervous wrecks, particularly since Katie was very anxious and was doubting herself. "What if I can't do this?"

"You'll be fine. We'll be right there watching you," Gina said, silently suppressing an urge for a big glass of wine (or six).

"Sit in the back!" commanded Katie. "You'll make me nervous."

But when she confidently entered the stage, Katie instantly put her parents at ease, flawlessly delivering her lines and picking up the cues. Gina and Mike (who were sitting in the front row) just sat there, stunned. They couldn't believe that shining under those lights was the same girl who desperately tried not to stand out.

During the performance, a proud Mike turned to Gina and said, "See what happens when you believe in a child?"

"I never doubted her for a second," Gina responded, crossing her fingers behind her back.

Since then, Katie's years at Willow Hill have been successful. She's made friends and blossomed in ways Gina and Mike never would have imagined. "Mike, can you believe our little girl is going on an overnight school trip?"

"No, I can't, Gina. She's gonna be all right. We've just gotta let her go. And speaking of letting go, can we get rid of Emmy for the night so that we can be kid-free?"

And though Katie would never admit it, she truly loves school.

"Katie, honey, I don't like the sound of that cough. I think you should stay home from school."

"No way, Mom. I have perfect attendance. I'm not blowing that."

"You know I hate to say this, Katie, but you're a nerd. You like school."

"I know. Please don't tell anyone, Mom. It's social suicide."

PART 4

Living the (Imperfect) Life

It really does take a village to raise a special child—a bartender, a pharmacist, and a taxi service.

—DIANE HAHN

CHAPTER 11

Anything Your Kid Can Do, Mine Can Do Differently

Giving It Back to Those Bragging Parents

Parenting a child with a disability is about letting go of your fantasies and learning to live with the reality. And one reality we must face is that parents who incessantly brag about their children ("perfect parents") will always be around. They have been since the beginning of time.

"Eve, do you realize that our son Abel hasn't lost one sheep yet? He's amazing."

"I know, Adam. And how about Cain? It's amazing how well they get along."

Us vs. Them

And despite the fact that we may live in the same neighborhood, attend the same church, or belong to the same book club as these braggers (excluding Adam and Eve), we often feel worlds apart from them. That's because we have different goals and ideas for success. For example:

THEM: "We only stay at hotels with the best accommodations."

US: "We only accept IEPs with the best accommodations."

THEM: "I was ecstatic to learn that Logan is at the head of the class."

US: "I was ecstatic to learn that John *went* to class."

THEM: "Princess is involved in many activities. She has ballet on Monday, soccer on Tuesday, and theater on Wednesday."

US: "Susie's involved, too. She has occupational therapy on Monday, counseling on Tuesday, and tutoring on Wednesday. And did I mention the new social skills workshop she's starting on Friday?"

US: "Last night my book club went over *Three Cups of Tea*."

THEM: "Last night my support group went through three bottles of wine."

THEM: "Thurston is in his third year at Penn State."

US: "Jennifer is on her third day of a manic state."

THEM: "Speed kills."

US: "Speed helps my kid focus."

THEM: "Harrison Jr. loves to play one-on-one."

US: "Kevin Jr. has a one-on-one."

See Imperfection in Action!

Tired of listening to those braggy parents drone on about their perfect kids? You're not alone. Check out our video *The Coffee Clash*. Just visit YouTube.com and search for *Shut Up About Your Perfect Kid*. If you like what you see, be sure to e-mail the link to your imperfect friends, colleagues, and family members.

Driving Home Our Point

If it's not bad enough that we have to listen to these bragging parents, we have to read their boastful bumper stickers on their minivans and SUVs, too. That's okay, because we've come up with a few of our own to showcase our imperfect pride.

THEIRS: Ask me about my honor student
OURS: Ask me about my Aspie

THEIRS: Baby on Board
OURS: Bipolar on Board

THEIRS: Honk if you love Jesus
OURS: Honk if you desperately need Jesus

THEIRS: My honor student loves me
OURS: My bipolar kid loves me *and* hates me

THEIRS: My child was Student of the Month
OURS: My child was Inpatient of the Month

THEIRS: I'm spending my kids' inheritance
OURS: I'm spending my kids' inheritance on therapists

THEIRS: This car climbed Mt. Washington
OURS: This car wants to drive off Mt. Washington

Holiday Braggings

During the holiday season, many of us have to experience an even more excruciating pain—reading those boastful newsletters that come from the perfect parents. You know them, those joyful holiday greetings in which parents share (in painful detail) every accomplishment their perfect children have made since conception. A typical "perfect" newsletter might look something like this:

Happy holidays to all our friends, family members, financial advisers, personal trainers, and fellow future National Honor Society parents.

We've had many blessings this year, beginning with Pandora's unexpected victory in the first grade spelling bee. We were ecstatic when she took home the prize on the word *perfection*. Winston Jr., or "Little Win" as we affectionately call him, continued to excel in preschool T-ball. Clearly, our investment in his strength and conditioning coach was a stroke of genius, giving him a clear advantage over the other toddlers. I'm busy running around with the kids and training for my fifth triathlon. I'm making great progress, but my personal trainer says I have a lot more weight gaining to do. "Big Win" has also had a fabulous year, earning his fifth promotion in two years. To celebrate, we'll be spending Christmas and New Year's in the Swiss Alps. We'll be looking down on you all, wishing you a happy, healthy, and perfect year.

The Not-So-Perfect Newsletter

We think it would be so much more interesting and fun to get an imperfect newsletter.

To our friends, family, neighbors, psychiatric professionals, pharmacists, advocates, and liquor store owners:

This year, our family saw more ups and downs than Kirstie Alley's bathroom scale, yet we still feel blessed to have survived it all and to have somehow found the positive (and the medicine cabinet) amid all the chaos. In January, Amelia, our ten-year-old, was diagnosed with anxiety, depression, and learning issues. Our psychiatrist put her on anti-anxiety medication, which unfortunately made her anxious and me depressed. Speaking of medication, we were ecstatic to learn that our family had earned "Family of the Year" honors at our pharmacy. Mark says it's because they know whom they work for. On a happy note, our accountant informed us that all our therapist co-pays and medication bills will give us a healthy tax refund. Instead of the actual money, we've asked for the refund to be paid in Klonopin, which should help us all sleep more soundly at night.

Candy has found her love of acting and has buried herself in research—now watching TV eight hours a day. Despite this, she's managed to care for five (count them) virtual families on The Sims. And to think we were worried about her life skills.

My business had a solid year despite the economic downturn. I actually had to hire an administrative assistant to keep up with all the calls (though most of them are still from the school). Mark is back to work following the layoff he experienced early in the year. I've never seen anyone work so hard to find a job. He said being home with the kids and me for six weeks gave him the motivation he needed.

That's all. Wishing you and yours a happy, healthy, hospitalization-free holiday season.

Sending the Wrong Message

We poke fun at the braggy newsletters, but we've actually met parents of special needs children who get depressed when they receive them. One wrote to us: "I had just put my daughter in the hospital and I came home to a newsletter from a friend. As I read about all the accomplishments of her perfect family, all I could think of was how much my family has struggled. I couldn't stop crying."

When parents of typically developing kids ask us whether they should not talk about their kids, we advise them to know their audience. For example, you wouldn't tell a parent of a child in a wheelchair how fast your child can run.

Shortly after our book came out, a mother e-mailed us this story, which so perfectly (if you'll pardon that word) illustrates this point. She wrote:

> We recently sent out an e-mail informing several friends that our daughter had been diagnosed with autism. Our daughter doesn't talk or communicate in other ways, or understand much of what we say. One friend, who has a daughter the same age, called to sympathize.
>
> To be polite, my husband asked his friend how things were going with his family. This guy could have told my husband anything. But what's the one thing he chose to tell my husband? He said he and his wife had begun speaking both English and Spanish in the home with the result that their daughter, the same age as ours, had become bilingual.
>
> How do you say "Shut Up About Your Perfect Kid" in Spanish?

A Few "Choice Words" for Bragging Parents

We really don't mean to be so hard on parents who brag endlessly about their children (okay, maybe we do). It's just hard to listen to how good their kid is on the baseball field when yours would rather catch real flies. Or how great their kid is doing in school when yours won't go to school.

But we're not foolish enough to believe these people are actually living perfect lives. We think it's all a matter of word choice. Some of us parents of imperfect children are guilty of creative phrasing of our own.

Like Meghan, the mother of two special needs children, who tells people she lives in a "gated community." **Translation:** She has to keep gates up all over her house to protect her children from falls.

Or us when we let it slip at cocktail parties that our money is "tied up in pharmaceuticals." **Translation:** Our kids are on a mix of meds.

Or our pal Susie, who tells people she has a "driver" take her daughter to school. **Translation:** Her kid gets picked up in a city-funded mini-van.

Then there's single mother Andrea, who tells people she's "seeing a handsome doctor." **Translation:** She's in therapy.

Even Gina has been known to play this game when she tells people, "I have to pick up Katie at the academy." **Translation:** It's a social skills group, Academy Metro West.

We're Just Sayin'

Though we can often feel worlds apart from parents of perfect kids, we do have something in common: We're all proud of our kids for one reason or another. It's just the reasons we're proud that differ. Unfortunately, we don't always realize that. Many parents of special kids feel angry that "perfect" parents brag about their kids. And many special parents assume that these perfect parents don't care about our kids.

We've found just the opposite. We think that people *do* care about our kids. It's just sometimes they forget to whom they are speaking to.

"Great to meet you, Gina. Is it true you wrote a book?"

"Yes, it's called *Shut Up About Your Perfect Kid*."

"Oh, you have kids, too? My little Mandy was the top tapper in her ballet school."

Or they don't know how to ask us about our kids without upsetting us. This is one of the reasons we openly talk about our kids, even before they ask.

"My daughter Jenn is sixteen. She tried out for the field hockey team and made it. I'm so proud of her because she's been through so much."

And as parents of special kids, we don't mind hearing "perfect" parents talk about their kids, though there are some who don't necessarily believe that. "Why would I want to hear two angry sisters speak about their kids?" The truth is, we like to hear about the success of every child. But if you brag about your kid, you have to be willing to hear us brag about ours.

"We're so happy that Jeffrey plans to study medicine."

"We're so happy that Katie remembered to take her medicine."

Celebrity Think-Alikes
FAMOUS PEOPLE WITH DISABILITIES

When we were young, we were always interested in the latest trends. Today, as adults, we're part of another growing trend we never imagined—having a child with a disability. With the great advances in diagnosing and treating learning disabilities and mental disorders, it's almost chic to have a kid with "issues," or to have issues yourself. Yes, over the years, we've discovered that our kids are in really good company, since many famous and highly successful people—actors, artists, entrepreneurs, inventors, musicians—have grown up with disabilities. The National Alliance on Mental Illness, a nationally recognized advocacy group, and realmentalhealth.com have identified the following celebrities with mental health issues:

Mike Wallace—television host
Ashley Judd—actress
Billy Joel—singer
Boris Yeltsin—Russian president
Britney Spears—singer
Brooke Shields—actress
Drew Carey—comedian
Gwyneth Paltrow—actress

BY GOLLY, LOOK WHO'S BIPOLAR
Patty Duke—actress
Buzz Aldrin—astronaut
Adam Ant—musician
Tim Burton—artist, director
Richard Dreyfus—actor
Connie Francis—singer
Jane Pauley—TV journalist
Ted Turner—businessman

According to greatschools.org, a program of Schwab Learning, the following celebrities have been diagnosed with learning disabilities, AD/HD, or dyslexia:

Charles Schwab—founder, chair, and CEO of the world's largest brokerage firm (dyslexia)

Joss Stone—British singer (dyslexia)

Princess Beatrice—daughter of Britain's Prince Andrew and fifth in line to the throne (dyslexia)

Ingvar Kamprad—Swedish founder and chairman of IKEA (dyslexia)

James Carville—political consultant (AD/HD)

Whoopi Goldberg—actress, comedian, and cohost of *The View* (dyslexia)

Michael Phelps—Olympic gold medalist (AD/HD)

Terry Bradshaw—actor, announcer, and former NFL quarterback (AD/HD)

Ty Pennington—host of ABC's *Extreme Makeover* (AD/HD)

Henry Winkler—actor, producer, and Yale graduate (dyslexia)

Tommy Hilfiger—fashion designer (dyslexia)

Richard Branson—entrepreneur and founder of Virgin Airlines (LD or AD/HD)

Orlando Bloom—actor (LD or AD/HD)

Cher—Academy Award–winning actress (LD or AD/HD)

Patrick Dempsey—actor (LD or AD/HD)

Woody Harrelson—actor (LD or AD/HD)

Anderson Cooper—news reporter (LD or AD/HD)

Harry Belafonte—singer and Academy Award–winning actor (LD or AD/HD)

William "Bell" Hewlett—cofounder of Hewlett-Packard (LD or AD/HD)

John T. Chambers—CEO of Cisco Systems (LD or AD/HD)

According to the epilepsyfoundation.org, the following people have epilepsy:

Agatha Christie—writer
Bonnie Franklin—actress
Florence Griffith Joyner (FloJo)—Olympian
Lindsey Buckingham—musician in Fleetwood Mac
Margeaux Hemingway—actress
Richard Burton—actor

CHAPTER 12

Coping Techniques and Therapy

Imperfect Strategies for Managing Stress for You and Your Child

We've repeatedly said we wanted our children to experience the same happy, carefree childhoods we did. Of course, that hasn't happened. In many ways, their childhoods are worlds apart from ours. One of the most obvious differences involves the need for therapy.

Growing up, our childhood experience with therapy was limited to the group sessions on *The Bob Newhart Show*. We were pretty much convinced therapy was meant for the likes of Elliot Carlin, the incurable neurotic who had a daily appointment with Dr. Bob.

Today, we and our kids have collectively logged more time on the couch than our husbands. ("Gene, do you mind if I stay home this weekend and watch this Rocky marathon?") In fact, counseling has become such a part of our normal lives, we don't even think about it anymore. ("Mommy, is the feelings doctor coming over for our Labor Day cookout?")

There's no question, we have a very different view of therapy today—one that Patty sums up well: "It's the people who aren't in therapy I worry about."

Taking Care of Ourselves

If we've learned anything about raising our imperfect children, it's about the importance of taking care of ourselves. Our wise friend Jane often reminds us of this.

"Gina and Patty, you all are the mothers of the house. You dictate the temperature of the house."

"So that's why I'm having hot flashes. It's stress. And all this time I thought it was because I was old."

The fact is, raising a child with a disability or a special need can be extremely stressful—on you and your entire family. That's why it's so important to take care of yourself, to do something that takes you away from the day-to-day stresses you face. But when you're busy battling school districts, waiting in line at the drive-up pharmacy, or trying to keep up with the Kardashians, that's not so easy to do.

It's something we forced ourselves to do because as MOHs (Mothers of Household) we are the epicenters of our familial life. The most complex and difficult problems run through us, making it critical for us to always be on top of our "emotional games."

"Mom! Help! I think someone deleted my virtual family on the computer."

"Calm down, Katie. We'll file a missing virtual persons report."

Gina's Way of Caring for Herself—Holding Court

As a former athlete, Gina finds basketball a great way to relieve stress. Two days a week, she carves out a few hours to play in an adult women's basketball league. For Gina, basketball has become an important activity, which allows her to run out stress and run through her problems on the court.

"So I really don't know what to do with my daughter. She had a really tough year in math and I'm worried she won't pass."

"Speaking of passing, do you think you could stop talking and pass the ball?"

Benefits of Basketball

Calories burned: 530
Time out of the house: Priceless

Patty's Favorite Coping Technique: Going for a Spin

Like Gina, Patty also chooses exercise for stress relief: She spins on a stationary bike at the gym. In fact, the more her life spins out of control, the more Patty spins.

"Pat, have you ever thought of switching to a non-stationary bike? Think how far away you could get from home."

Patty's favorite coping technique, however, is a lot less strenuous. It's driving. Or driving away, to be exact. What began as a little spin around the block soon became a way of life when things got a little too stressful at home.

"There goes Mom again," said Patty's son, Mikey, looking out the window.

"That reminds me, I need to take her car in for an oil change," said Patty's husband.

Patty's favorite place to drive to is the beach. There's something about the warm sand and the vast ocean that soothes her. Of course, it could also be the poor cell phone reception that draws her there. ("Patty, where have you been? I've been trying to call you to tell on the kids.")

Gina shares Patty's love for the ocean. To both of us, the ocean is a relaxing and spiritual place that takes us away from our day-to-day problems and reminds us there's something much bigger and more important than the two of us.

"That's a fine-looking sand castle, Pat."

"Your sand angel is pretty cool, too, Gene."

Join Us on Facebook and Twitter

You can become a fan of *Shut Up About Your Perfect Kid* on Facebook to learn about our speaking engagements and other late-breaking news in the ever-changing, wide world of imperfection. You can also follow us on Twitter at shutupaboutcom. (If you do decide to follow us, keep in mind that neither of us is very good with directions.)

Ideas for Taking Care of Yourself

Spending time on yourself is like putting money in the bank—the sanity bank. Here are some ways we and other parents make regular deposits.

Yoga. There's nothing like a good pretzel to help relieve stress. (We particularly like the kind with mustard.) Yoga not only provides physical benefits, such as increased flexibility and improved muscle tone, but also is said to decrease anxiety, depression, and hostility.

Running. We won't lie; neither of us is a big fan of running (though we can often be seen running to the liquor store). Many parents of children with disabilities find running to be a great way to relieve stress and maintain good mental and physical health.

Book Clubs. A book club is a great way to exercise your mind and get out of the house. If you do join a club, be sure to do your homework and read the book. If you don't have the time to do so, at least rent the movie or buy the CliffsNotes.

Knitting/Needlepoint. When we speak at conferences, we often meet parents of special needs children who tell us about the relaxation involved in knitting. Many times, they'll knit while we're speaking. We've found this a valuable way to gauge the length of our speeches. ("Gene, I think we might have gone on a little too long. That lady made an entire afghan during our talk.")

Reiki. Reiki is an ancient Japanese laying-on-of-hands healing technique that uses the life force energy to heal and balance the energies within the body. Gina was skeptical about Reiki, until a friend who is a Reiki practitioner invited her to a session in her home. She had Gina lie down on a cot in her

The Support Group

In addition to finding activities to take you away from your problems, it's important to find people who understand the challenges and struggles you face. The last thing you want to do is be around a group of people who don't understand you or your children.

"And yesterday, I came home to Jenn attempting to put Mikey through the spin cycle."

"Ma'am, I'm sorry. I think you have the wrong group. This is for parents of kids in drama, not parents who *live in* drama."

The way to find parents who understand your unique challenges

---

Ideas for Taking Care of Yourself (continued)

dining room, put on soft meditative music, and then placed her hands above the areas on Gina's body where she thought Gina needed healing. Gina, who was extremely tense before the session, walked away feeling light, free, and unburdened.

Music. We've both found listening to music to be a healthy way to relax. It's not uncommon to find either one of us walking around the house with an iPod singing aloud, "I will survive. As long as I know how to love, I know I'll stay alive. Hey. Hey."

Social Networking. Advances in technology have also brought us a new coping technique—writing on Facebook and Twitter. We've personally found Facebook to be a great way to reach out to friends and family. For those who don't know, these are social networking websites that allow you to notify your friends, family members, and colleagues about the status of your life. We like to use it to share milestones and frustrations about our kids and other family members. Facebook is great way to connect with other parents of children with disabilities to obtain support and assistance.

is to join a support group. Patty had great success with a local NAMI mental illness support group. (Visit nami.org for more information.)

"Gene, it was so good to know I'm not alone. The people are wonderful. Everyone has a story. There's no judgment; just real people dealing with real challenges. And despite all they have to go through in their own lives, people are always willing to help."

Finding the right support group may take time. One of our friends, for example, attended a support group, only to discover it was too depressing for her. "I couldn't wait to get home. All these women were sitting around and crying. I can cry alone. Why would I want to do it with them?"

You might say that finding the right support group is a lot like finding the right partner (though you don't have to worry about kissing anyone good night).

Gina found the perfect support group for her—on her very first "date." It was one our cousin Jodi, the mother of a young boy with pervasive developmental disorder, invited us to attend. This particular group combined all the things we both love—our cousin, an evening away from our homes, and one of our most effective coping mechanisms: wine.

When we arrived at Jodi's house, the group was gathered around the kitchen island, already engaged in deep and meaningful conversation. "So do you prefer Cool Ranch– or Nacho-flavored Doritos?"

Jodi, a wonderful hostess, introduced us to the group ("Say hello to my cousins Patty and Gina, or bipolar and Asperger's") and offered us a glass of wine. Eager to overcome our nervousness at meeting new people, and to continue our family's age-old tradition of never refusing alcohol, we graciously accepted. "Why not? Surely, it will take the edge off."

One glass led to another, and before we knew it, the entire group (PDD, autism, Asperger's, bipolar, and cerebral palsy) had jelled, holding up our glasses in unison and calling out, "Hey, PDD! More support over here, please!"

At the end of the evening, Gina turned to Patty and said, "Wow! You were right, Pat. These support groups are very helpful."

"I told you, Gene."

"And to think, all this time I thought we had to talk about the kids. I'm not sure some of them even had kids."

Online Resources and Forums

Despite what our mother might think ("Stay off the Internet; it's loaded with perverts"), we believe the Internet offers a wealth of helpful information and support for parents of children with disabilities. In particular, we've found a number of online forums to be helpful. On a forum, you can post questions and topics to connect with other parents. There are forums available for every type of disability. See the Resources section on page 249 for a list of popular forums and online resources.

Laughing Our Way to Sanity

Of all the coping techniques we've employed, we've found laughter to be one of the most effective. We are not the only ones who have benefited from this strategy. As many parents of special needs kids often say, we have two choices—to laugh or to cry. We prefer laughter. It doesn't create puffy eyes, and it offers some serious health benefits.

Laughter is said to do the following:

✔ Improve breathing
✔ Trigger endorphins, the body's natural painkillers
✔ Improve brain functioning

We also have heard that laughter strengthens and tones abdominal muscles, though there is no evidence to support this in us.

"Gene, do you ever think I'll lose this baby fat in my stomach?"

"Well, considering the baby is now thirteen, I'm gonna say probably not."

We received this story from a mother of a then-ten-year-old girl with Asperger's syndrome, which demonstrates our point about laughter. She wrote:

> One Sunday my daughter was with me at church when she started picking at her eye. She said it was hurting her, which is one of her many sensory issues. I was constantly asking her to stop. Finally, she excused herself to use the restroom.
>
> We had a wonderful speaker that Sunday who was telling a moving story about stewardship. The entire congregation was

near tears. I noticed my daughter had quietly come into church, though through the front of the church, of course. It took me several seconds to process what I was seeing. My daughter had carefully wrapped paper towels around her head several times, covering the entire top of her head and her one eye. She literally looked like she had just returned from the battle of Gettysburg, like she had just had brain surgery, or as if we were under attack. I pulled her down into the pew and asked, "What did you do?" She stated quite proudly, "My eye was hurting. I wanted to hold a cold towel to it, but I didn't want to hold my hand on my eye. People would look at me funny if I did that." I looked at my daughter, who looked pleased as punch with nearly three yards of paper towel covering her head, and did the only thing I could do: I laughed. I laughed so hard I thought I would break the pew. Not many people at church said anything, except for one man who quietly came up to me and said, "I guess Halloween came early this year." I just smiled. When you have a child with a disability, you know that every day something will happen that will make you laugh or cry. Thank God for the blessing of humor. Sometimes it's the only thing that keeps you sane.

Though Patty struggled with Jennifer's bouts of anger, there were times when Jennifer's behavior was humorous. It's not that Patty wasn't taking Jennifer's anger seriously; it's just that some of the ways Jenn chose to showcase her anger were funny. One Sunday morning, for example, Jennifer was extremely agitated and fighting with her older sister, Jules, as Patty prepared to take her children to church.

"I hate you, Julie!" Jenn screeched at her older sister for borrowing one of her shirts.

"I don't know why you don't just run away for good, Jennifer!" fired back Jules.

"Shut up!" Patty screamed, unknowingly giving our book a plug. "Jules and Mikey, get into the car. We're leaving for church!"

On the way out, Patty approached Jennifer with what she thought was an outstanding solution. "Jenn, why don't you try to write down your feelings while we're gone? We'll put your story in the book," Patty said, desperately hoping to calm Jenn down.

[**Authors' Note:** During these explosive episodes, it's always best to leave Jennifer alone at home, where she can have time to calm down. Clearly, putting her feelings in writing would be the perfect therapy. At least that's what Patty thought.]

When Patty and her other two kids returned home an hour later, they realized Jennifer had taken her mother's advice, but not in the manner Patty intended. There, wedged inside the storm door, was the latest draft of *Shut Up About Your Perfect Kid*. Attached to the manuscript was a yellow Post-it note with the scrawled words, "I hate this piece of $%#@!"

Instinctively, Patty placed a call to Gina.

"Well, we just got our first negative review of the manuscript," Patty said.

"What? Who doesn't like our book?" asked the highly oversensitive Gina.

As Patty proceeded to tell Gina about her fun-filled morning, Jules and Mikey ran up to Patty.

"Mom, Jenn was really busy while we were at church," said Jules, showing Patty a Post-it note that read, "I hate you."

"Yeah, Mom, she definitely did some writing," Mikey said as he handed Patty two more Post-its with the words "I hate you!" scribbled in black marker.

Before Patty knew it, Jules and Mikey were finding "I hate you" Post-its on the toilet, the refrigerator, the lamps, the dog, and everywhere you could possibly imagine.

Jules exclaimed, "Whoa! It's like a scavenger hunt! Okay, Mikey, I've got like seven. How many can you find?"

Patty couldn't help but smile when she saw Jules and Mikey having so much fun. It felt good to hear them really laughing. When Jennifer calmed down later on, *she* even laughed about it. ("All right, I know, it was funny. I was just so mad.")

It may not have been a very green solution, but it was harmless, and Jennifer was able to work through her anger and frustration.

Bringing in the Professionals

Of course, there's always the option of seeking professional help from a therapist. Many people find therapy a productive way to share their feelings with an unbiased source. However, Gina had an experience with one therapist who was not at all unbiased, at least when it came to the abilities and strengths of himself and his "perfect" daughter.

Gina found him at one of the lowest points of her life—when Katie started having social difficulties at school and became very sad. Gina was sad, too, something Patty was quick to pick up on. "Look, Gene, you're depressing the hell out of me. I think it's time you get therapy."

Gina took Patty's advice and started calling therapists from the Yellow Pages.

"Sure, I'll take you. You can come right now if you like," the first doctor she called responded.

"That's okay, Doctor; sometime this week would be fine," Gina replied, impressed by his responsiveness.

When Gina arrived for her appointment, the doctor said, "Have a seat. Sorry if I seem a little tired; I just got back from the White House."

"You did?" Gina asked, impressed with the man she had carefully selected.

"Yes, I take photographs as a hobby. The president was so impressed by one I did of the American flag he invited me to the White House."

"Wonderful," Gina politely replied, waiting for him to get around to talking about her life. "So I have this daughter . . ."

"I have a daughter, too," he blurted out. "She's amazing."

"That's great, but . . ."

"In fact, she graduated at the top of her class. On parents' night they told me she was one of the brightest students to graduate."

"Terrific. You must be proud," Gina said, wondering what new, innovative form of therapy he was using. Surely it would only be a matter of time till he turned things back to her.

"She's on a full scholarship, you know."

Gina listened to him drone on and on, and then before she knew it, her time was up. When she returned home, she recounted this twisted tale to her husband, who always sees the good in people.

"Well, Gene, maybe he was caught up in the excitement of the White House. I think you should give him another chance."

Like a fool, Gina took his advice and went back for her next appointment. "I'm worried about my daughter's academic future and whether she will ever be able to go to college," Gina confessed.

"Speaking of college," he interrupted. "I teach at the local state college. During the graduation ceremony, a student gave a speech about the one person that's influenced her life the most. I was shocked when she said it was me."

You Know You've Got a Bad Therapist When . . .

Apparently, Gina wasn't the only one who encountered a bad therapist. At our website, shutupabout.com, we received these responses to the following phrase:

YOU KNOW YOU'VE GOT A BAD THERAPIST WHEN . . .

✔ You have to tell him your time is up.
✔ She cancels your appointment and never calls to reschedule.
✔ He finds your life so very difficult and depressing that he suggests you write a book or a Lifetime movie.
✔ You have to console *him*.
✔ Her alter ego shows up for group therapy.
✔ He cries throughout your entire session and asks you for tissues.
✔ You start to wonder why you aren't the one being paid.
✔ She says nothing during your entire session and just hands you a bill.
✔ You end up giving him more advice than he gives you.
✔ You say something and he gasps.
✔ She keeps yawning during your session.
✔ He continually asks you, "How does that make you feel?" while you're crying.
✔ He's lying down on the couch.

"Wow," Gina said, silently scanning the room for an escape hatch.

"Do you want to see the video? I have it on tape."

"Sure, why not?" Gina said.

As she watched him search for the video, Gina experienced a remarkable moment of clarity. *Hey, my life's not so bad. He's a psychologist and he's crazy as a loon. My problems are nothing compared to his!*

By golly, his innovative therapy had actually worked.

Kid-Friendly Therapy

Just as professional therapists can help adults, they can also help children. Finding a good child therapist is challenging enough; getting your child to go to one is even harder.

"Come on, Katie. Time to go to the therapist."

"Oh, Mom, it's so boring. All we do is sit around and talk about feelings, feelings, feelings. He doesn't even have a TV."

In contrast, Gina's younger daughter, Emily, who has anxiety

Tips on Finding a Good Therapist for Your Child

(Condensed from kargacademy.com)

Finding a therapist that best fits your child's needs and personality, and your budget, can take time and effort. Here are some tips to make the process easier:

✔ **Identify your child's needs** both in school and at home, to give the therapist an idea of your child's issues.

✔ **Look for direct referrals** from trusted physicians, other therapists, family members, or close friends. When a clinician is highly regarded, they are usually well known in the community.

✔ **Plan for long-term care** by making sure therapists are covered by your insurance or have a pay scale you can afford.

Tips on Finding a Good Therapist (continued)

✔ **Verify credentials** through the professional organizations that offer psychotherapist directories and reliably verify psychotherapists' basic qualifications:
  - ✔ The American Psychological Association: apa.org
  - ✔ International OCD Foundation: ocfoundation.org
  - ✔ Association for Behavioral and Cognitive Therapies: aabt.org
  - ✔ Academy of Cognitive Therapy: academyofct.org
  - ✔ Anxiety Disorders Association of America: adaa.org
  - ✔ American Academy of Child and Adolescent Psychiatry: aacap.org
  - ✔ *Psychology Today*: therapists.psychologytoday.com

✔ **Schedule a consult visit** to interview the therapist yourself before you bring in your child. Good therapists will welcome the chance to answer any questions you have in an engaged, responsive, straightforward, and professional manner.
  - ✔ Discuss your child's issues with the therapist and find out what experience he or she has in dealing with similar problems.
  - ✔ Ask for details on his or her therapeutic philosophy and treatment methods.
  - ✔ Find out how the therapist establishes trust relationships.
  - ✔ Make sure the therapist is willing to work with your child's current physicians, especially if your child is on a medication regimen.
  - ✔ Discuss basic time estimations for progress.
  - ✔ Make sure the therapist has a solid action plan for emergencies or crisis intervention.

Most Important Tip from Gina and Patty
Find a therapist who accepts credit cards. That way you can earn reward points and go to Disney World on your issues.

and learning issues, loves seeing her therapist, and is quite vocal about it.

"Hi, Mrs. Wallace. Can Amanda come out to play? I just got back from seeing my therapist, Anita."

Emily is also quick to seek help. "Mom, can you please make me a therapist appointment? I promise I'll be good."

She's also blurred the lines between the professional and the personal. "Mom, can I invite Anita to my birthday party?"

"Oh, honey, I think that's really sweet, but Anita may be too big for the ball pit."

As children grow older and wiser, having a therapist they like is not always a good thing. ("Mom, I can't believe you forgot to pick me up at school. I'm telling my therapist.")

Child Coping Techniques

Parents aren't the only ones who need to work their problems out. Here are some coping techniques that have proven effective for children.

FACEBOOK. With parental supervision, our daughters have both found Facebook therapeutic. It's particularly helped Katie, who has difficulty picking up the phone and initiating conversations with friends.

To ensure Katie's safety (and allow Gina to spy on her), Gina requested that Katie accept her as a friend. She was pleasantly surprised that Katie didn't protest.

"Honey, that's so nice of you to include me as a Facebook friend."

"Yeah, I'm just trying to get my friend count up. As soon as I get 101 friends, I'm dropping you."

[**Authors' Note:** Neither of us has friended our mother. Not because we're embarrassed of her, but more because she's not that techno savvy. "Patty, will you MyFace your brother and ask him to come to dinner?"]

Gina has also found Facebook to be a great tool in helping determine Katie's emotional state, since Katie often keeps her feelings to herself. One day, for example, Katie came home from school and quietly said, "Mom, I'm going to my room, okay?"

A few moments later, Gina logged on to Facebook and read Katie's status line, which said: "Katie Gallagher is not talking to anyone today!"

Almost instantly, Gina's maternal instincts kicked in. *Hmm. I'm not entirely certain, but I think something might be wrong with Katie.*

She raced up the stairs to Katie's room and asked if anything was wrong. Katie broke down and confided she was having friend difficulty that day. Gina gave her a hug and a pep talk and left Katie alone.

Later on, Gina called Patty to get her thoughts on the situation.

"Patty, poor Katie was all upset today."

"I know, but she's fine now."

"How do you know?"

"'Cause her Facebook status says: 'Katie Gallagher is fine now.'"

EXERCISE. Jennifer has found running and Rollerblading to be outstanding ways to relieve stress. Often, she can be found skating around Patty's cul-de-sac late into the evening. Patty's neighbors are no longer fazed by this, though Jenn's older sister, Jules, has feelings of her own.

"Look at her, Mom! She's such a freak!"

Jennifer also finds swinging on the swing set or jumping on the trampoline an effective way to relieve stress. No wonder she maintains her girlish figure.

For a list of other coping techniques from LeeAnn Karg, see our Resources on page 249.

CHAPTER 13

A Different Way of Thinking

Seeing the World in a New and Different Way

Parents love to share their knowledge and wisdom with their children. Our parents, in particular, are always ready and willing to give advice (most of it unsolicited). In fact, in the course of a day, they dish out more than Martha Stewart. And though the subjects of their ongoing lecture series vary, they constantly tell us to "stop and smell the roses": "Your lives are too busy; you need to slow down, enjoy your life, and balance your checkbooks."

We know they're right, but with special kids, it's pretty hard to do. It's a common theme among most parents, especially parents who have children with disabilities. That's because children with disabilities are often on their own schedules—schedules that generally aren't conducive to meeting a school bus in time or evacuating the house in a family fire drill.

"Katie! The bus is almost here! What are you doing in the bathroom so long?"

"Oh, nothing. I was just counting my teeth."

Yes, Katie and a lot of other special children seem to have no trouble stopping and smelling the roses. And though it can sometimes be trying when their parents have a schedule to keep (or a plane to catch), there's something to be learned from these children who know how to appreciate the little things in life.

A then-eight-year-old Katie demonstrated this point one morning when Gina asked her to retrieve the Sunday paper, which was at the very bottom of Gina's long, hilly, and winding driveway.

Gina kissed Katie at the door and watched her make her journey down the stairs. Katie walked a few steps and then stopped to follow a bird.

Several minutes later, Katie continued down the front walk, pausing to catch up with a caterpillar. When she finally hit asphalt, she stopped again, picking up a piece of sidewalk chalk and writing, "I love Mom." Touched, Gina went inside the house. Twenty minutes later, Gina heard the doorbell ring. "Here's your paper, Mom," Katie proudly declared.

A part of Gina was frustrated it took so long, but then she reflected on the previous day, when she was sitting in a Starbucks waiting to meet a colleague. She remembered the harried businesspeople racing in and out and furiously texting and talking on their phones. Clearly they weren't stopping to smell the mocha latte.

Gina couldn't help but think, *I'm like those silly people in Starbucks. I rush around and look ridiculous, yet I think there's something wrong with my daughter for stopping to enjoy the beauty of nature? Katie's fine. It's the rest of us who are crazy.*

A Different View of Life

Being singled out for their differences is one of the hardest things children with special needs and disabilities have to experience. Often their differences make them appear strange to other children and adults, who aren't always willing to look beyond their quirks. But over the years, we've learned that it's our children's differences that give them a unique and refreshing perspective on life.

Yes, we like to think of our children as Macintosh computers operating in a world full of PCs; they get the same answers but process things differently.

Our friend Andy, a teen with AD/HD, is living proof of that. We find his unique outlook on life refreshing. One evening, for example, Andy was looking at his Halloween candy stash when he picked up a small Snickers bar and said to his parents, "Mom and Dad, I just don't get it."

"Get what, Andy?" his dad asked.

"This candy bar. Why do they call it 'fun size'? There's nothing fun about it. Now a candy bar this big," he said, stretching his arms as far apart as they could go, "*that's* what I call fun size."

There's no question our children see the world differently. Sometimes they amaze us with their brilliance, and sometimes they just make us laugh with their innocence, as this story, sent to us from a Pennsylvania mother, indicates:

> When my daughter Morgan was five, we went to a Mom and Tots camp. We did everything together. Morgan, who has high-functioning autism, was obsessed with the movie A Bug's Life. At one point in the movie, one bug slaps another bug on the butt and says, "Hey, nice butt." Our two daughters had taken to slapping each other at bath time and other times. One day at camp, we had gotten really dirty. Just as I was putting Morgan in the shower, a naked woman got out of the shower next to us. Morgan, seeing a naked butt, slapped the other mother on the butt and remarked, "Hey, nice butt!" If I could have slid down the drain, I would have. I later apologized to the other woman, and she said she took it as a compliment.

Extreme Makeover

When you have a child with a mental illness, there's really nothing that surprises you. With two teenagers, one of whom is bipolar, Patty has pretty much seen and heard it all. There's never a dull (or quiet) moment in Patty's house.

Over the years, Patty has learned that when Jenn is having a "bipolar bender," the best thing to do is to leave her alone. This gives Jennifer a chance to cool down and work through her difficulties.

One day, when Patty's family was planning to attend a birthday party, Jenn was particularly anxious, forcing Patty and Michael to come to the difficult decision to leave her alone. ("Hurry up, Michael. Start the car before she comes out!")

When they returned home several hours later, Patty and Michael had no idea what they would find in the house, or even if the house would still be standing. But, much to their surprise, Jennifer had cleaned the house. She had not only dusted and vacuumed, but had also reorganized the silverware drawer, facing all the utensils in the same direction.

Patty was even more shocked to see that Jennifer (a slight girl) had single-handedly moved a solid cherry, full-length bookcase from one end of the living room to another.

Patty was impressed and said to Michael, "You know, Michael, I just never thought of putting it there, but it looks great."

In fact, Patty and Michael were so impressed by Jenn's work that Patty later wondered, "Michael, we have your friends coming over next Saturday. Do you think we should schedule a meltdown with Jenn?"

Patty and Michael joked about it, but the truth was, Jennifer had once again taken her negative feelings and channeled them in a positive way. It was so effective that Patty is thinking about pitching a new show to ABC—*Extreme Makeover: Bipolar Edition*.

Black and Whitehead

Often, children with special needs and language-based learning disabilities are very concrete and literal thinkers. Gina's younger daughter, Emily, demonstrated this one day during a drive to the store with Gina and her sister, Katie.

Katie was sitting in the passenger seat, staring at her face in the mirror when she whined, "Ugh! I hate whiteheads."

Hearing her sister complain, Emily admonished, "Katie stop that! Dad's a whitehead!" referring to Gina's husband, Mike, who has gray hair.

CHAPTER 14

Field of (Day) Dreaming

Lessons and Stories from the
Wide World of Imperfect Sports
and Other Activities

When we were children, sports and activities were designed to develop coordination, team building, and, most important, self-esteem. Today, you can pretty much pitch that idea away like a Curt Schilling fastball. Children of all ages are now taking to the baseball diamonds, soccer fields, and ballet stages with a single goal—to please their parents.

The competitiveness of sports and activities today is difficult for a lot of children, especially those with special needs.

But we question whether our imperfect children, the kids who seem distracted or confused on the field or onstage, simply prefer not to get caught up in the insanity of it all. No, maybe they would rather just kick back, enjoy their time in the sun, and follow a butterfly.

And that's not easy for a parent to accept, particularly if they excelled at the activity in which their child is participating. As a former athlete, Gina couldn't wait to enroll Katie in soccer when she reached first grade.

While Katie liked being on the team, she had very little interest in how the game was actually played—a fact that was somewhat obvious on the field. ("Okay, honey, put down the pussy willows! Here comes the ball!") Gina found Katie's lack of interest quite unsettling, particularly when she noticed the looks the mothers of the perfect kids were giving Gina. They may have been smiling, but Gina knew what they were thinking. *Lady, your kid stinks. You have no right to be here.*

What upset Gina most was that they didn't appear to be the athletes Gina was. No sir, many of them were nonathletes trying to live through their children. Gina felt like challenging them to a race around the track to show them just who they were judging. *Don't look at me like that, Blondie. Do you know I took home the gold in my fifth-grade 220 and I had two 100 patches on my candlepin bowling jacket?*

But she never said anything. She just sat there quietly, bursting on the inside. In her mind, everyone was judging her daughter.

She of course did try to improve Katie, dragging her out to the yard for some healthy, spirited practice competition. ("Mom, do I have to play against the cat?") And though Katie did okay in practice, it was a completely different story during the actual games.

Generally, if the ball was on one side of the field, Katie was on the other, usually in a different time zone altogether. But she wasn't the type to just stand around; she made the most of her playing time either by following butterflies or by gathering a bouquet of dandelions for Gina.

To inspire her to get into the game, Gina developed a complex rewards system early in the season.

"Okay, honey, every time you touch the ball, Mommy will pay you a quarter."

"Awesome! Let's play!"

Midway into the season, Katie had accrued twenty-five cents, which she got on a technicality. She was sitting on the sidelines eating orange slices when someone kicked the ball into her.

"Mom," she called, holding out her hand, "you never said I had to be on the field."

At the final game of the season, as Gina watched Katie take the field in her clean uniform, she realized Katie probably would never touch the ball, let alone score a goal. But when the half ended and Katie came to her with tears in her eyes, Gina realized *Katie* wanted more.

"What's wrong, baby?" Gina asked.

"Everyone scored a goal but me. The kids say I'm not very good."

Heartbroken, Gina got down to her level and gave Katie a speech that would have made Knute Rockne proud. "Well, it's the last game of the season. And you probably won't play next year," Gina said (silently thanking God). "So just go out there and have fun. Don't worry about what anyone thinks. And if you do well, I'll buy you that Barbie beauty parlor you've always wanted."

When Gina watched Katie take her position on the field, she knew something was different "Look, Mike! She's on the same side of the field as the ball," Gina yelled to her husband. Then, she ran to the ball and started kicking it down the field. One, two, three times. "Mike, she's kicking the ball! Look at her go! She's up to seventy-five cents!"

"Gina! She's going the wrong way!"

Then something happened that Gina never expected.

Katie was standing in front of the opponent's net when the ball came her way. In a Hokey Pokey–like motion, she put her right foot out. The ball bounced off her foot and started rolling toward the left goalpost. Gina and Mike jumped out of their seats and watched as the ball ever so slowly bounced off the post and trickled in.

Then Gina's little "soccer star" came rushing toward her with open arms. It was a Kodak moment—and one of the greatest of Gina's entire life.

Gina looked at Mike, who had tears in his eyes, and the reality hit her. That one goal meant more than the hundreds of goals, hits, and baskets Gina had made. But that's just one of the gifts of having a child like Katie. They make us appreciate the little things in life.

For information on sports and extracurricular activities appropriate for children with disabilities, see our Resources section, page 249.

The View from the Sidelines

As special parents, we often try to guide our children along in life. But when they're on the basketball court or the soccer field, sometimes we just have to sit back and watch, as Candy, mother of Tory, a bright boy with AD/HD, shared with us when she wrote:

We couldn't believe it when Tory's recreational basketball team made it to the finals. My husband and I were so happy for him.

During the game, he even got to hold the ball a few times (though he immediately threw it away like a hot potato).

The last five minutes of the game were very tense, and Tory, who is dramatic and sometimes has difficulty keeping his emotions in check, got down on his knees and started praying and blessing himself on the sidelines. We were horrified.

"Candy! Do something!" my husband screamed.

"What am I supposed to do?" I shouted back.

We were so concerned that others might be watching Tory that we stopped watching the game altogether.

As parents, we want our kids to fit in so badly that we get embarrassed when they act out of the ordinary. But what I failed to realize is that Tory is a loving and emotional kid who wears his heart on his sleeve. He's the kind of kid who will stop whatever he's doing to come and give me a hug. How many twelve-year-old boys do that in front of their friends?

Ballet Blunders

Special needs parents are often encouraged to enroll their children in activities that assist with motor planning and coordination. One activity that Gina and many other parents have tried is ballet. What Gina failed to realize about ballet was the mental toughness it required. Not just on the part of the special children, but on the parents who must watch their children struggle.

When Gina discovered that ballet might help Katie, she didn't hesitate to sign her up, even though she had no interest in the activity herself. In fact, her ballet experience was limited to the ballerina who performed in her childhood jewelry box (home of her baseball cards). But the truth was, Gina would have signed Katie up for pole dancing if the experts said it would help her.

At first, Katie didn't seem to mind ballet, but toward the end of the long season, her interest began to wane and Gina's began to perk up, especially after Gina invested in Katie's recital costume (the equivalent of the GNP of some countries).

"I don't want to be in the recital! Ballet is too hard," she protested when Gina asked her to try on her costume the first time.

"Are you crazy?" Gina fired back. "Do you have any idea how much I spent for that costume?"

"But Mom, I don't want to do ballet anymore, and the costume is too itchy."

Gina had suffered through nine months of ballet and was not about to back down. "Oh, you're not quitting," Gina warned.

On the day of the recital, Katie continued to protest. "I'm not getting out of this car, Mom!"

At that moment, Gina's childhood friend Kim, mother of a fellow ballerina, decided to get involved.

"Gina, get lost!" Kim said.

"Excuse me?" Gina repeated, sure she was hearing things.

"Go away. As long as you're here, she won't go on. Let me take her backstage."

Reluctantly, Gina went to sit down with the eighty-nine other family members on hand.

Feeling helpless and disappointed, Gina sat back and prepared to watch the recital, which sadly would not include her daughter. As Gina watched all the performers, she wondered *Why isn't Katie like all these other girls? Why does she have to make things so difficult?*

After what seemed like three years, Gina heard the familiar song and watched as members of Katie's troupe filed out onto the floor. Gina was shocked to find Katie bringing up the rear. Instinctively, she notified our family members. "Mom! Dad! Everyone! Wake up! Katie's on the stage!"

Katie kept right up with the girls, mirroring the steps she had learned over all those grueling weeks. Gina was instantly flooded with fond memories of her jewelry box ballerina, with one minor difference—Katie didn't face the audience. During the entire performance, she faced the back wall, never once looking out at us.

It didn't matter; Gina was ecstatic.

"Honey, you did great. I'm so proud of you. And the back of your head looked beautiful."

"Yeah, now get me out of this itchy costume. I don't ever want to wear it again."

Gina wasn't alone in getting bitten by the ballet bug. Susan, the mother of an adorable daughter, Lexie, with **developmental coordination disorder,** also shared a humorous ballet story.

Like Gina, Susan found it painful to watch her daughter through the glass window. Lexie rarely paid attention and was often out of sync with the other girls.

One day, while getting ready for class, Lexie told her mother she didn't want to wear her leotard. Knowing when to pick her battles, Susan decided to grant Lexie her wish, dressing her only in leggings and a T-shirt. *I don't see the harm,* she thought.

During class, Lexie kept putting her hands inside the back of her leggings, thinking they were her pockets. The result was that, for the entire class, Lexie mooned the crowd of parents watching outside the window.

The parents were all laughing hysterically. And even Susan, who felt like crawling under the carpet, couldn't help but laugh at her adorable daughter, who was putting on quite a performance.

PART 5

Lessons in Love and Imperfection

Life is not about waiting for the
storms to pass. It's about learning
to dance in the rain.

—VIVIAN GREENE

CHAPTER 15

Change Will Do You Good

Going Beyond Your Own
Expectations

What if?

W At some point in our lives, we all ask ourselves this question. When our children were conceived and we had dreams of perfection, we pondered a number of "what if" questions:

What if our children are star athletes? What if they become Rhodes scholars? What if they have thin legs, unlike us?

But when we faced the reality our children had disabilities, we focused on a set of different scenarios:

What if our kids didn't have disabilities? Would their lives be easier? Would they have more friends? Be better in school? Have busier social calendars? Probably.

And what would our lives as their parents be like if they didn't have disabilities? Would we have more money? Drive better cars? Be invited to more parties?

We used to wonder about all of this. But now, after the journey of writing this book, we've learned to view things from a different perspective, and now we ask ourselves a completely new set of questions:

What if our children didn't have disabilities? Would we be as compassionate? Would we look beyond other people's differences? Would we take the time to help others? And be less quick to judge people?

We'd like to say wisdom and maturity led us to this change in thinking. But by now, you know us well enough to not buy that.

The truth is, it just happened.

We were, after all, just two frustrated, imperfect mothers trying to get to a good place with our daughters' disabilities. We never imagined the journey our children would take us on, or the amazing people we would meet along the way—like all the disabled adults and children who have told us what it was like to grow up feeling different. And countless parents, grandparents, foster parents, siblings, advocates, and other professionals who have dedicated their lives to making life better for the disabled. And people like our dear friend Mark, who sadly lost his only son, Tony, to bipolar disorder and suicide just days before Tony's twenty-ninth birthday. Mark was quite proud of his son and was devastated by his death.

> *"Tony could have been called a genius. Without a high school diploma, he still became a very talented and self-taught computer engineer. He worked developing computer hardware and software and conducting testing and technical support. He was getting lucrative job offers long after his death in 2001. His talents were much in demand in the computer industry, although in the last couple of months of his life he was working selling cars, as his illness was causing him such problems."*

Despite this incredible loss, which he will never get over, Mark has taken something positive out of it. He's dedicated his life to helping other families affected by mental illness. Mark knows that through his son, he has been given an incredible gift. We'll never forget when he shared with us, "Patty and Gina, the greatest gift you can give someone is the gift of compassion. It says to a person, 'I care that you are hurting; let me share your pain with you.'"

Yes, it was all these extraordinary experiences with extraordinary people like this dear man that have made us stop and take a closer look at our lives and our values, and see the world in a new and different way.

One day, Gina was telling a close friend about the people we have met when her friend commented, "Gina, I worry about you and Patty. Being around people with such sad stories can make you depressed."

"Depressed?" Gina responded. "These people don't *depress* us; they *inspire* us. They remind us of what's really important and have changed our lives."

Of course, we mustn't forget the people who set us out on the path of change—our "special" daughters, Jennifer and Katie. Through all their tears and fears and hospitalizations and tribulations, they have shown us—and all our family—the true meaning of love and acceptance.

How Katie Has Changed Gina

There's no question, Gina and Katie are complete opposites. In fact, when Gina was young, she probably would have been classified as a "perfect kid," though Patty doesn't necessarily agree. ("Look at that stupid bowl haircut you had. There's no way you were perfect.") But the fact is, Gina was a star athlete, an excellent student, and a kid other kids wanted to be around.

> [**Authors' Note:** Gina's popularity may or may not have been due to our family's having a swimming pool.]

And unlike Katie, who takes a very laid-back approach to life ("Mom, I don't have to get a hundred on every test; that's so boring"), Gina was constantly driven to succeed, never stopping to enjoy her successes along the way. For Gina Terrasi, failure was definitely not an option, which is why she was devastated when she learned about Katie's disability.

"I'm not strong enough for this. I never should have become a mother. I wish I didn't have kids."

Watching Katie struggle at all the things Gina was good at— playing sports, getting good grades, making friends—was enough to leave Gina, a classic overachiever and a chronic worrier, awake night after night pondering the same burning question:

How will my little girl get her self-esteem?

But what Gina failed to notice was that despite all her difficulties, Katie was happier and more self-confident than Gina ever was. Katie has taught Gina to appreciate the little things in life—things that most people take for granted.

"Daddy, guess what? I answered a question right today at school!"

"You'll never believe this, Mom. I got invited to a birthday party!"

"I told a joke today and all the kids laughed."

These days, Gina appreciates Katie's teen milestones, though some keep her up at night.

"Mom, I got invited to a pool party. Can I wear this little bikini?"

"Mom, I'm not gonna lie to you. A boy at school asked me out today, and I said yes."

But perhaps what Gina admires most about her daughter is Katie's resilience. Despite all the difficulties she's had to endure in her young life (and she's had more than her share), Katie has always managed to bounce back. She demonstrated this resilience when she was young.

"Mom, the kids on the bus all made fun of me today because I flap my hands."

"Well, it's settled, then. I'm driving you to school."

"No way, Mom. I love to ride the bus. If I don't ride the bus, then that's letting them win."

And she continues to be resilient as a teenager.

"Katie, I'm sorry you and your boyfriend broke up," Gina said, crossing her fingers behind her back.

"It's okay, Mom. I was really sad, but now I'm just gonna focus my time on my friends."

Over the years, Katie has never given up on herself or lowered her expectations. Her view of herself and of her future has always been positive, even when her parents had their doubts.

"Mom and Dad, I'll be driving soon. I'm almost sixteen."

"Yeah, about that. Maybe you should wait until you're older—like forty-five."

"Yeah, Katie. That Barbie car you had hasn't been the same since you drove it into that tree."

"Mom and Dad, I can do it. You gotta trust me."

Gina would have loved to have seen all these positive qualities in Katie from the beginning, but instead, she was blinded by her daughter's "failures." She would have done anything to make Katie's Asperger's go away. ("Mike, I wish I could take her to be cured. What's that healing place in France?")

But during this amazing journey, Gina changed the way she saw her daughter. Somewhere along the line, she learned to stop seeing Katie through society's ridiculous looking glass of perfection and to see Katie through Katie's eyes. And what she saw has truly changed Gina's life.

To cure Katie of her Asperger's would take away all the things Gina loves most about her daughter—her innocence, her wonderful sense of humor, her fighting spirit, even her quirkiness. Anyone who knows Gina, a lifetime subscriber to *Popular Pessimist* magazine, can't believe she sees her daughter this way. She no longer thinks about what Katie *won't* become, but dreams about what she *will* become. She doesn't dwell on what Katie *can't* do, but celebrates all the amazing things Katie *can* do.

How Jennifer Has Changed Patty

It's never easy for a parent to hear there's something wrong with their child. So it's not surprising that when Jennifer was diagnosed with a serious mental illness, Patty realized her life would never again be "normal."

And in many ways, it never will be.

But over the years, Patty's discovered that Jennifer and her struggles with bipolar disorder have changed Patty in ways she'd never imagined. She didn't realize the magnitude of this until one night when Jenn came to her with a question. "Mom, why would you want to write a book about me? I feel like all I ever did was disrupt this family."

Patty could understand her question. Jennifer's illness definitely *had* disrupted the family. There were days when Patty didn't think her family would make it through Jenn's bouts of sadness and hostility. Days when Jenn threatened to run away and Patty secretly hoped she would. ("Quick, Michael! Lock the doors before she comes back!")

Patty also recognized that Jennifer's difficulties were compounded by another factor: Jennifer was the middle child, sandwiched between her high-achieving older sister, Jules, and her adorable little brother, Mikey.

Sometimes Jennifer felt like she had no place in the family. But the truth was, Patty was proud of all her kids for different reasons. With Jennifer it was for her courage, strength, and compassion, which she displayed when she was released from one of her hospital stays on a day when she had a youth basketball game. Patty was shocked when Jennifer came to her and asked, "Mom, can I play in my game today? Please?"

Patty was frightened at the thought. But how could she deny this child, who had already experienced more pain than any child should have to experience?

"Okay, Jenn, if you're up to it," Patty responded, thinking how tired and drawn Jennifer looked. She couldn't imagine Jennifer staying awake, let alone playing in a physical game like basketball.

When Gina and our parents heard Jenn was playing in the game, they drove up to show support. We all huddled together in the stands, each of us nervous about Jennifer's first public experience. Would she pass out? Would she break down and cry? Did other people know what she had gone through? What if someone said something to upset her?

We sat in silence, not knowing what to expect, until five minutes into the game, when Jennifer came onto the court. She ran her heart out, chasing after loose balls and tightly guarding her opponents. Looking at her, you would never have known what this child had been through over the past few weeks.

A minute later, we watched in amazement as she stole the ball from her opponent, dribbled down the court, and put in a perfect layup. Our entire family—Patty, Michael, Gina, Mike, our parents, and all the kids—jumped up, hugging each other and drawing strange looks from the people around us, who were probably thinking, *Look at that family of goons! What do they think this is, the WNBA?*

None of us cared, especially Patty. Jennifer had the game of her career, and Patty, who had looked so exhausted over the past few weeks, was exhilarated. She couldn't have been any prouder. She also could not have loved and admired her daughter any more.

But how could she convey her feelings to Jennifer, who felt so terrible for what she had put the family through? "Mom, I'm so sorry. I don't know why I act this way. I hate myself for hurting you."

That evening, when Jennifer asked her mother about why Patty would write a book about her, Patty finally found the words to tell her daughter what she meant to her.

"Jennifer, I want to write a book about you because you have made me a better person."

"Why do you say that?" asked Jenn.

"Because of all the gifts you've given me, Jenn."

"Like what?" Jenn asked, wiping her eyes.

"Well, thanks to you I'm not as materialistic as I once was.

"I've learned to take each day one day at a time.

"I no longer sweat the small stuff.

"I'm not so quick to judge or talk about people.

"I've learned to appreciate the wonderful family we have.

"I've met some amazing people whom I never would have met otherwise.

"Jennifer, you have not only made me better, you've made the world better just by being in it."

Jennifer hugged her mother and said, "Thank you, Mom. I love you."

Changing Together

Though we may not always realize it (especially when they make fun of us), it's not uncommon for children to mirror the behavior of their parents. Jennifer and Katie certainly do, despite what their "teenittudes" may lead us to believe. "When I'm a mother, I'm not gonna be anything like you."

Yes, over the years, they've copied many of our behaviors, including some of our bad ones.

"Katie, it's late. Are you still on Facebook?"

"Are you, Mom?"

But what we didn't expect them to mirror was our change in perspective on their disabilities. Yet when we began evolving, they evolved right with us.

How Katie Has Changed

Throughout her life, Katie has only known what it's like to be different. Though at times she can come off as aloof and socially awkward, she has always wanted nothing more than to be like "everybody else"—to fit in and to find her place. ("But Mom, why can't I ride my bike around the block without you? All the other kids can.") Part of fitting in meant not being singled out, which is why she's always preferred to fly under the radar.

Today, at age fifteen, Katie no longer feels the same way. She doesn't ignore her differences; she talks about them, which is pretty amazing for a teenager who wants to be like everybody else.

"Katie, the parents' association wants us to speak at your school. I don't want to do it if you're not comfortable."

"Hey, I don't care. Do it. Kids will think I'm famous."

When she was younger, Katie hated her differences, often crying herself to sleep. ("I hate this stupid Asperger's. I hate it!") Like her mother, she would have done anything to make it all just go away.

But when Gina started to accept Katie's disability, Katie followed her lead, recognizing that her Asperger's has made her the strong, resilient person she is today. This doesn't mean she doesn't have days when she wishes some of her quirks were less noticeable or that she was more social. "Mom, I wish I could call my friends on the phone. It's just hard for me. I get nervous and don't know what to say. It's part of my Asperger's."

She's more aware of her limitations than anyone else, yet she's so proud of herself for the young woman she's become. "You know, Mom, I wouldn't want to be anyone else."

And unlike a lot of teens, she's no longer preoccupied with what people and other kids think. In fact, she's constantly scolding Gina and her husband, Mike, for caring too much.

"Mom and Dad, why do you care if that lady doesn't like you? You guys care too much about what people think. Lots of people don't like me. I could care less."

She also tries to console her little sister, Emily, who got her parents' oversensitivity gene.

"Emmy, you have to stop taking everything so seriously. Laugh at yourself. I do it all the time. Well . . . wait . . . that's because I'm really funny."

Katie has also learned something her mother didn't growing up:

that life isn't about having hundreds of friends. It's about having a few good ones who will stand by you. Katie's true friends—including our neighbor Jake and his little brother, Luke, who are the same ages as Katie and Emily, respectively—don't just accept her differences, they embrace them.

Over the years, we've watched these boys blossom into handsome, athletic, and popular young men. Gina and Mike liked them instantly, especially since they welcomed Katie into their circle of neighborhood friends. ("Yeah, she can play with us. Come on.")

As they grew older, Gina sadly expected Katie and Jake to drift apart, particularly since Jake has lots of friends and is involved in many sports.

"You know, Gene, one day Luke and Jake probably won't wanna hang out with Katie," said Mike. "They really have nothing in common."

"I know. I'll be so sad when that happens."

But Jake and Luke have surprised us with their loyalty to Katie. To this day, they both come over to our house to hang out with Katie—to talk to her about what's going on at school and see what's happening in her life.

When Jake and Luke discovered that Katie was playing basketball (one of their favorite sports) at her new school, they were ecstatic. "Katie, you gotta get out here and practice! Your dribbling is awful."

"Yeah, you don't even dribble," added Luke, showing his devilish smile.

Because she's so comfortable with both boys, Katie is completely herself, as she often demonstrates when the boys come over to visit her.

"Katie! Jake and Luke are here."

"Hi, guys. I don't feel like hanging out. I'm playing The Sims."

Sometimes, this makes Gina cringe.

"Let me get this straight. A popular, handsome boy your age just came to hang out with you and you said no?"

"Uh, sorry, Mom. I just don't feel like hanging out."

But this never stops them from coming back to see her. And when they do hang out, Katie and Jake like to tease each other.

"Hey Katie, where'd you get that big zit on your face?"

"Shut up, Jake! Yours is bigger than mine."

To Jake and Luke, Katie's not a kid with a label of Asperger's; she's Katie. They're not afraid of her differences, but fascinated by them.

"Katie, try another French fry. That's so weird how you choke on them."

"All right, one more, then I'm done gagging for the night."

Whenever Katie performs in school plays, Luke and Jake can always be found in the audience, sitting with our family, whistling and chanting, "Katie! Katie! Katie" during curtain calls.

When Katie talks about her difficulties being herself with some of her friends, Gina often asks her, "Well, how come you do so well with Luke and Jake?"

"Mom, Luke and Jake accept me for who I am."

How Jennifer Has Changed

Like her younger cousin Katie, Jennifer has always preferred to be under the radar, particularly when it came to sharing news of her disability. But one day, when Patty approached her about speaking at a fund-raiser for a local organization, Families for Depression Awareness (ffda.org), Jennifer surprised her with her answer.

"Sure, Mom, I'll do it."

"You will?" asked a stunned Patty.

Patty was thrilled. But on the evening of the event, Jennifer was overcome with anxiety.

"I'm not going! And you can't make me!" cried a defiant Jennifer.

"Oh, you're goin'. You told them you'd do this. You made a commitment!" asserted Patty.

"Mom, *I'll* do it," said Patty's son, Mikey, running into the house to write a speech.

Ten minutes later, Patty and Mikey were backing out of the driveway when a sandal came flying out of the house, crashing into Patty's windshield.

It was no ordinary sandal. It was from the pair Jennifer had picked out to wear for the event—and a subtle signal to Patty that said, "Yes, Mother. I will be going with you, after all."

On the drive to the fund-raiser, a disheveled Jennifer crawled into the cargo area of Patty's car, while Mikey put the finishing touches on his speech. During the entire thirty-five-minute drive, Jennifer was quiet, until Mikey called from the backseat, "Mom, how do you spell obnoxious?"

Jennifer hissed at Mikey, reminding Patty that she was, indeed, still with them. A stressed Patty spent the drive pondering ways to explain this to Rebecca, the lovely woman who had organized the event. All Rebecca had to do was take a look at Jenn to know something wasn't right. Jenn's hair, which had been perfectly brushed earlier, was a mess, and her makeup had run down her cheeks. If Patty hadn't known better, she would have thought she had brought Alice Cooper to the event.

When they arrived, Patty found Rebecca and explained the situation. Rebecca immediately grabbed Jenn and said, "Jenn, let me show you some of the cool stuff we have here." From her experience working with depressed children, Rebecca knew that distracting Jennifer and getting her away from Patty and Mikey would be the best solution.

After Rebecca and Jennifer left, Mikey handed his mother his "carefully crafted" speech. Patty couldn't help but wonder, "How come you did that so fast but your homework takes three hours?"

When she read the words he'd written, Patty was deeply touched and pleasantly surprised. ("Wow! I've never seen his writing this neat.")

Hello. My name is Mikey Konjoian. I am almost eleven years old and I am a fifth-grader at High Plain Elementary. When I found out my sister Jenn was diagnosed with bipolar disorder, I was terrified. She had mood swings every day. One day she would be happy, the next she would be all angry. Then when she got hospitalized I would pray at night and make cards for her. Jenn has made me a better person, along with my family. My other sister and I tend to gang up on her sometimes when she gets obnoxious, but we don't really mean it. I felt really bad for her and I tried to help her as much as I could. I understand that she really doesn't mean to say hurtful things. That is just the way bipolar disorder works, and I am really happy to have her as my sister.

Patty was about to show the speech to Rebecca when Jennifer, looking fresh as a daisy, appeared in front of Patty and casually announced, "I want to do it."

"You want to do what?" Patty asked, fully expecting her to say she wanted to run away or find a new mother.

"I want to speak. Duh!" she responded in her normal teenage tone.

"But I thought I was gonna speak!" cried Mikey.

Patty, who at this point was thinking about running away, went to Rebecca with her dilemma.

"They can both do it," Rebecca pleasantly responded.

So that evening our family watched as Jennifer, with her little brother at her side, stood up and spoke about her battle with bipolar disorder. She talked about her good days and her bad days and how she was managing to live with her illness. When she was finished, Mikey gave her a thumbs-up and read his speech.

Together, they exited the stage to healthy applause. Patty and our entire family were in tears.

It's not surprising that Jennifer had the courage to make the speech. Throughout her battle with bipolar disorder, she has shown a fighting spirit. Patty and Michael didn't realize how strong it was until they went to pick her up at the hospital after her first stay.

As they nervously walked the corridor to Jennifer's room, a teenage girl jumped out in front, blocking their path.

"Wait! I have to tell you something! Your daughter saved my life."

Patty and Michael stared blankly at each other as she explained. "Well, this really scary kid, Zachary, was mad at me and was just about to punch me in the face when Jenn stepped right in front of his fist."

"That's great. Thanks for telling us," Michael said, nudging Patty along toward Jennifer's room. Obviously, this girl was delusional. But when they stepped into Jennifer's room and saw their little "Rocky" sporting her first shiner, they were in shock. Here Jennifer had been through so much, yet she still took the time to help someone else. While that shiner would have been horrifying for a perfect parent to see, to Patty it showed just how strong her daughter was. *If anyone can persevere through the struggles of bipolar disorder, it's Jennifer,* Patty thought.

How the Rest of Our Imperfect Clan Has Changed

It's pretty obvious that when you have a child with a disability, the whole household is affected. We've documented the struggles our families have had with our daughters' disabilities. But what we haven't talked about is the positive impact their disabilities have had on our other children.

In Patty's house, it's had a profound positive impact on her two other children, especially her older daughter, Jules, who believes Jennifer's struggles have made her realize what's important in life.

"Mom, it's like this thing with Jennifer is so bad that sometimes I don't want to come home. But you know what, Mom? I see kids at school worrying about such stupid stuff. We're the lucky ones because we know what's really important."

Jules summed up her feelings for Jenn one day when she came home and announced, "Mom, here's my college essay. I wrote it about Jenn." As Patty read the words on the page, her heart soared. Over the years, she had felt so guilty about what her children had to go through with Jennifer's illness, but when she learned it had helped shape Jules into a more compassionate person, Patty was elated.

Jennifer's disability has also helped Patty's son, Mikey, view the world differently, as he showed to Patty one evening at Mother/Son Night at the batting cages. They were waiting in line for their turn when another boy cut in front of them.

"Mikey, did you see that? That kid just cut in line! I'm gonna say something to him!"

"Mom, chill! That kid has special needs. You should know from your book."

"Uh, yeah, right."

The Ride of a Lifetime

College Essay by Julianne Konjoian

Upon returning home from church one pleasant Sunday morning, my mother, brother, and I are greeted at the front door with a dozen colorful Post-it notes reading, "I hate you!" While some may find this unsettling, unexpected, or unusual, it comes as no surprise to any of us. As we enter the house quite stealthily, it becomes apparent that my younger sister, Jenn, has done some serious work while we were at church. It didn't take very long for her message to "stick" with us, as everything from the kitchen cabinets to the toilet seats is covered in "I hate you" Post-it notes.

A week later, I open the front door to welcome my cousins and aunt into the house, briefly recalling the last time I saw them. This time is different, however. As I open the door hastily, I see the apprehension in my aunt's face instantly. I see my two young cousins glance at me quickly, but they immediately look away. I sense their confusion and fear but do not have the strength to say a word. Seconds later, our awkward greeting is interrupted by piercing screams. I step back, shielding my younger brother, and watch as my mother and father frantically carry my sister down the stairs. She is thrashing violently, grabbing at the railing, and lashing out at my parents. "I hate you both!" she shrieks. "You're ruining my life, and it's not fair that I have to go away!" My knees feel weak, and my palms are sweating profusely. I want to help or run away: anything to stop the screams. Instead, I silently watch. I watch my parents drag my sister out to the driveway, where there is an ambulance waiting to take her away. I want to run to my parents and tell them they're making a mistake, or grab my sister and tell her everything will be okay. But deep down I know they aren't making a mistake, and I know everything isn't okay, so I continue to watch. Now my aunt directs my brother and cousins into her car and drives away. Once alone, I remember my friends will be over shortly. Tonight is the Kiss concert, the concert I have been looking forward to for months. Suddenly, however, I don't feel much like loud music, garish makeup, or even being around anyone.

Two years later, I sit in my car, which is parked in the same spot the ambulance was that day. I bang on the horn and impatiently yell, "Hurry up, Jenn! We're going to be late for school!" Seconds later, she runs out of the house and throws herself into the car. "Geez, Jules. I couldn't find my lip gloss. You're such a pain," she says curtly. As a rude comment begins to form on my tongue, I stop myself. I look at my sister and think, "Jenn is such an obnoxious, annoying little sister. Boy, am I lucky." Sometimes, living with Jenn seems unbearable. But when I remember that day—the day I almost lost her forever—I realize how lucky I am to have her.

Growing up with a bipolar sister has been everything but easy. After nearly eight years of ongoing chaos, there is not much I haven't seen or felt. Jenn's unreasonable meltdowns, her bouts of sadness and anxiety, and her unruly mood swings make our lives resemble a roller coaster. Nonetheless, her illness has also made us stronger. Watching Jenn as she scuttles out the door to the car, yelling at me for being impatient, I am able to reflect on the aspects of my life that she has changed for the better. I think back to one of the happiest days of my life: the day I got my driver's license. The wind gracefully twirls through my hair; I've never felt so alive. I take my eyes off the road for a moment and turn to the passenger's seat. My first official copilot is my sister, during a trip to the mall. No, it's not the inexorable freedom that makes this day exceptional. It's having my little sister beside me.

Another Child, Another Challenge

In Gina's house, things have been a little different. During the process of writing this book, Gina's baby, Emily, was diagnosed with learning disabilities and anxiety. Gina was crushed, as she thought Emily was her link to the elusive world of typically developing children. "Mike, why do both our kids have to suffer? It's not fair."

Though Gina had learned to see the positive side of raising a child with a disability through Katie, she had to go through the mourning process all over again with Emily.

She was, as she was when Katie was diagnosed, devastated.

All she could do was cry, which probably wasn't doing Emily much good.

Surprisingly, the person who showed the most strength and support for Emily was Katie. Katie's strength helped us all.

"Emmy, you're imperfect like me. I understand. Everything is gonna be okay.

"And Mom and Dad, you saved me. Now you've got to save Emmy. She needs you more than I do right now."

Gina and Mike couldn't believe what they had heard, especially since their daughters had both carried on the tradition we set in our childhood—they couldn't stand each other. In many ways, Katie and Emily are complete opposites.

"Mom, she's driving me crazy! Tell her to leave me alone! I'm on Katie Time."

"Mom, Katie's so mean! She never plays with me."

Yet when Emily had her worst days struggling in school or having difficulties with friends, the person she asked for was Katie. "Mommy, I think I'm stupid. I don't like myself," she sobbed.

"Don't ever say that! You're not stupid. You're smart and beautiful."

"Mommy, I need Katie."

Gina was more shocked when Katie, who rations her hugs, took Emmy in her arms and said, "Emmy, don't say that. You're not stupid. People used to say that about me. Don't believe them. Look at how good I'm doing."

With Our Issues Comes a Stronger Bond

Our daughters' disabilities have strengthened not only the bond between us, but also those among all our kids. Jennifer, in particular, is
always reaching out to Katie to see how she's doing. She's become the
big sister Katie will never have.

And given that they share the common bond of anxiety, Jennifer
and Emily are especially close. Jennifer, who was blessed with the gift
of empathy, is always there for Emmy.

"Emmy, don't worry. I feel worried sometimes, too. It's gonna be
okay."

Whenever our families gather, Jennifer and Emily are always
together. Jennifer, who is quite slight in stature, is often seen giving
Emily a piggyback ride. ("Go faster, Jenn! Giddyup!")

Jennifer's love and compassion for both of Gina's kids has given
her a special place in Gina's heart. It's why when Jennifer was hospitalized, Gina needed to be there for Jenn. "Pat, you and Michael take a
night off. I want to go see Jenn tonight."

"Okay, Gene, but she's really not herself."

Gina didn't care. She just wanted to hold her niece—to tell her how
much she meant to her. "Jenn, stay strong. We all love you so much!
You can get through this," Gina said while rocking an exhausted,
medicated Jennifer in her arms and fighting back her own tears.

Today, when Gina sees Jennifer running track or when Jenn excitedly asks Gina for pointers on field hockey while they hit shots in
Jennifer's backyard, Gina is reminded of how far Jennifer has come.

There's no one Gina admires more.

Jennifer shares Gina's admiration, as she demonstrated when she
came home from school one day and summoned Patty.

"Mom, can you help me with this?" she said, handing Patty a piece
of paper.

"Okay, Jenn, but if it's math homework, you know my cutoff is
third grade. Once they start combining the alphabet with numbers,
I'm lost."

"Don't worry, Mom. It's not algebra," Jenn responded, giving Patty
the sweet smile Patty had learned to cherish.

When Patty scanned the title, "The Person Whom I Most Admire," she secretly hoped the essay was about her—the person who constantly advocates for Jennifer.

Instead, it was about Gina. Patty wasn't surprised Jenn chose Gina; they have always had a close relationship. It was why she chose Gina that caught her off guard.

> My aunt is tall and humorous and always has a positive attitude toward life. She and my mom are in the process of writing a book. It is about kids with different kinds of disabilities and uses humor to let people feel that they are not alone in this world. I thought it was very thoughtful of my aunt and my mom to take the time to create a fabulous book that makes kids with learning differences and illnesses feel more comfortable. Reading the book that my mom and my aunt had put such tremendous effort in made me want to contribute to it.

The Imperfection Connection

Our journey with this book has brought us closer not only to our families, but to complete strangers as well. Wherever we travel, across town or across the country, we meet people who face incredible challenges. People from all different socioeconomic brackets, races, and education levels. Caring, compassionate people whom we never would have met if our daughters didn't have disabilities.

Yes, even in our perfection-crazed world, we have managed to find warm, wonderful people who have the courage to be real and to face challenges. Mothers, fathers, and grandparents with the strength to discuss their greatest fears, joys, challenges, and failures to offer hope and comfort to others, even complete strangers.

In our imperfect circles, we like to call this bond the "Imperfection Connection."

While we were attending the NAMI Pennsylvania state conference, the father of a child with Asperger's broke down and sobbed to Gina about his daughter's struggles. Instinctively, Gina put her arms around him, silently letting him know he wasn't alone.

Hugging a complete stranger, especially a man, was not something

Gina did very often. But at that moment, it just seemed the right thing to do. Though she had just met him and never even learned his name, Gina felt a connection to this man, who had trusted her with his pain. In those brief moments, he had let Gina into his heart—and she had let him into hers, something Gina had not even done with many friends and family members she's known her entire life.

It's ironic that we are invited to speak to people like this about our learning experiences when it's their experiences that have taught us. They have shown us the blessings of our family and given us valuable insights, which we simply were unable to discover on our own. Our friend Jane often reminds Gina of this.

"Gina, of course you couldn't see how your own stress is negatively affecting your kids. You're too close to things. You're in a snit."

Sometimes, for example, we get so caught up in our own struggles and pain that we forget to ask our husbands how *they* feel.

A wonderful man we met at a parent meeting came up to us and enlightened us about this topic. He said, "Thank you for your presentation. It really helped me know I wasn't alone. My wife goes to her support group with other mothers and gets her feelings out. Guys don't do that kind of thing. We don't sit around the water bubbler and discuss our feelings or what's wrong with our kids." With tears flowing down his cheeks, he told Gina how he felt when his five-year-old daughter with autism was being bullied. "I wish she was a boy. That way I could teach her to hit back. I'm her daddy, and there's nothing I can do to protect my little girl."

After hearing that, Gina started thinking about her husband, Mike. Did she ever ask him how he felt about the kids' struggles? How he was handling things? Or even thank him for standing by her and the kids?

She was saddened to realize she never had.

When she got home, Gina immediately hugged Mike and said, "Mike, I'm so sorry."

"What did you do now? Did you back into the garage door again?"

"No, it's just that tonight I met this wonderful man who helped me realize that I forget to ask you how you feel about the kids' disabilities."

"Well, Gene, don't worry about me. I know how hard it is for you. You're the mother. You get the worst of it."

"Yes, but how do *you* feel?"

"Do you want the truth? It breaks my heart to see my little girls struggle. When kids tease them, I want to hit someone. Sometimes I think it's just not fair," Mike confessed, his eyes filling up with tears.

The fact is, Mike never imagined this life for his kids, either. A loving and religious man, Mike planned for a life that was much easier.

"Gene, I'm a pretty simple guy. I just like life to be like this," he said, drawing a straight line.

Gina had to laugh. "Well, Mike, that's not gonna happen with two special needs kids. Your life is more like this," she responded, drawing a line with more ups and downs than the Dow Jones in 2008.

But like Gina, Mike acknowledges the gifts both his children have brought to his family. "You know, Gene, I was thinking. I wouldn't trade Katie or Emily for the world. Issues and all."

"Since you feel this way, maybe we should have another child, Mike."

"Are you kidding? Our gene pool is more polluted than Love Canal!"

CHAPTER 16

Loving the Reality

Celebrating the Gifts
of Special Children

Though we recognize the gifts our children have brought us, we'll never fully get over the loss of our dreams for them—those shattered plans and expectations we had even before they were born. It's that fantasy trip to Italy that Emily Perl Kingsley so eloquently captured in her essay "Welcome to Holland" (page 8).

Yes, there have been and will continue to be days when the loss of our dreams is very real.

Gina experienced this a few months ago when she went to see our brother's daughter, Jessica, in her dress before her prom. It was a bittersweet moment for Gina, who was so proud of the beautiful, mature young woman Jessica had become.

Yet when Gina saw the look of pride and excitement in Jessica's mother's eyes at seeing her daughter, she felt a deep sadness. Just a year before, she had seen that same look on Patty's face when her daughter, Jules, attended the prom. *I'll never get to see my daughter attend a real prom like this*, Gina thought.

Later that evening, our mother, who had also gone to see Jessica, phoned Gina.

"Gina," she asked, "are you okay?"

"Yeah, Mom, I'm fine. Jess looked so beautiful. I loved her dress," Gina responded, not wanting our mother to pick up on her sadness.

"Yes, she sure did. But I didn't call you to talk about that. I want to talk about you. You looked sad."

Almost instantly, Gina's eyes filled with tears. "Well, Mom, it was kind of hard, to tell the truth. I don't want to take anything away from Jess. I'm so proud of her. It's just a little sad when I think my daughter will never experience this. That I won't experience this with her. It's not fair, Mom."

"I know, Gene. I thought you might be thinking that. But look at how well Katie's doing. We're all so proud of her. Look at how much you and Katie are helping people. She's a gift, Gina. I know you might not experience things like this, but you've experienced other things. Remember when she got up in front of all those people for that play? We were all so proud of her."

That was all Gina needed to hear. "You're right, Mom. Thank you for reminding me. It's just so hard sometimes."

"Don't you think I know that? But Gina, would you trade Katie for any other child?"

"No, Mom. I wouldn't trade either Katie or Emmy for the world. It's just so hard to watch them both struggle."

"Just remember, your girls are special, and they were given to you for a reason."

"Thank you, Mom. You're always there for me."

"Hey, Gene, that's a mother's job. We never stop worrying about our kids—even when they don't have disabilities."

"I love you, Mom."

"I love you, too. Now do me a favor and stop crying. You'll wake up with bags under your eyes."

So though we may never get to Italy with Jennifer, Katie, or even Emily via the perfect kid way, we'll get there someday by plane. And in the meantime, we'll take our time to enjoy all the beautiful sights in Holland.

"Gene, do these Dutch shoes make my feet look too big?"

"No, but you're crushing the tulips with them, you buffoon."

A Happy Ending?

One evening at a local speaking event, a woman approached us after our presentation and remarked, "Your story was nice. But the ending was too happy. What about all the parents who aren't as happy? Did you think about them?"

We looked this woman straight in the eye and replied, "We think about them every day."

We know that while our children have had struggles, there are children who have struggled far more than ours. There are parents who have to live with much harsher realities than we do; many will never see their children talk, walk, or even grow up. Our challenges pale in comparison to theirs.

And while we have learned to accept—and even cherish—our children's disabilities, many parents can only pray for a cure. And who could blame them?

One of Gina's friends reminded her of this when she told Gina about her nonverbal autistic son. "When he screams, I don't know if he's in pain. How does that make me feel as a mother? I don't even know my own child."

It's hard to see the positive side of life when you must constantly watch your children suffer. But we also know that like us, these parents have learned to stop and appreciate the little things in life—like the joy in watching an autistic child utter a word or draw a beautiful picture. Or seeing a child with bipolar disorder smile from ear to ear. Our hearts soared one day when our friend Meghan captured her young autistic son, Kevin, singing *Hey There Delilah* on video. Kevin, who uses words sparingly, knew all the words and sang the song beautifully.

And though these may not be the milestones we experience with our kids, we can relate to the joy that comes from witnessing them. An inner joy that's like no other—that money could never buy.

Gina will never forget a joy she and other parents witnessed one day while watching a high school team play basketball. She was there to see Katie's friend Jake play and was sitting in the stands with Jake's parents, Juli and Bob, and their friends. The game was close, and the parents were all tense, especially when Jake's team started losing. With the game in hand, the other team's coach sent a child with Down syndrome into the game. The entire gym was mesmerized.

With just a few minutes left in the game, the Down syndrome child got the ball. His defender, a solid and aggressive player, took a small step backward. It wasn't an obvious step—just enough to show his heart, and his desire to see this kid shoot. Recognizing this opportunity, the boy with Down syndrome raised the ball over his head and released a perfect shot that swished through the center of the net.

The entire gym, including everyone on Jake's team (the opponents), stood up and cheered. Then we watched as the boy ran off the court onto the sidelines and into the arms of another Down's child on the junior varsity team who was waiting for him.

As Gina looked around the gym, through her tearstained eyes she saw people grinning from ear-to-ear and high-fiving each other. In that brief and beautiful moment, those two boys gave the entire crowd a tremendous gift. They reminded us that life is not about winning; it's about having a winning heart.

After the game, Gina went down to talk to Jake, who had a big grin on his face, despite his team's bad loss to their rivals.

"Gene," he said. "Did you see that kid's shot? And when he went to hug his friend? Wasn't it awesome?"

"It sure was, Jake. That was a *SportsCenter* moment."

Gina was pretty sure that every person in the gym left that game with a lighter heart. She certainly did.

Imperfect Life Goes On

Though we are currently in good places with Jennifer and Katie, we have no idea if our stories will have happy endings. What we have learned is to take one day at a time, and to do everything we can to help our children through whatever challenges may lie ahead.

We have listened to too many stories with sad endings to ever be certain that ours will end happily. Our lives may remain as they always have—full of unpredictable highs and lows. Gina, for example, has had to come to grips with the fact she's facing a life of uncertainty with not just Katie, but also with Emily, her baby.

And many of the future-related questions she used to ask about Katie are still present in her mind. *Will she marry? Drive a car? Live away at college? Ever leave home?*

Gina used to stay up at night and worry about this until she had coffee with her neighbor Tom one day. Tom, who is an author and the father of an adult son with autism, said, "My son will be with us until the day I die. Aren't I lucky? Most parents have to let go of their children and watch them move away. I get to keep my Michael."

Tom helped Gina see a different perspective. "You're right, Tom. Katie's such a joy. I love having her around." Gina has learned from so many people like Tom. Just recently, after one of our speaking engagements, a quiet, soft-spoken woman approached Gina. She said, "I have to tell you three things. First, if I were a kid today, I would have been diagnosed with Asperger's. Second, my childhood was miserable. I hated it and would never want to go back. Last, I love my life as an adult. It's so much better than my childhood. I'm very happy." Gina was thrilled to hear this and was amazed when the woman said, "And by the way, I have a nonverbal autistic son and two foster children with issues."

Parental Anxiety

Patty's accepted that her worries with Jennifer will always be present. Over the past few years, Jennifer has been managing her disability well for the most part. Patty attributed this to her medication. But one day, Patty was devastated when Jennifer made a startling confession.

"Jenn, isn't it time to refill your medication?"

"Uh, Mom, I haven't taken my medication in weeks."

This wasn't just any medication; it was lithium. Jenn's psychiatrist had repeatedly informed Patty about the dangers of abruptly stopping the drug.

"It could lead to suicide," he warned.

Patty was shocked—and furious.

"Jennifer, why didn't you tell me? You can't make this decision on your own."

"Well, Mom, I knew you wouldn't agree with me. You think I'm bipolar and I'm not. I'm fine. I don't need medication."

Patty felt like she'd been kicked in the stomach. She had always listened to Jennifer's concerns, and relayed them to the doctor. When Jennifer asked to be taken off anti-anxiety medication, Patty conveyed

Jenn's feelings to the doctor and they weaned her off. But now her daughter was making this life-alternating decision—without consulting her.

Patty immediately called the doctor and told him about the situation. The doctor was concerned, particularly since Jennifer hadn't been to therapy. While he understood and respected Jennifer's decision, he cautioned her.

"Jennifer, if you choose to do this, you must see your therapist regularly and promise to go back on the meds if you feel sad."

"Okay, I will. Thank you," responded Jennifer, who was ecstatic that the doctor was treating her like an adult.

Patty knew the day would come when Jennifer would have to make her own choices about her treatment. She just didn't expect it to come so soon—at sixteen.

For Patty, it was a painful reminder that we can never predict what new direction our children's disabilities will take us in. We'll have new and different worries and challenges, as well as joys and milestones on their imperfect journeys through life.

"Pat, the day Katie graduates from high school, I'm gonna have a parade in the city."

"Okay, but I insist on paying for the fireworks. She is, after all, my godchild."

We'll worry about who our children will marry, or if they even will marry. And if they have children, we'll have a completely different set of worries and "What ifs?" to keep us busy. *What if their children have disabilities? Will we have to experience this all over again? Will they be strong enough to care for them?*

Only time will tell.

But isn't that what parenting is about for *every* parent? Managing the unexpected. We know that better than anyone, and have learned from our own mother that every child comes with their own set of worries. Motherhood, after all, is a life sentence.

"Hi, Mom. Can I talk to you about something?"

"What's wrong now? You girls are always calling with bad news."

There's no question, parenting a child with a disability is not as Gina's husband would like it to be—a smooth ride. It's a roller-coaster ride, filled with sudden drops and unexpected twists and turns. But it's those exhilarating highs that make us feel alive and inspire us to stay on the ride, and to hold on to our children for dear life.

The Movement of Imperfection Has Just Begun

So all of this has brought us to this point in our lives. There's no question, we are not the same imperfect people who began this journey. Oh, we still have our share of imperfections; our husbands can attest to that. And we're still not that bright. ("Gina and Patty, when I told you my father was in the European theater in World War II, I didn't mean he was an actor.")

It's our values that have changed.

Our heroes are no longer star athletes, talented performers, or beautiful movie stars. Our dreams are no longer about big houses, exotic vacations, and giant bank accounts. No, on this journey, we've been given something bigger and better than all of that: We've been given the gift of awareness—of ourselves, our children, and others with differences. It's a consciousness of a greater joy and purpose we never would have experienced if Jennifer and Katie hadn't brought us into the light.

When you think about this whole experience, it's pretty amazing. What started out as something small—two imperfect mothers looking to cope with their kids' struggles—has now grown into a powerful Movement of Imperfection that's no longer just about the two of us.

Yes, somewhere on this remarkable journey, we decided we no longer wanted to change our daughters—we wanted to change the world. And we've started to travel around the country to share Katie's and Jenn's stories so that others may see what is now crystal clear to us—and that's the incredible beauty, spirit, and individuality of all children, even imperfect ones.

But as our favorite imperfect singer of the 1970s, the late Karen Carpenter sang, "We've only just begun."

GLOSSARY

(Condensed from
kargacademy.com)

AD/HD: Attention deficit hyperactivity disorder is a neurodevelopmental disorder involving the areas of the brain involved in regulating behavior, including the prefrontal cortex. AD/HD is characterized by consistent impulsivity, hyperactivity, and/or inattention sufficient to disrupt everyday life that does not fluctuate with emotional states. Divided into four category subtypes, AD/HD can be **predominantly hyperactive/impulsive** (fidgeting, restlessness, climbing, running, interrupting, or intruding, and difficulty with patience, waiting, sharing, or taking turns); **predominantly inattentive** (difficulty sustaining attention, listening, following directions or routines, and organizing tasks; misplacing items; and distractibility); **combined hyperactive/ impulsive and inattentive** (meeting both inattentive and hyperactive/ impulsive criteria); and **not otherwise specified/NOS** (insufficient number of symptoms to reach a full diagnosis). To be accurately diagnosed with the disorder, at least six out of the nine symptoms included in each subtype category must be demonstrated for at least six months to a *degree that is significantly greater than that of typically developing children of the same age.* Causal factors include genetic, neurological, and environmental components. Genetically, one diagnosed parent can increase the risk of inheritance in their children by as much as 50 percent, siblings of diagnosed children are five times more likely to develop the disorder, and as many as 80 percent of identical twins share the diagnosis of AD/HD. Environmentally, prenatal exposure to toxic substances (tobacco, alcohol, lead) and/or specific damage to the executive functioning areas of the brain can increase the risk of AD/HD. Neurologically, overproduction of the neurotransmitter dopamine in the prefrontal regions of the brain results in the inability to control or inhibit responses. An increased number of dopamine receptors in males may be the reason boys are diagnosed with AD/ HD almost four times more often than girls.

Agitation: A clinical state of extreme emotional disturbance in bipolar disorder, occurring during both manic and depressive episodes, that involves nonproductive, repetitive physical actions (e.g., restlessness; pulling or rubbing on hair, skin, or clothing; changing positions; pacing; fidgeting; unusual throat-nose-mouth noises; or any other compulsive motor activity) accompanied by emotional outbursts or inner tension (e.g., racing thoughts or speech, yelling, crying, hallucinations, guilt, frustration, anxiety, panic, aggression, anger, abnormal sensations, paranoia, confusion, uncharacteristic language, morbid or suicidal ideation), increased energy or strength, marked insensitivity or oversensitivity to pain, and a significant lack of safety awareness.

Anorexia: An eating disorder involving significantly reduced body weight (at least 15 percent below normal body weight), a distorted body image, an obsessive fear of gaining weight or being fat, and extended menstrual cycle disruption (amenorrhea) typically manifesting during early adolescence in approximately 4 percent of middle- to upper-middle-class Caucasian women (about one out of every hundred teenage girls). Neurological factors suggested by anorexia studies have included genetic components, hypothalamus dysfunction, neurotransmitter imbalance, serotonin disturbances, and/or reduced blood flow to the temporal lobes. Psychological factors suggested have included high levels of anxiety and depression, obsessive-compulsive disorders, personality disorders, mood disorders, childhood abuse, poor self-image, and a possible link to autism.

Apgar: The method to quickly evaluate the health of babies immediately after birth developed in 1952 by anesthesiologist Virginia Apgar, involving a simple scoring system (on a scale of 0 to 2, resulting in an Apgar score ranging from 0 to 10) of the five criteria making up the Apgar mnemonic acronym: activity, pulse, grimace, appearance, and respiration.

Asperger's syndrome: A neurodevelopmental disorder involving the left hemisphere of the brain included in the category of pervasive developmental disorders (PDDs) that was first described in 1944 by Austrian pediatrician Dr. Hans Asperger. Always diagnosed after the age of three, Asperger's is characterized by qualitative impairments in social interaction, social communication, abstract imagination, sensory processing, and executive functioning, accompanied by a significant intolerance to change, obsessive/inflexible interests, unusual speech patterns, delayed motor development, and a compulsive need for perfection, despite normal to advanced cognitive and language development. Although they share the same diagnostic category and similar criteria, Asperger's differs from autism both genetically and neurologically. Genetically, children with Asperger's are more likely to have relatives with depression and schizophrenia. Neurologically, Asperger's is defined more by abnormal brain function than by abnormal growth, with reduced frontal lobe activity noted during tasks involving social judgment and emotional expression, and abnormal levels of specific proteins similar to those found in obsessive-compulsive disorders. Boys are diagnosed with Asperger's at a rate almost four times greater than girls, and twin studies have suggested a possible genetic component.

Assistive technology (AT): An assistive technology device can be any item, piece of equipment, or product system—excluding surgically implanted medical devices—that can be used to increase, maintain, or improve the functional capabilities of a child with a disability (e.g., service animals, wheelchairs, hearing aids, voice recognition software, etc.). As such, assistive technology devices are the tools used to compensate for any disability that interferes with any activity of daily living in order to perform functions that might otherwise be difficult or impossible. Universal access assistive technology is designed to benefit the entire population. For example, dropped curbs at street crossings serve to increase the maneuverability of any type of mobility device with wheels, including wheelchairs, strollers, shopping carts, and wheeled briefcases and luggage. An assistive technology service is any service that directly assists a child with a disability in the selection, acquisition, or use of an assistive technology device. Federal regulations for assistive technology in special education dictate that the public school district assess the student's AT needs, acquire the necessary AT devices, coordinate the AT use with all of the student's teachers and other service providers, and provide the training for the student, the student's family, and the school personnel to ensure that the AT device is being used effectively.

Autism: A neurodevelopmental disorder involving a pattern of deficits indicative of a significant left hemisphere dysfunction included in the category of pervasive developmental disorders (PDDs). The symptoms of autism can begin as early as birth, are always present before the age of three, and vary widely from person to person. Symptoms are characterized by qualitative impairments in social interaction, social communication, abstract imagination, sensory processing, and executive functioning, accompanied by a significant intolerance to change, obsessive/inflexible interests and attachments, unusual speech patterns, and significantly delayed motor, cognitive, and language development. Autism affects all races, ethnic groups, and socioeconomic levels, with boys being diagnosed at a rate approximately four times greater than girls. Suggested causal factors for autism include genetic, environmental, and neurological components. Genetically, one diagnosed sibling increases the risk of a second sibling's developing autism from one in five hundred to one in twenty; two diagnosed siblings increases the risk of a third sibling's developing autism to one in three, and if one identical twin is autistic, there's a 90 percent chance that the other twin will also have the disorder. Genetic mutations can be inherited or spontaneous, with placental growth pattern abnormalities one of the first indicators of abnormal growth patterns in the brain. Preterm birth (before thirty-three weeks) and low birth weight (under five and a half pounds) seem to increase the risk of autism more for girls than for boys. Environmentally, pre- and postnatal exposure to toxins (including mercury and artificial sweeteners) and food allergies (especially to wheat and dairy) have been found to increase the severity of symptoms, as have vitamin and nutritional deficiencies from gastrointestinal malabsorption, viral infections, and immune system deficiencies. Increased age of the father and psychiatric disorders diagnosed in the mother are also thought to increase the risk of autism. Neurological components include abnormalities in pre- and postnatal brain growth, structure, and function (especially involving the cerebral cortex and the amygdala), and metabolic imbalances.

Autism Spectrum Disorders: The diagnostic category of pervasive developmental disorders (PDDs) refers to a group of neurodevelopmental disorders.

Bipolar disorder: A neurological disorder involving the cerebral cortex and the limbic system of the brain that causes unusual patterns of mood, energy, and activity levels that significantly disrupt daily activities. Causal factors include genetic, neurological, and environmental components, with specific stressors often responsible for triggering latent symptoms. Genetically, about 50 percent of people diagnosed with bipolar disorder have been found to have at least one family member diagnosed with some type of mood disorder; one parent diagnosed with bipolar disorder can increase the risk of inheritance by as much as 25 percent, and identical twins share bipolar disorder eight times more often than do fraternal twins. Neurologically, both specific and related levels of neurotransmitters (especially norepinephrine, dopamine, and serotonin) are indicated in the progression of bipolar disorder, as are increased sensitivities of the neuroreceptors of nerve cells and overproduction of the stress hormone cortisol. Environmental factors act primarily as triggers for latent genetic or neurological predispositions for bipolar disorder, with significant life stressors, altered health habits, alcohol or drug abuse, hormonal imbalances, and certain medications triggering its onset.

Central auditory processing disorder (CAPD): A neurodevelopmental disorder involving the central nervous system and the speech/auditory processing centers in the left temporal lobe of the brain that has a direct effect on the ability of the brain to process auditory information. Unfavorable acoustic environments and competing background noise significantly increase the negative effects of CAPD on receptive language comprehension, expressive language production, and learning. Causal factors include genetic, environmental, and neurological components impacting the development or maturation of the central auditory pathway, such as preterm births, low birth weights, traumatic and acquired brain injuries, viral encephalitis, pre- and postnatal exposure to environmental toxins (especially cigarette smoke and alcohol), Lyme disease, and or pre- or postnatal anoxia.

CT scan: Computerized axial tomography scans (CT scans; also known as CAT scans) use a rotating X-ray device to create detailed cross-sectional images (or slices) of the area being scanned, to be used in identifying neurological injuries, conditions, and diseases, and in determining the progress of a previously diagnosed disease.

Depression: A neurological disorder involving a chemical imbalance of neurotransmitters in the cerebral cortex and the limbic system of the brain that causes excessively low levels of mood, energy, and activity that significantly interfere with daily activities. Otherwise known as major depressive disorder. The diagnosis of this disorder requires at least five of the criteria symptoms (fatigue; lack of energy; restlessness; agitation; irritability; difficulty concentrating or making decisions; disturbed sleep and eating patterns; feelings of anger, inadequacy, discouragement, hopelessness, helplessness, worthlessness, and guilt; morbid thoughts of death; suicidal ideation; and a marked decrease in interest or pleasure in previously enjoyed activities) experienced every day for at least two weeks. Severe episodes can include psychotic symptoms such as paranoia, delusions, or hallucinations. Depression affects up to 5 percent of men and women of all ages, races, and economic levels; however, it is more often diagnosed in women. There are several subtypes to this disorder, including **seasonal affective disorder** (the recurrence of the symptoms during certain seasons), **postpartum depression** (occurring within the first year after giving birth), and **dysthymia** (chronic depression with often less severe symptoms lasting nearly every day for at least two years).

Developmental coordination disorder: A neurodevelopmental disorder involving the motor cortex, the cerebellum, and the vestibular systems of the brain, characterized by serious impairments in the ability to use visual, spatial, and sensory motor information to plan and execute movement that significantly interfere with activities of daily living and academic achievement, despite normal or advanced cognitive development. Clinical symptoms indicate deficient or delayed neuromotor development, including a general unsteadiness or shaking, an at-rest muscle tone that is below normal despite an active muscle tone that is above normal, awkward styles of movement, poor coordination, unusual strategies for performing tasks, perceptual-motor difficulties, and motor learning deficits not due to an otherwise recognized medical condition or pervasive developmental disorder. Prevalence and causal factors are quite similar to those for AD/HD, and include genetic, environmental, and neurological components.

DSM-IV *(Diagnostic and Statistical Manual of Mental Disorders):* The manual published by the American Psychiatric Association and utilized by mental health professionals that contains a listing of psychiatric disorders and their diagnostic codes, accompanied by a set of diagnostic criteria and information about the disorder, such as associated features, prevalence, familial patterns, age-, culture-, and gender-specific features, and differential diagnosis. No information about treatment or presumed etiology is included.

Dynamic theory of development: Development is shaped by a process of selection through which children develop the skills that are necessary for functioning in their specific environment, stimulated by the interaction challenges presented by the environment. Areas of development that are delayed must be stimulated through planned, appropriate environmental opportunity to learn and practice new skills that are as important to overall functional ability as intrinsic genetic capacities.

Dyslexia: A neurological learning disability involving specific dysfunction in the left hemisphere of the brain critical for translating visual and auditory information into understandable language, with accompanying efforts to compensate from less efficient systems in the right hemisphere. Also known as developmental reading disorder (DRD), dyslexia is the most commonly diagnosed learning disability, affecting up to 80 percent of school-age children. Dyslexia is diagnosed when children with otherwise normal vision, hearing, and intelligence have specific difficulty interpreting the spoken and written components of language, despite the capacity to think and understand complex ideas. Symptoms of dyslexia can include significantly below age level reading; difficulty with processing rapid or complicated speech and/or multistep directions; difficulty with sequencing, organization, spelling, decoding, rhyming, letter-sound relationships, contextual cues, and calculation; and letter/number reversals past the age of eight. Dyslexia can also include the inability to effectively translate thought into written language and/or correctly sequence written symbols (numbers/letters). Dyslexia affects all races, ethnic groups, and socioeconomic levels, with boys being diagnosed more often than girls. Causal factors include genetic and neurological components, though environmental factors can exacerbate the severity of symptoms. Genetically, one parent diagnosed with dyslexia can increase the risk of inheritance by as much as 50 percent, while one diagnosed sibling can increase the risk by as much as 60 percent, and a diagnosed identical twin can increase the risk by more than 80 percent. Neurologically, dyslexic brains have been found to have specific structural differences in the left hemisphere; and while the dominant hemisphere of the brain is typically larger than the nondominant hemisphere, dyslexic brains have a tendency for the dominant hemisphere to be of an equal or smaller size than the nondominant hemisphere.

Dyspraxia: A neurodevelopmental disorder involving the motor cortex, cerebellum, and vestibular system of the brain characterized by serious impairments in the ability to use visual spatial and sensory motor information to organize, plan, initiate, and execute purposeful movement.

Educational consultant: A licensed teacher with a graduate degree in education, focused on accurately interpreting state and federal special education regulations and researching the most effective evidence-based teaching methods, supports, services, and assistive technology to be used in developing appropriate Individualized Education Plans for children with disabilities. Educational consultants also create and conduct professional development workshops and training for parents and teachers, participate in education committees and conferences, monitor progress, and administer functional behavior assessments (FBAs), all in the interest of promoting the intellectual, social, and physical welfare of students.

EEG: Electroencephalographs (EEGs) document abnormal electrical brain-wave activity or patterns in the cerebral hemispheres and can be used to identify neurological dysfunction.

Environmental accommodations: Physical devices or physical changes to the educational environment specifically designed to improve the inclusion, independence, and productivity of students with disabilities. Environmental accommodations can include changes in space (size of classroom, arrangement of equipment and supplies, number of children), position (proximity to teacher or chalkboard, type of seating or support), and/or environmental stimulation (reduced or increased auditory and/or visual information), as well as assistive technology devices that will increase the student's access and participation in the general curriculum.

Executive functioning: Governed by the cerebral cortex—the "command and control" center of the brain—executive functioning involves the higher order processes of the brain, including but not limited to impulse control, decision making, planning and executing movement, regulating emotion, prioritizing, sequencing, establishing goals, monitoring progress, paying attention, remembering details, beginning, starting, and completing tasks, strategizing, and problem solving.

504 plan: The rights of students with disabilities who need environmental accommodations to succeed in their Free and Appropriate Public Education (FAPE) are covered under Section 504 of the Americans with Disabilities Act (ADA) and require a 504 plan. 504 plans are written plans developed by the 504 committee, including the parents of the student for whom the 504 plan is written. They identify the student's specific disabilities and the specific accommodations that will be implemented by the school to address the disabilities. 504 plans are updated at least annually. The 504 coordinator is responsible for contacting all of the school staff involved in the implementation of the specific disability accommodations for each student with a 504 plan.

Grandiosity: An exaggerated sense of superiority in importance, power, knowledge, or identity, often with religious overtones, experienced by those in a manic episode.

Hyperlexia: A neurodevelopmental disorder involving the left hemisphere of the brain characterized by an almost spontaneous and exceedingly advanced ability to decode or read words with little or no formal instruction or reading comprehension, an intense fascination with letters or numbers, and unusually strong auditory and visual memory, accompanied by marked deficits in sensory processing, verbal and nonverbal communication, language acquisition, sensory processing, abstract comprehension, and social interaction. Children with hyperlexia demonstrate many of the symptoms often associated with autism spectrum disorders, including ritualized, repetitive self-stimulatory behaviors; unusual resistance to change; difficulty with transitions; echolalia; and unusual and intense phobias and anxieties. Causal factors include genetic and neurological components, though environmental factors can exacerbate the severity of symptoms. Genetically, twin studies have suggested a possible link to high-functioning autism spectrum disorders in some variants of hyperlexia. Neurologically, some studies have shown higher levels of activity in the left hemisphere of hyperlexic brains, while other studies have suggested that hyperlexia may be the true opposite of dyslexia.

Hypersexuality: A symptom of bipolar mania characterized by obsessive thoughts about sex, often accompanied by compulsively seeking and/or engaging in sexual activity to the point of addictive behaviors, or neglecting important social, occupational, or recreational activities in favor of continual sexual activity despite the negative consequences involved, including loss of health, job, marriage, or freedom.

Independent educational evaluation (IEE): The United States Code of Federal Regulations for Special Education defines an *independent educational evaluation* as "an evaluation conducted by a qualified examiner who is not employed by the public agency responsible for the education of the child in question." (34 C.F.R. 300.503)

Individual Education Plan (IEP): The rights of students with disabilities who need specialized instructional modifications to the general curriculum *as well as* environmental accommodations to succeed in their Free and Appropriate Public Education (FAPE) are covered by the Individuals with Disabilities Education Act (IDEA), and require an Individualized Education Plan (IEP). IEPs are written plans developed by the IEP team, including the parents of the student with the disability for whom the IEP is written. They are more involved than 504 plans because in addition to the student's disabilities and the environmental accommodations, they have to identify the specific instructional modifications to the general curriculum that will be implemented to address the disability, and the specific special/regular educator or service provider responsible for implementing each of the environmental accommodations and instructional modifications included in the IEP. IEPs are updated annually. It is the responsibility of the special and regular educators, administrators, and service providers to thoroughly familiarize themselves with the provisions of the IEP for each of their students with disabilities throughout the school year.

Instructional modifications: A change in instructional routine, method, or approach specifically designed to compensate for cognitive skills or abilities that an individual lacks, with the goal of improving the inclusion, independence, and productivity of students with disabilities. Instructional modifications can include but are not limited to: calculators, spell-checking or grammar-correcting software, reduced assignments, graphic organizers, study guides, digitally recorded lessons, tutoring, and the use of concept integrity reading material presented at a reduced level of reading difficulty.

Invisible disabilities: The U.S. Department of Education Office of Special Education and Rehabilitative Services (OSERS) refers to neurodevelopmental disabilities such as AD/HD, dyslexia, and Asperger's syndrome as "invisible disabilities." Symptoms or characteristics of "invisible disabilities" are often very subtle or can appear very similar to those of other types of disabilities, making accurate identification difficult. Neuropsychological assessments are necessary to identify any significant deficits of attention, reasoning, processing, memory, communication, and coordination.

Jaundice: A condition in 50 to 60 percent of all newborn babies, and more often with prematurely born babies, characterized by yellowish discoloration of the skin and conjunctival membranes of the eyes caused by the inability of the newborn liver to sufficiently filter bilirubin out of the blood. Normally, jaundice is resolved quickly as the newborn liver adjusts to the task of filtering the blood, but excessive bilirubin levels can cause permanent damage to the nervous system and, very rarely, can result in a condition called kernicterus, which can result in deafness, delayed development, or a form of cerebral palsy.

Language pragmatics: The ability to understand and use the rules of social language appropriately and successfully in social situations. The social use of language is divided into three main categories: *when and how to use language for specific purposes* (e.g., greeting, providing information, giving directions, making requests); *when and how to change language to meet personal or situational needs* (e.g., formal, informal, age appropriate, respectful, or protective language); and *when and how to follow the rules for conversation* (e.g., taking turns, introducing topics, staying on topic, using both verbal and nonverbal communication, observing personal space, interpreting facial expressions, and maintaining eye contact).

Learning disability: A disorder characterized by an inability to process and store information caused by specific areas of neurological dysfunction and/or an inability of the brain to form new connections and generate new brain cells in response to experience and learning. Learning disabilities are usually divided into respective areas of processing: motor disorders (dyspraxia), math disorders (dyscalculia), written and spoken language disorders (dyslexia), and writing disorders (dysgraphia), as well as sensory processing disorders, auditory processing disorders, and visual processing disorders.

Mania: The manic phase of bipolar disorder, during which chemical imbalances of neurotransmitters in the cerebral cortex and the limbic system of the brain cause excessively high levels of mood, energy, and activity that significantly interfere with daily activities. Mania is characterized by physical hyperactivity, highly disorganized thoughts and behaviors, and abnormally elevated states of mood, arousal, and energy levels, with rapid speech, hypersexuality, euphoria, impulsiveness, grandiosity, and an obsessive interest in completing egocentric, goal-directed activities with very little thought or consideration for negative consequences, and therefore very little restraint exercised. Racing thoughts can cause excessive distractibility and preoccupation with seemingly trivial or unimportant stimuli, which makes keeping track of time difficult, adding to the decreased ability or need for sleep.

Midline crossing: If you imagine the "midline" as a straight line down the center of your body dividing the right side from the left, then "crossing the midline" means extending your reach or vision from one side of the body into the space of the other side. Crossing the midline requires effective bilateral coordination skills (the ability to use both sides of the body at the same time) and cross-lateral motion skills (the ability to move opposing limbs—left arm and right leg or right arm and left leg—at the same time). Children who experience difficulty with crossing the midline of their body often have trouble with reading and writing.

Mood swings: The frequent and intense fluctuations of mood from mania to depression common in those with bipolar disorder.

MRI: Magnetic resonance imaging uses powerful magnetic fields and radio frequency pulses to produce detailed pictures of the different soft tissues of the body, creating much higher resolutions and much clearer images than are possible from X-rays and CT scans.

Neurodevelopmental disorders: Any disability that results from delayed or compromised growth and development of the brain or central nervous system. These can have numerous causes, including genetic and congenital disorders, metabolic disease, immune system disorders, nutritional factors, environmental toxins, and/or acquired or traumatic neurological damage. Early identification of neurodevelopmental disorders is essential for early intervention to prevent or limit sustained impact on intellectual and functional capacity.

Neurologist: A neurologist is a medical doctor (MD) who is board certified in neurology, a specialty field of medicine. Neurologists study the structural and physiological aspects of brain injury, brain damage, and brain disease, and utilize a pharmacological regimen of treatment to address the functional impact of such neurological conditions.

Neuropsychologist: A neuropsychologist has a doctoral degree in highly specialized disciplines of psychology (PsyD) or philosophy (PhD). Neuropsychologists are licensed to provide clinical and diagnostic opinions regarding the presence, scope, and treatment of cognitive and behavioral disorders and mental illness that result from neurological injury, disease, or dysfunction in relation to short- and long-term memory functioning; verbal and nonverbal problem-solving and reasoning abilities; attention span and orientation to time, place, and space; expressive and receptive language function; visual-motor and sensory-motor coordination; and the ability to plan, abstract, and synthesize information in all sensory modalities.

Nonverbal learning disorder (NLD): A neurodevelopmental disorder involving the right hemisphere of the brain, characterized by advanced auditory processing skills and verbal IQs in comparison to marked deficits in visual processing, executive functioning, social interaction and communication, sensory processing, motor coordination, and fine and gross motor development that significantly impairs academic performance, social functioning, and emotional well-being. In comparison, nonverbal learning disorders seem to be diagnosed much less frequently than the language-based learning disabilities, and also seem to be diagnosed more often in girls than in boys. Causal factors include genetic and neurological components, though environmental factors can exacerbate the severity of symptoms. Genetically, family studies support a possible genetic link with NLD. Neurologically, studies have indicated both damage to the right hemisphere and insufficient or dysfunctional white matter, resulting in inefficient communication between the right and left cerebral hemispheres, with the severity of symptoms relative to the amount of damage or dysfunction.

Obsessive-compulsive disorder (OCD): A neurological disorder involving a chemical imbalance of neurotransmitters in the brain (specifically serotonin) characterized by recurrent, unwanted, anxiety-producing thought patterns that can be controlled only by performing repetitive, ritualistic behaviors (compulsions) that consume both time and concentration to the point of disrupting normal activities of daily life. Unfortunately, relief from the obsessive thought patterns lasts only as long as the compulsive behaviors are being performed. Obsessions and compulsions often center on themes, the most common of which are fear of contamination, the need for order and symmetry, and the preoccupation with sex, religion, or aggressive/horrific acts. OCD sufferers often recognize their thoughts and subsequent actions as irrational, increasing their anxiety and perpetuating the cycle. More than 2 percent of the U.S. population suffers from OCD, making it more prevalent than both schizophrenia and bipolar disorder. Early-onset obsessive-compulsive disorder often begins around the age of ten, while adult-onset OCD typically begins around the age of twenty-one. Causal factors include genetic and neurological components, although symptoms can be triggered or exacerbated by environmental stressors. Genetically, familial and twin studies have suggested an increased risk of OCD with diagnosed parents, siblings, or other family members. Neurologically, OCD brains often have significantly less white matter beneath the cerebral cortex than do normal brains, suggesting a widely distributed brain abnormality resulting in less intracranial communication. OCD brains also exhibit increased rates of metabolic activity in direct proportion to the severity of the disorder in the frontal lobe and the orbital cortex (the worry center of the brain). The serotonin deficiency has been supported by the success of OCD medications that enhance the action of serotonin.

Panic disorder: Panic disorders involve panic attacks, a feeling of sudden terror accompanied by physical sensations such as a pounding heart, sweating, nausea, chest pain or compression, and faintness or dizziness. If left untreated, panic disorders can lead to a pattern of avoidance of places or situations where panic attacks have occurred, leading to elective isolation and/or agoraphobia. Panic disorder is one of the most treatable forms of anxiety disorders, responding effectively to medications and psychotherapy.

Pervasive developmental disorder (PDD): The diagnostic category of pervasive developmental disorders (PDDs) refers to a group of neurodevelopmental disorders, also known as autism spectrum disorders (ASDs), involving a pattern of deficits indicative of a significant left hemisphere dysfunction. Symptoms vary widely from person to person, are usually present before the age of three, and are most often characterized by qualitative impairments in social interaction, social communication, abstract imagination, sensory processing, motor development, and executive functioning, accompanied by intolerance to change, abnormal interests and attachments, unusual speech patterns, self-stimulatory behaviors, and varying language and cognitive development. Autism is the most well known and researched of the pervasive developmental disorders, which currently include Asperger's syndrome, childhood disintegrative disorder, Rett syndrome, and PDD/NOS.

Psychiatrist: A medical doctor (MD) who specializes in the physical and neurological foundations of emotional and mental disorders and follows the medical model of treatment: mental disorders result from physical dysfunction, and so should be treated medically. Psychiatrists' level of education and training provides them with an in-depth knowledge of the benefits and limitations of specific types of medications in treating specific types of mental illness, allowing them to prescribe medication as a treatment modality.

Psychologist: Psychologists have doctoral degrees in philosophy (PhD) or psychology (PsyD), and specialize in the psychotherapy mode of treatment: negative thought and behavior patterns are resolved through cognitive and behavioral intervention. Clinical psychologists have the most rigorous training in psychotherapy, and can administer and report the results of psychological testing.

Psychotic episode: An isolated episode during which a loss of contact with reality occurs, typically including delusions (false ideas about what is taking place or who one is), hallucinations (seeing or hearing things that aren't there), and/or paranoia (unusual or unrealistic fears).

Social workers: Social workers have graduate degrees in the field of social work and specialize in the social foundations of emotional and mental disorders. Treatment plans involve all social aspects of their client's lives and can include advocating and educating, teaching effective problem-solving and coping skills, and providing direct links to essential community resources, as well as counseling and protecting the rights of their clients.

Team meeting: IDEA regulations for special education define the Individualized Education Plan (IEP) team as a group of individuals (including the parents, regular and special education teachers, a representative of the district knowledgeable about the district resources and qualified to supervise the provision of special education services, individuals who can interpret the instructional implications of evaluation results, and—at the discretion of the parents—any other individuals who have knowledge or special expertise regarding the child) who are responsible for developing, reviewing, or revising an IEP for a child with a disability.

Tourette's syndrome: A neurodevelopmental disorder involving abnormalities in certain regions of the brain (including the frontal lobes and the cerebral cortex) first diagnosed in 1885 by French neurologist Georges Gilles de la Tourette and characterized by repetitive, stereotyped, involuntary movements, and vocalizations called tics. Tourette's is categorized as part of the spectrum of tic disorders, which also includes transient and chronic tics. Though most often associated with the relatively rare vocal tics composed of altering socially inappropriate and derogatory words or remarks, Tourette's usually involves the more common tics of eye blinking, coughing, throat clearing, sniffing, and facial movements. It is diagnosed approximately four times more often in boys than girls, the onset of symptoms most often occurs between the ages of seven and ten, and the disorder affects people from all ethnic groups. Most people with this disorder experience their worst symptoms in their early teens, with improvement occurring in the late teens and continuing into adulthood. However, approximately 10 percent of childhood Tourette disorders continue to progress into adulthood. Tics are classified as either simple (involving a limited number of muscle groups, such as eye blinking or throat clearing) or complex (distinct, coordinated patterns of movements involving several muscle groups, such as jumping or uttering words or phrases), with the most severe forms involving involuntary self-injury, yelling out inappropriate words, and echolalia (repeating words or phrases). Tics can be preceded by a sensation of urgency or a premonitory urge in the affected muscle group that may require several tic repetitions to relieve. Causal factors include both genetic and neurological components, although environmental stressors may trigger or exacerbate symptoms. Genetically, twin and family studies have both suggested that Tourette's is inheritable and that it has a possible link to AD/HD. Neurologically, inefficient neurotransmitters seem to be responsible for miscommunication among nerve cells and between regions of the brain.

Vision therapy: A type of neurological physical therapy designed to train the entire visual system to effectively recognize, interpret, and respond to visual information. In this manner, vision therapy is an effective strategy to address reading and learning disabilities related to visual motor and visual perceptual deficiencies.

WISC: The Wechsler Intelligence Scale for Children is an individual test for children six to sixteen years of age that does not require reading or writing ability from the test subject to assess the intellectual functioning in verbal comprehension, perceptual reasoning, working memory, and processing speed, and which provides a composite score that represents a child's general intellectual ability.

RESOURCES

RECOMMENDED BY LeeAnn Karg, MEd. For further information, visit kargacademy.com.

More Tips for Getting Your Child the Support They May Need

✔ To create the best education plan for your child, seek independent, unbiased evaluations from the top pediatric specialists in your area. You can't ask your child's school for any service that hasn't been recommended by an accepted, standardized assessment administered by a licensed medical doctor or therapist.

✔ Remember that your public school is first and foremost a business. To stay within their budget, school districts choose evaluations that will recommend the supports and services they already provide. Your independent educational evaluations (IEEs) will provide the proof your district needs to qualify for emergency Office of Special Education Programs funding earmarked for providing public school services for children with specific disabilities.

✔ Document everything, and make sure you have the paper trail to back up every conversation. Ask for every notice in writing. Choose e-mail correspondence over phone calls.

✔ Your school is only required to provide the specific therapy services (OT, PT, speech, social skills, counseling, etc.) written on the "Special Education and Related Service(s)" page of your child's IEP. Pay special attention to this page, noting the specific terminology, provider, frequency, and location used to describe the service being provided to your child. *You don't have to accept the IEP if you don't agree with the services to be provided to your child exactly as they are written.*

✔ Your school is only required to provide the instructional modifications and environmental accommodations written in the "Supplemental Aids and Services" section of your child's IEP. Pay special attention to the exact language used, and any change to the strategies for presenting curriculum instruction (e.g., extended time for processing directions or completing assignments, reduction in workload, graphic organizers or other assistance with organizing or sequencing instructional materials) *and* the exact environmental accommodations (e.g., preferential seating, the use of assistive technology, sensory breaks, specialized chairs or desks, writing implements or assistance, or any device to help your child hear the teacher or see the material better) your child needs to access and progress in the general curriculum in the same manner as their nondisabled peers. *You don't have to accept the IEP if you don't agree with the supplemental aids and services to be provided to your child exactly as they are written.*

✔ Remember that school districts get separate funding for assistive technology. As defined in the Assistive Technology Act Amendments of 2004 (or the "AT Act of 2004"), *assistive technology includes "any device or adaptation to existing devices that facilitates activities of daily living to significantly benefit individuals with disabilities of all ages . . .* by increasing involvement in, and reducing expenditures associated with, programs and activities that facilitate communication, ensure independent functioning, enable early childhood development, support educational achievement, provide and enhance employment options, and enable full participation in community living for individuals with disabilities."

✔ Remember that social skills groups are effective only if the group is appropriate for *all* of its members. This is the only way to ensure that evidence-based, researched, and proven social skill interventions are accurately targeted. *You have the right to know exactly which reliable interventions, methods, and strategies are being used to increase and monitor the progress of your child's social language and social skill development.*

Other Methods of Therapy for Kids
(Condensed from kargacademy.com)

Here are just a few of the effective therapy programs LeeAnn Karg has used with great success:

- ✔ **HOW DOES YOUR ENGINE RUN?:** An innovative program that supports children, teachers, parents, and therapists to choose appropriate strategies to change or maintain optimal states of alertness. Increasing awareness of how important self-regulation is for basic functioning helps adults teach highly effective, developmentally appropriate self-regulation skills to help children independently recognize their own states of awareness and maintain their own level of optimal functioning. (alertprogram.com)

- ✔ **HANDWRITING WITHOUT TEARS (HWT):** Developed by occupational therapist Jan Olsen to facilitate her own son's handwriting, HWT is easy to learn, easy to teach, developmentally appropriate, and inclusive. (hwtears.com)

- ✔ **BRAIN GYM:** A nonprofit organization committed to the principle that intentional movement is the door to optimal living and learning, Brain Gym International offers exercises that enhance and encourage midline crossing and cross-lateral motion to help to jump-start the brain's natural development for bilateral coordination. (braingym.org)

- ✔ **PLAY THERAPY:** Allowing children to work through emotional conflicts through directed play with themes that develop coping strategies and positive problem-solving skills offers children a safe medium for expressing feelings and both disclosing and describing negative or traumatic experiences. The use of toys enables children to transfer anxieties, fears, fantasies, and guilt to objects rather than people. In the process, children are safe from their own feelings and reactions because play enables children to distance themselves from traumatic events and experiences. (a4pt.org)

Sports and Extracurricular Activities for Children with Disabilities
(Condensed from kargacademy.com)

Finding hobbies and activities appropriate for special children can be a challenging task for many parents. Here are a few of the links suggested by LeeAnn Karg, MEd, to help you help your children find their interests.

✔ **Adaptive Adventures** takes pride in creating sports and recreation opportunities for youth by providing access to the outdoors and by helping families work toward inclusion in their local communities. (adaptiveadventures.org)

✔ **Dreams for Kids** is a volunteer-based, nonprofit children's charity that works to break down social barriers and end the isolation of children in need. Their mission is to empower young people of all abilities through dynamic leadership programs and life-changing activities that inspire them to fearlessly pursue their dreams and compassionately change the world. (dreamsforkids .org)

✔ **Adaptive Sports Association (ASA)** is a program that helps enrich and transform the lives of people with disabilities through sports and recreation. By working with students to overcome physical and cognitive challenges in a safe, supportive environment, ASA helps students "explore possibilities." (asadurango.com)

✔ **The American Association of Adapted SPORTS Programs** works in partnership with education agencies in the United States to establish programs, policies, procedures, and regulations in interscholastic adapted sports for students with physical disabilities to enhance educational outcomes. (adaptedsports .org)

✔ **Summer Camps Directory** offers a list of special needs summer camps throughout the United States and in Canada. (summercampsinfo.com)

Where to Find the Help You Need Online
(Condensed from kargacademy.com)

- ✔ **CHADD (Children and Adults with AD/HD):** Provides a professional directory that is an invaluable resource to find professionals, products, or others providing services for families and individuals living with AD/HD. (chadd.org)
- ✔ **NAMI (National Alliance on Mental Illness):** Provides information and services focused on improving the lives of individuals and families affected by mental illness. (nami.org)
- ✔ **Live in the Balance:** The nonprofit Web home of Dr. Ross Greene and the Collaborative Problem Solving Model he originated and describes in his books *The Explosive Child* and *Lost at School*. (liveinthebalance.org)
- ✔ **Our-Kids:** Provides information on everything from indefinite developmental delays and sensory integration problems to cerebral palsy and rare genetic disorders. (our-kids.org)
- ✔ **American Self-Help Clearinghouse:** Provides keyword-searchable database of self-help support groups for addictions, bereavement, health, mental health, disabilities, abuse, parenting, caregiver concerns, and other stressful life situations. (mentalhelp.net/selfhelp)
- ✔ **Parent to Parent USA (P2PUSA):** Provides emotional and informational support to families of children who have special needs, highlighting statewide organizations and evidence-based practices. (p2pusa.org)
- ✔ **Uniquely Gifted:** Provides a resource page specifically for "twice-exceptional" children (intellectually gifted children with special needs). (uniquelygifted.org)
- ✔ **The Council for Exceptional Children (CEC):** An international professional organization dedicated to improving educational outcomes for individuals with exceptionalities, students with disabilities, and/or the gifted. (cec.sped.org)
- ✔ **LD Online:** The world's leading website on learning disabilities and AD/HD, providing accurate and up-to-date information and advice, a comprehensive resource guide, and a "Yellow Pages" referral directory of professionals, schools, and products. (ldonline.org)

✔ **Learning Disabilities Association of America:** Provides cutting-edge information on learning disabilities, practical solutions, and a comprehensive network of resources. (ldanatl.org)

✔ **Special Education Resources on the Internet (SERI):** Provides information and resources for those involved in special education. (seriweb.com)

✔ **The National Information Center for Children and Youth with Disabilities (NICHCY):** Provides information on disability-related issues for families, educators, and other professionals, with a special emphasis on birth to twenty-two years. (nichcy.org)

✔ **Educational Resources Information Center (ERIC):** Provides subject-specific clearinghouses and support components, and a variety of services and products on a broad range of education-related issues. (eric.ed.gov)

✔ **AskERIC:** Provides education information to teachers, librarians, counselors, administrators, parents, and anyone interested in education. (ericir.syr.edu)

✔ **Autism Society of America (ASA):** Strives to offer only credible and reliable resources by employing the nationwide network of ASA chapters and collaborating with other autism organizations and professionals throughout the United States. (autism-society.org)

✔ **Autism Source:** Provides a searchable database of nationwide autism-related services and supports by location or service type. (autismsource.org)

✔ **Autism Speaks:** Provides research into the cause, prevention, and treatment for autism, increasing awareness of autism spectrum disorders and advocating for the needs of individuals with autism and their families. (autismspeaks.org)

✔ **BellaOnline:** Provides research, information, an online forum and live chat discussions, and an extensive resource listing and links to products and sites geared to autism spectrum disorders. (autismspectrumdisorders.bellaonline.com)

✔ **ASAT (Association for Science in Autism Treatment):** Provides accurate, scientifically sound information about autism and treatments for autism. (asatonline.org/helpdesk/helpdesk.htm)

✔ **National Autism Association:** Educates and empowers families affected by autism and other neurological disorders, while advocating on behalf of those who cannot fight for their own rights. (nationalautismassociation.org)

✔ **(ARI) Autism Research Institute:** Provides research-based information to parents and professionals on the triggers, methods of diagnosing, and treatment of autism. (autism.com)

✔ **PAL (Parent/Professional Advocacy League):** Advocates for support, treatment, and policies that enable families to live in their communities in an environment of stability and respect. (http://ppal.net)

✔ **ADDitude magazine:** Provides clear, accurate, user-friendly information and advice from the leading experts and practitioners in AD/HD, mental health, education, and learning disabilities. (additudemag.com)

✔ **DBSA (Depression and Bipolar Support Alliance):** Provides up-to-date, scientifically based tools and information on mood disorders. (dbsalliance.org)

✔ **MDJunction:** An online support group offering a comfort zone for people to discuss their feelings, questions, and hopes with like-minded friends dealing with the same health challenges. (mdjunction.com)

✔ **Bipolar support.org:** Provides details about bipolar disorder, resources, recommended books, service provider links, and supportive forums and chat rooms. (bipolarsupport.org)

✔ **BPChildren:** Provides resources and information for teachers, parents, kids, and teens about childhood bipolar disorder. (bpchildren.org)

ACKNOWLEDGMENTS

There are so many people who have helped us find our way on this incredible journey. And when you're not that bright, you tend to rely on them.

First, to Jenny Frost for finding us imperfect zirconias in the rough.

To our wonderful and gracious agent, Vicky Bijur. Your responsiveness, support, and belief in us means more than you'll ever know. To our former editors, Lucinda Bartley and Lindsay Orman, whose valuable insights have made this book a powerful tool to empower special parents. To Emily Timberlake, who won us over with her incredible heart and mind, and to Stephanie Chan, who helped see this through.

To Dr. Ross Greene for all your work with "special" children and for taking time out of your busy schedule to help us.

To Jane Lynn, who was there from the beginning with Bipolar, By Golly. You poured your beautiful heart and soul into this project, and we will be eternally grateful for your support, advice, honesty, and friendship.

To LeeAnn Karg, MEd. Your incredible mind is surpassed only by your enormous heart. And to Alex K. for sharing your mom to help others.

To our young and talented illustrators, Emily Gallagher, Katie Gallagher, Brendan Moody, Austyn Lavertue, Shawn Moody, and Grace Kane.

To Dayna, thank you for helping Jenn through some very difficult times and for teaching her to accept the beautiful person she is. Your warm smile and tremendous heart will be forever missed but not forgotten.

To Jackie MacMullan, bestselling author of *When the Game Was Ours.* Thank you for your invaluable writing advice and support and for putting up with Gina's imperfect play on the basketball court.

To the Raptors for not fining Gina for missing so many games and for still considering her for Raptor of the Month honors. To the

Sunday-morning crew who provide much-needed stress relief for Gina.

To all former and current pals at PAL—Joanne, Stephany, Cindy, Yvette, Mary, and the wonderful Janet Hodges, who will always be our favorite Hero. Special thanks to Rina C., who got The Movement of Imperfҽction rolling.

To Rhonda Taft Farrell and all the exceptional teachers, administrators, and staff members at Willow Hill School who work tirelessly to help our children reach their fullest potential. Special thanks to Pat, Pete, and Rachael for the support you've given Katie, and to the amazing Margot Law, for giving Katie the gift of theater.

To the Willow Hill moms, Tracy, Bill, Mary, Greta, and Barclay for all your support with the book.

To our friends at NAMI, including Darcy Gruttadaro, Lynda Cuttrell, Karen Mcgravey-Gajera, Cara Falconi, and Laurie Martinelli. And to Lady Jane Roennigke and the PIAT crew.

To Jim, Dr. Shah, Ellen, and Claudia, our Pennsylvania NAMI pals. And to Gary M. Sandy, and Gary in Montana.

To the Breakfast/Weight Watchers Bunch (no conflict there)—Urs and Cheryl—and all our loving and supportive friends.

To the MHS crew for your wonderful support—Marcy, Chrissi, Mary, Lisa, Emily, Jane, Irene, Debbie, Rosalie, Dani, and Karen.

To all our talented YouTube actors, Laurel, Polly, Dawn, Mike, Kristen, Tony V., Anna V., and especially The Director.

To the lovable Anthony V. We know you will go on and do great things in the world.

To Luke and Jake Goulet for helping spread The Movement of Imperfҽction with your kind hearts. To Juli and Bob for raising such compassionate kids.

To our generous and talented designer friends, Fran Cloonan and Mike Surabian.

To the amazing friends we've collected on this journey, including Diane (the Southcoast Stalker), Schmoopie, Rebecca, Darcy, Debbie S., Lois, Angel, Joanna, Liz H., and Martha, who had us at hello with their stories. To our dear friend Mark Anderson, who has given us the privilege of hearing Tony's story.

To the Midwest Stalkers—Lori, Pam, Louise, and Susan.

To Laurel, we love you always.

To Jessica and Daniel. We're so proud to be your aunts. Follow your dreams wherever they take you.

To Bob, the Shut Up brother; we will always be here for you.

To Vera, for sharing your wisdom and experience and for always listening and believing in us.

To Mom and Dad (our Senior Shippers) for surrounding us with your love and support. Sharing this journey with you has been our greatest joy.

To Jules, an amazing kid with an incredible heart and talent for writing. The world is your oyster.

To Mikey, who has the compassion, drive, and financial wizardry to take over the Shut Up empire someday.

To our husbands, Mike and Michael, who have given us the freedom to take this journey where it would lead us, even to the brink of bankruptcy.

And lastly, to Jenn, Katie, and Emmy. You amaze us every day with your courage, strength, and resilience. You have helped so many people with your stories and have taught us both the true meaning of love and acceptance. We could not be any prouder of you.

God bless you all!

INDEX

Academy of Cognitive Therapy, 185
acceptance
    of bipolar disorder, 54–59, 225–26
    and change, 202–3
    by community, 90
    of disability by children, 105–6, 108,
        113
    by grandparents, 90
    and happy endings, 223
    and parental anxiety, 225–26
    and placement, 150
    and response to negative comments, 80
accommodations. *See* environmental
    accommodations
action plan, 144
AD/HD, 64, 110, 114, 171, 190–91, 195–96,
    229, 253, 255
Adaptive Adventures, 252
Adaptive Sports Association (ASA), 252
ADDitude magazine, 255
advocates, 94–95, 127
American Academy of Child and
    Adolescent Psychiatry, 185
American Association of Adapted SPORTS
    Programs, 252
American Psychological Association, 185
American Self-Help Clearinghouse, 253
anger, 48, 111, 180–81
anorexia, 47, 230
anxiety
    change as trigger for, 106
    coping with, 176
    of Emily, 109, 111, 213, 216
    and grieving for loss of perfect child,
        48
    and importance of consistency, 90
    of Jennifer, 32, 149–50
    parental, 101, 139, 225–27
    separation, 32
    stimming as response to, 99
Anxiety Disorders Association of America,
    185
Apgar, 2, 230
AskERIC, 254
Asperger's syndrome
    children's book about, 110
    and comorbid, 149
    definition and characteristics of, 231
    diagnosis of, 27–29
    early signs of, 22–24, 30–31
    facing the challenge of, 47–53
    as high-functioning autism, 29
    and knowing you've got issues, 6
    learning about, 49–50

pride in children with, 3
strategy for dealing with, 70–74
See also Gina; Katie
assistive technology (AT), 231–32, 250
Association for Behavioral and Cognitive
    Therapies, 185
Association for Science in Autism
    Treatment (ASAT), 254
autism, 5, 30–31, 64–65, 68–70, 191, 232–
    33, 254–55. *See also specific type of autism
    or organization*
autism gear, 68, 69
Autism Research Institute (ARI), 255
Autism Society of America (ASA), 69,
    254
Autism Speaks, 254
autism spectrum disorders, 233

ballet school, 65, 196–98
bathroom wall, writing on, 141
BellaOnline, 70, 254
bipolar disorder
    acceptance of, 54–59
    children's book about, 110
    and comorbid, 149
    confirmation of, 56–57
    definition and characteristics of, 16–18,
        34, 44–45, 105, 233
    diagnosis of, 33–34
    and different way of thinking, 191–92
    early signs of, 32–33, 34, 35–39, 41
    famous people with, 170
    medications for, 57, 58, 225–26
    preparing the family for, 41–43
    pride in children with, 3
    resources about, 76, 255
    and suicide, 202
    telling others about, 64, 74–75
    and testing, 37
    thoughts on early childhood, 44–45
    See also Jennifer; Patty; *specific organization*
Bipolar support.org, 255
birthday parties, 71–72, 113–14
blame, 49, 91
bonding, 216–18
book clubs, 176
books
    about disabilities, 110–11
    See also resources
BPChildren, 255
bragging, 136, 163–69
Brain Gym, 251
bumper stickers, 164–65
Buttons and More, 69

ABOUT THE AUTHORS

PATRICIA KONJOIAN lives in Andover, Massachusetts, with her husband and their three children. She owns Champion Video Productions, which offers sports recruitment videos and event videography.

GINA GALLAGHER is a freelance copywriter. She lives in Marlborough, Massachusetts, with her husband and their two daughters.

Praise for SHUT UP ABOUT YOUR PERFECT KID

"Know, work with, or love a child with special needs? If so, Gina Gallagher and Patricia Konjoian's SHUT UP ABOUT YOUR PERFECT KID is the latest 'must-read' book on the subject. The sisters, whose wit and delivery could have landed them a gig on the stand-up circuit, share facts and funny stories about raising kids with disabilities while providing practical advice and identifying helpful resources. You'll laugh, you'll cry, you'll learn a lot about living well with challenge. Buy a copy for yourself . . . and two or three more for your friends with perfect kids!"

KATE McLAUGHLIN, author of *Mommy I'm Still in Here: One Family's Journey with Bipolar Disease*

"SHUT UP ABOUT YOUR PERFECT KID is the perfect antidote to a society obsessed with perfection. It was written by two sisters who both have children with unique challenges. Gina Gallagher and Patricia Konjoian have created an honest, humorous, and touching book that will make you laugh and cry, but most of all it will make you reevaluate how you look at other people in this world. Their journey is similar to that of many parents who have been filled with conflicting feelings about their children. But at the end of the day, instead of seeing their children's differences, they see their determination and spirit. It's that determination and spirit that has changed their lives in every way. It's also what they would like the rest of the world to embrace. This book is a breath of fresh air to parents of kids with all sorts of abilities."

TRACY ANGLADA, executive director of BPChildren and author of *Intense Minds: Through the Eyes of Young People with Bipolar Disorder*

"This survival guide is a must-read for families of children with emerging and existing mental health conditions. Not only does this book provide highly practical advice, but it infuses that advice with real-life stories of families who have faced unthinkable challenges and come out on top. It offers hope to every family who has faced the dark side of stigma and the struggle of securing effective services and supports for their child. Families who read this book will truly understand that they are not alone. The road can be long and hard, but this book reminds us that on our journey, humor provides a powerful role in the struggle. Ordinary families will find themselves reading and rereading this guide as they come to appreciate the beauty of their unique and special child."

DARCY GRUTTADARO, director of the NAMI
National Child and Adolescent Action Center

"Thank you, Gina and Patty, for reminding the world that our most cherished human qualities, courage and resilience among them, can never be captured by a test score or grade on a report card. Your book, your message, and your 'Movement of Imperfəction' could not have arrived at a better time. Thanks to you, countless numbers of people, children and adults alike, will come to see their differences in a hopeful new light."

MARK KATZ, PhD, clinical and consulting psychologist, San Diego, California, and author of *On Playing a Poor Hand Well*